www.wadsworth.com

wadsworth.com is the World Wide Web site for Wadsworth Publishing Company and is your direct source to dozens of online resources.

At *wadsworth.com* you can find out about supplements, demonstration software, and student resources. You can also send e-mail to many of our authors and preview new publications and exciting new technologies.

wadsworth.com
Changing the way the world learns®

The Contemporary Congress

A Bicameral Approach

MATTHEW C. MOEN
University of Maine

GARY W. COPELAND
University of Oklahoma

West/Wadsworth
ITP® An International Thomson Publishing Company

Belmont, CA • Albany, NY • Boston • Cincinnati • Johannesburg • London • Madrid • Melbourne
Mexico City • New York • Pacific Grove, CA • Scottsdale, AZ • Singapore • Tokyo • Toronto

Political Science Editor: Clark Baxter
Senior Developmental Editor: Sharon Adams Poore
Editorial Assistants: Melissa Gleason and Amy Guastello
Marketing Manager: Jay Hu
Print Buyer: Barbara Britton
Permissions Editor: Bob Kauser
Cover Design: Ark Stein/The Visual Group
Cover Photographs: capitol: Norman Rothschild/The Stock Market; people: Tony Stone Images
Copy Editor: Thomas L. Briggs
Illustrations: Joan Carol
Production and Composition: Vicki Moran/Publishing Support Services
Printer: Webcom Ltd.

Printed in Canada
1 2 3 4 5 6 7 8 9 10

For more information, contact: Wadsworth Publishing Company, 10 Davis Drive,
Belmont, California 94002, or electronically at http://www.wadsworth.com

International Thomson Publishing Europe
Berkshire House
168-173 High Holborn
London, WC1V 7AA, United Kingdom

International Thomson Editores
Seneca, 53
Colonia Polanco
11560 México D.F. México

Nelson ITP, Australia
102 Dodds Street
South Melbourne
Victoria 3205 Australia

International Thomson Publishing Asia
60 Albert Street
#15-01 Albert Complex
Singapore 189969

Nelson Canada
1120 Birchmount Road
Scarborough, Ontario
Canada M1K 5G4

International Thomson Publishing Japan
Hirakawa-cho Kyowa Building, 3F
2-2-1 Hirakawa-cho, Chiyoda-ku
Tokyo 102 Japan

International Thomson Publishing Southern Africa
Building 18, Constantia Square
138 Sixteenth Road, P. O. Box 2459
Halfway House, 1685 South Africa

Library of Congress Cataloging-in-Publication Data
Moen, Matthew C., 1958–
        The Contemporary Congress / Matthew C. Moen, Gary W. Copeland.
            p. cm.
        Includes bibliographical references and index.
        ISBN 0–314–12804–2
        1. United States. Congress.   I. Copeland, Gary W.   II. Title.
JK1021.M64   1998
328.73—dc21
                                                               98–31602

To my daughter, Erika Lynn Moen

&

To my family, Chris, Casie, Kellie, and Cory Copeland

Contents

Illustrations

Tables

Preface

William Everett represented a Massachusetts district in the House of Representatives in the 1890s. When asked if he enjoyed serving in Congress, Everett quipped: "In the House they have got things fixed so that you can't get anything in, and in the Senate they have arranged things so that you can't get anything out." He obviously believed the two chambers differed.

The Contemporary Congress explains the operations and politics of the legislative branch through the prism of House and Senate similarities and differences. Although no single framework can convey the complexity of Capitol Hill, our focus on bicameralism captures an important and enduring dimension of the institution. It encourages readers to look beyond simple facts. We therefore present a bicameralism theme whenever it is appropriate, without twisting information to fit it.

We are indebted to many people for their assistance in this project. Supportive colleagues at our home institutions provided valuable insights. Students offered excellent research assistance and insightful comments, with special thanks owed to the following people: Chris Cookson, Barbara Greening, Daniel Hemberger, Colleen Johnson, Mary Alice Johnson, Jocelyn Jones, Jeannie Matava, Jennifer O'Leary, Amanda Roth-Lewis, Hans Seidenstucker, Marshall Tracy, Kellye Walker, and Elizabeth Watson. At UMaine, Ms. Deborah Grant assisted in many ways.

Many excellent scholars have provided helpful comments and suggestions: Jon R. Bond, Texas A&M University; Eileen Burgin, University of Vermont; Richard A. Champaigne, University of Wisconsin; Kenneth M. Cosgrove, Bethany College; Christopher J. Deering, George Washington University; Georgia

Duerst-Lahti, Beloit College; Charles W. Dunn, Clemson University; Jim Graves, Kentucky State University; Roger Hambug, Indiana University–South Bend; Bradford Jones, University of Arizona; Henry C. Kenski, University of Arizona; Rhonda Kinney, Eastern Michigan University; Robin Kolodny, Temple University; Thomas S. Langston, Tulane University; Michael J. Laslovich, The University of Montana; Arthur B. Levy, University of South Florida; John M. Lewis, Indiana University–South Bend; Stan Luger, University of Northern Colorado; Carl Lutrin, California Polytechnic State University; H. R. Mahood, The University of Memphis; Michael D. Martinez, University of Florida; Karen M. McCurdy, University of Missouri; Rosanna Perotti, Hofstra University; Lilliard Richardson, University of Tennessee; Sean J. Savage, St. Mary's College; Harvey L. Schantz, State University of New York–College of Plattsburgh. In a broader sense, we are deeply indebted to the community of congressional scholars whose ideas, suggestions, and research make books such as this one possible.

Finally, we have had the opportunity to work with consummate professionals at West/Wadsworth. Clark Baxter has combined diligence and knowledge with gracious good humor. Amy Guastello has done a superb job of guiding the manuscript into production. We warmly appreciate their efforts.

Matthew C. Moen, University of Maine
Gary W. Copeland, University of Oklahoma

1

~

A Bicameral Institution

The House of Representatives convened for the historic 100th Congress at high noon on January 6, 1987. In keeping with long-standing tradition, the House chaplain delivered a prayer, and the newly elected members took their oath of office. The House passed a resolution informing President Reagan and the Senate that it had convened. The 100th Congress was off to a quiet start.

Within minutes, though, House members were confronted with a sweeping proposal—one that sought to alter a procedural rule first crafted by Thomas Jefferson in 1797 and then followed in the House for more than 150 years. The proposal was sponsored by the second-ranking Democrat in the House, Majority Leader Tom Foley (D., Wash.); it was described by Martin Frost (D., Tex.), a member of the House Rules Committee, as "the only proposed change [in the rules for the 100th Congress] that will significantly alter the way we do business in the House of Representatives."[1] Despite the heritage of Jefferson's rule and the sweeping nature of the proposal, it passed with virtually no debate.

What new rule was inaugurated at the beginning of the 100th Congress? What change in Clause 1 of Rule XIV of "Jefferson's Manual of the Rules and Procedures of the House of Representatives" was instituted?[2] Although it sounds odd, House members gave themselves the right to refer to the Senate by name during debates on the House floor!

Prior to the rules change, House members were expected to refer euphemistically to the Senate as "the other body" during floor debates. That practice represented part of a much larger effort to promote harmony between the two chambers by making references as impersonal as possible. In addition, use of this euphemism contributed to the image of a House that debated weighty public issues and arrived at its own decisions without reference to the actions of the Senate. These lofty reasons were summarized by Jefferson in his procedural manual, which reminded members that "each house [of Congress] should be left to its own independency, not to be influenced by the proceedings of the other; and the quoting them might beget reflections leading to a misunderstanding between the two houses."[3]

The expectation that House members would refer to the Senate as "the other body" created some humorous moments over the years. In 1986, Representative Barney Frank (D., Mass.) was championing a housing bill that had been derailed in the Senate. Widely known for his keen intellect and quick wit, Frank was tongue-tied this particular time, unable to produce the proper euphemism of "the other body" in the midst of debate. He blurted out that for the bill to become law, "something has to happen somewhere else," a reference to the Senate so vague that his House colleagues were genuinely puzzled. Frank paused momentarily, sensing their confusion, but he was still unable to recall the proper phrase. Finally, in lieu of the proper expression, he produced a variation of the first line of Judy Garland's famous song in *The Wizard of Oz,* singing, "Somewhere Over the Rotunda [Rainbow]."[4] That oblique reference to "the other body" in the capitol building drew howls of laughter from his colleagues on the floor.

The sensitivity of members of Congress to a *bicameral* (two-house) legislature is expressed in an epic struggle between the House and Senate Appropriations Committees.[5] In September 1961, in the midst of an intense disagreement with the Senate, House Appropriations Committee Chair Clarence Cannon (D., Mo.) pushed a spending bill through the House before it adjourned, effectively telling the Senate to take it "as is." He followed up that impertinent act with a telephone call to Carl Hayden (D., Ariz.), head of the Senate Appropriations Committee, informing him that all future meetings of the two committees would rotate between the House and Senate sides of the capitol building. In doing so, Cannon was ending the long-standing practice of House members walking to the Senate side. Hayden rebuffed that idea, and for months the two committees refused to meet because they could not agree on a site. Institutional and personal honor were at stake. Finally, on the brink of a government shutdown caused by the lack of an appropriations bill, the two committees met in a room just slightly on the Senate side. A coin toss determined that a representative, not a senator, would lead the meeting. At last, the impasse was ended.

Although the personal conduct of the participants in that episode may seem petty, their behavior graphically illustrates the abiding tension that exists between the House and Senate. Bicameral wrangling is particularly evident when Republicans control one chamber while Democrats control another, as in the 97th to 99th Congresses (1981–1986). Yet, bicameral tensions persist no matter which political party controls which chamber at any particular time. Since 1995, Democratic President Bill Clinton has faced a Republican majority in both chambers. Even in those political circumstances, when we might expect close cooperation between House and Senate, bicameral differences still emerge.[6] In the 104th

Congress (1995–1996), for instance, the House and Senate split sharply over the ten-point "Contract With America," despite Republican majorities in both chambers. By the end of 1995, the House had acted on all ten items contained in the contract.[7] In contrast, the Senate finished work on only six, substantially amending the original bills produced by the House in most cases.[8] Bicameral differences resurfaced in the first session of the 105th Congress (1997), on issues such as trade, the Endangered Species Act, and reform of the Internal Revenue Service.[9] Cooperation usually prevails over conflict when the same party controls both chambers, but rivalry between the House and Senate still exists.

The bicameral character of the U.S. Congress, illuminated by the preceding vignettes, is specified in Article I of the U.S. Constitution: "All legislative powers herein granted shall be vested in a Congress of the United States, which shall consist of a Senate and a House of Representatives." Clearly, members often think in bicameral terms, and perhaps even in a chauvinistic way about their own chamber. Former presidential candidate and Senate Majority Leader Bob Dole (R., Kans.) once gently ribbed his House counterparts for their chamber loyalty during negotiations over a bill: "I suggest that my colleagues in the House recognize that the U.S. Senate is part of the Congress [too]. . . ."[10] A more poignant reminder was offered by former House Speaker Jim Wright (D., Tex.) when he resigned in 1989 amidst ethics charges. He spoke movingly of his affection for the House of Representatives:

> I love this institution. I want to assure each of you that under no circumstances, having spent more than half my life here, this House being my home, would I ever knowingly or intentionally do or say anything to violate its rules or detract from its standards. . . . I do not want to be a party to tearing up this institution. I love it.[11]

Chamber loyalty may be particularly intense among members who spend their entire careers in only one of the two chambers.

This book explains the U.S. Congress through the perspective of bicameralism, which is a principal and enduring feature of the institution. It chronicles House and Senate differences en route to explaining how Congress functions. Daniel Wirls has noted that "although bicameralism is one of the fundamental and distinguishing features of American government, the literature on legislatures and Congress contains no sustained treatment of the impact of bicameralism on the legislative process, let alone American government and politics more generally."[12] Ross Baker offers an analogous view: "A sustained comparison of the House and Senate is something that most people assume to exist. They are usually surprised to find that such a book is not to be found."[13] This book helps redress that situation.

Obviously, no single framework can explain a highly complex institution like Congress. Scholars have tried with themes like institutional change and persistence, legislative structures and individual behavior, and centralization/decentralization.[14] The bicameralism paradigm gives readers another alternative, one that springs from theory, tradition, and practical politics. The theme is revisited when it is appropriate to do so, without imposing it artificially in places where it does not fit.

THE THEORY OF BICAMERALISM

The men who wrote Article I of our Constitution, creating a House of Representatives and a Senate, borrowed heavily from the work of French political philosopher Charles de Montesquieu. His influential book, *Spirit of the Laws,* was published a generation before the Constitutional Convention of 1787. Montesquieu argued for the principle of tripartite government, composed of a legislative, executive, and judicial branch. Furthermore, he suggested, the legislature ought to consist of two chambers with "separate views and interests."[15] What better way to ensure that divergent perspectives were brought to bear on public policy issues than to have two distinctive chambers? What better way to avoid rash and poor decisions than to have issues percolate in two chambers?

Yet, the principal virtue of bicameralism was its protection against legislative tyranny. Because people were imperfect, Montesquieu reasoned, they might employ their governing institutions to oppress others. One way to decrease the possibility was to split the legislature into two chambers and to give each "the mutual privilege of rejecting" the other's proposals.

Montesquieu's fondness for bicameralism was informed by the practical experiences of Great Britain, which for centuries had used a bicameral Parliament, consisting of a hereditary House of Lords and a popularly elected House of Commons. To Montesquieu, that formula made sense. The elected assembly would reflect the wishes and passions of the ordinary people, while the unelected nobility would temper their excesses. The net result might be a constant tussle between the chambers, but also a healthy balance between the people's short-term desires and the nation's long-term needs.

Although Montesquieu cannot be credited with originating the concept of bicameralism, he certainly popularized it to America's Founding Fathers. James Madison acknowledged Montesquieu's important contribution in Federalist 47: "If he [Montesquieu] be not the author of this invaluable precept in the science of politics, he has the merit at least of displaying and recommending it most effectually to the attention of mankind."[16]

BICAMERALISM IN THE UNITED STATES

When Americans constructed their colonial legislatures, they basically adopted the principle of bicameralism and accepted the idea of two distinctive chambers, with one more oriented than the other toward the short-term passions of the people. They followed that formula for ten of the thirteen colonial legislatures.[17] The framers of the Constitution also copied it when they created the U.S. Congress. They adopted bicameralism, with the House closely tied to popular sentiment through direct election and the Senate more independent by virtue of indirect election through the state legislatures. (Indirect election of senators was ended in 1913 by the Seventeenth Amendment.) In a story with apocryphal overtones, President George Washington remarked to Thomas Jefferson that just

---

BOX 1.1   The Vulgar Demeanor of a Great Assembly

In the 1830s, a young French aristocrat and public official named Alexis de Tocqueville visited the United States. Over the course of many months, he traveled extensively around the newly emerging nation, and he eventually produced a classic book entitled *Democracy in America*. It is considered by many to be the most penetrating account ever written of the fundamental character of American civilization.

Tocqueville became an early witness to the bicameral nature of Congress, as it was proposed by Montesquieu and instituted by the Founding Fathers. He voiced strong opinions about the suitability of each chamber, believing that the members of the House were markedly inferior to their Senate counterparts. According to Tocqueville:

> When one enters the House of Representatives at Washington, one is struck by the vulgar demeanor of that great assembly. One can often look in vain for a single famous man. Almost all of the members are obscure people whose names form no picture in one's mind. They are mostly village lawyers, tradesmen, or even men of the lowest classes. In a country where education is spread almost universally, it is said that the people's representatives do not always know how to write correctly.[1]

Tocqueville blamed direct popular election of House members for the lowly character of the institution.

In stark contrast, he believed that senators were first-rate public officials. He argued that their indirect election (in the days prior to the Seventeenth Amendment) via state legislatures refined and even purified the choices of the masses. His accolades for senators rivaled his criticism of representatives:

> A couple of paces [away from the House] is the entrance to the Senate, whose narrow precincts contain a large proportion of the famous men of America. There is scarcely a man to be seen there whose name does not recall some recent claim to fame. They are eloquent advocates, distinguished generals, wise magistrates, and noted statesmen. Every word uttered in this assembly would add luster to the greatest parliamentary debates in Europe.[2]

Tocqueville's description was fair, if melodramatic. Yet, it was also time-bound. Tocqueville witnessed bicameralism at a time when the Senate happened to be the more vigorous and influential of the two chambers. At other times in American history, the same could be said of the House.[3] The perception of the Senate as the more important chamber endures, but the reality is more complex.

---

1. Alexis de Tocqueville, *Democracy in America*, trans. George Lawrence, ed. J. P. Mayer (Garden City, N.Y.: Doubleday 1969), 200.
2. Ibid., 200–201.
3. Ross Baker, *House and Senate*, 2d ed. (New York: Norton, 1995), 40–49.

---

as he poured coffee into a saucer to cool it, the Constitution would pour "legislation [from the House] into the senatorial saucer to cool it."[18]

Although many Americans agreed with the principle of an "upper house" checking a popularly elected "lower house," as Montesquieu envisioned, they were not enthusiastic about his preference for a hereditary body of nobles. The idea was contrary to their egalitarian instincts. Thousands of them had fled from nations where kings or nobles exercised power over average people, or they traced their lineage to such people. They refused to accept a new privileged class. Delegates to the Constitutional Convention therefore had to work out some other arrangement than an "upper house" of nobles.

One of the first items of business for the delegates to the Constitutional Convention was the design of Congress. Edmund Randolph began the discussion when he submitted his *Virginia Plan* for consideration. The plan provided for a bicameral legislature, with a House of Delegates elected by the people and a Senate chosen by the members of the House. Randolph's plan was a variation of the British Parliament, with its two chambers and its conception of a "lower" and "upper" house; it was modeled after the Virginia legislature.[19] Its most controversial component was its emphasis on proportional representation in both houses, which meant states would receive seats in Congress according to their population.

The concept of proportional representation did not appeal to the delegates from less populous states. They worried about being dominated by their larger counterparts, a legitimate issue because Virginia, Pennsylvania, and Massachusetts alone would have controlled 46 percent of the seats in both houses of Congress under Randolph's plan.[20] A bicameral legislature with proportional representation in both chambers consigned the less populated states to a minuscule role. In response, "small-state" delegates drafted an alternative called the *New Jersey Plan,* which proposed unicameralism with equal representation for each state—the design of the Articles of Confederation.[21] However, this plan was not taken seriously because the Articles of Confederation had been considered a failure, and the concept of equal representation was manifestly unfair to the more populous states. Yet, the New Jersey Plan served a purpose: It triggered negotiations.

The logjam over bicameralism required concessions by both sides. The delegates tried to reach agreement by asking a committee to study the matter and issue recommendations. The committee proposed this compromise: a House of Representatives, based on the principle of proportional representation, along with a Senate, based on the principle of state equality. In short, the committee simply split the difference. Supporters of the Virginia Plan prevailed on the bicameralism issue and gained proportional representation in the House; those favoring the New Jersey Plan secured equal representation for each state in the Senate. As another part of the compromise, the less populous states were guaranteed a minimum of one representative, while the larger states secured the right to have money bills originate in the House. The latter provision guaranteed that the states with the most resources had the most say over how federal funds would be spent.

This *Great Compromise,* as it is often called, finalized our bicameral congressional structure. The Founding Fathers built on the theoretical arguments and practical experiments of colonial legislatures, but ultimately they negotiated away their political differences. Yet, they still faced the job of convincing Americans to accept their handiwork.

The Federalist Papers were a series of eighty-five essays, written by James Madison, Alexander Hamilton, and John Jay under the alias of "Publius," in support of ratifying the Constitution. Generally, the essays offered intellectual justification for key concepts like tripartite government. Yet, a subset of the papers dealt quite specifically with the organization of Congress, and particularly with the need for bicameralism. The authors' message reflected Montesquieu's earlier arguments. Federalist 62, for instance, pointed out that two distinctive chambers "doubles the security to the [ordinary] people, by requiring the concurrence of

---

BOX 1.2   The First Congress

The House of Representatives convened on April 1, 1789, when the thirtieth member of the fifty-nine member institution arrived in Washington, D.C., thereby creating a quorum. The House wasted no time getting down to business. On that same day, it elected Frederick Muhlenberg from Pennsylvania to the speakership, by a vote of 23–7. His election partly reflected his qualifications as the former Speaker of the Pennsylvania House and as a member of the earlier Continental Congress; his election also was a consolation prize for the large and powerful state of Pennsylvania, which had lost out on both the location of the capital and the presidency and vice-presidency (filled by George Washington from Virginia and John Adams from Massachusetts, respectively).[1]

The next day, Speaker Muhlenberg appointed an informal group of eleven members to draw up rules of procedure, which the entire House adopted a week later. The House also created its very first committee—the Committee on Elections—to certify the election results of the duly elected members. Before that formality was completed, however, the House was already debating a tariff bill.[2]

In contrast, the Senate immediately bogged down. Vice-President-elect John Adams, who under the newly adopted Constitution was to serve as president of the Senate, did not arrive in the Capitol until April 23. A proper and principled man, Adams insisted that the Senate begin its work by establishing appropriate titles for government officials. For instance, he believed the title "president" lacked stature, because it was used in too many circumstances, so he implored his colleagues to consider an alternative phrase. A Senate committee suggested the phrase, "His Highness, the President of the United States of America and Protector of the Rights of the Same."[3] That awkward phrase was soon jettisoned, but not before House members ribbed their Senate colleagues by referring to them individually as "Your Highness of the Senate." For more than three weeks, the Senate lurched from one ceremonial discussion to another, getting almost nowhere with the people's business.

The different character of the House and Senate surfaced in that 1st Congress. Although the Senate long ago completed its debate over titles, its differences from the House endure.

---

1. Ronald M. Peters, Jr., *The American Speakership* (Baltimore: Johns Hopkins University Press, 1990), 24–25.
2. *Origins and Development of Congress* (Washington, D.C.: Congressional Quarterly, 1976), 81.
3. Alvin M. Josephy, Jr., *On the Hill: A History of the American Congress* (New York: Touchstone, 1979), 44–47.

---

two distinct bodies in schemes of usurpation or perfidy . . ."[22] Federalist 51 provided an unrivaled description of separation of powers and of "checks and balances" in government. In it, Madison readily acknowledged the problem of legislative tyranny and then offered bicameralism as the solution:

> In republican government, the legislative authority necessarily predominates. The remedy for this inconveniency is to divide the legislature into different branches; and to render them, by different modes of election and different principles of action, as little connected with each other as the nature of their common functions and their common dependence on the society will admit.[23]

From a different angle, Madison voiced concern in Federalist 48 over a Congress too "inspired by a supposed influence over the people, with an intrepid confidence in its strength."[24]

Clearly, the framers instituted bicameralism to temper the powerful legislature they created. Their design offers a useful framework for examining the operations of the modern Congress.

HOUSE AND SENATE

The House and Senate share obvious affinities, such as "one person, one vote" in each chamber. They also process legislation in a similar way, usually passing it through committees or subcommittees before debating and voting on the floor. Further, they are somewhat similar in terms of their legislative efficiency.[25] Bicameralism does not automatically translate into institutional differences. In spite of obvious affinities, however, the House and Senate are more distinctive than alike, just as the framers hoped.

Table 1.1 summarizes their numerous and significant differences. Among other things, the House and Senate vary in size, electoral cycles, constitutional responsibilities, and rules/procedures. They have different leadership and committee structures and different staffing needs. The Senate is the more prestigious, or "upper house," of the bicameral legislature. It is also the body in which personal ties between members are particularly important. Although the list of differences is not comprehensive, it is sufficient to justify the view "that the Congress is indeed comprised of two fundamentally different institutions," whose differences "thoroughly overshadow their similarities."[26] The same view is expressed by someone who served in both chambers and who traced institutional differences back to the founding period: "The Founding Fathers intended the two [chambers] to be unlike, and their intentions have been very influential to this very day. Although we are physically close together, the House and Senate are far apart in reality."[27]

The differences between the House and Senate are so numerous and fundamental that they sometimes prevent Congress from working efficiently and effectively. A bicameral legislature composed of two distinctive chambers may be a fine hedge against tyranny, but it is also a prescription for deadlock. The inevitable trade-off between security for the citizenry and legislative stalemate was recognized by Publius in Federalist 62: "It must be acknowledged that this complicated check on legislation may in some instances be injurious as well as beneficial."[28] Ultimately, the framers of the Constitution chose security over stalemate, and liberty over efficiency. Their fear of tyranny, fueled by years of conflict with the English king and Parliament, took precedence over their concern with legislative gridlock. In modern times, the opposite may be true. Citizens seem less worried about legislative tyranny than they are about legislative failure to fix the nation's major problems.

In fact, Congress faces a skeptical, even hostile citizenry. People complain that Congress is dominated by special interests, wracked by partisan conflict, and staffed by self-serving elites. Voter hostility has been evident in the 1990s in ballot measures aimed at limiting the number of terms served by members[29] and in challenges to legislative pay and perquisites. In 1992, citizens pressured members

Table 1.1   Selected House–Senate Differences

	House	Senate
Formal		
Membership	435	100
Term of office	2 years	6 years
Minimum age for service	25 years	30 years
Electoral arena	district	state
Leadership	speaker	vice-president
Exclusive powers	raise revenue	advise and consent
Informal		
Institutional prestige	lower	higher
Level of comity	lower	higher
Reliance on staff	lower	higher
Degree of hierarchy	higher	lower
Degree of partisanship	higher	lower
Member accessibility	higher	lower

of Congress to agree to a constitutional amendment drafted in 1789, but dormant for over 200 years, that prevents them from raising their own pay without an intervening election.[30]

Members of Congress seemed to share the public's concern in the early 1990s. Their distress over legislative gridlock contributed to a record number of voluntary retirements during the 102nd Congress (1991–1992).[31] Although many factors explain the sizable number of retirements, including a "check-kiting" scandal in the House, even those untouched by controversy seemed ready to leave out of concern that the institution was "not functioning."[32] Retiring Representative William Broomfield (R., Mich.) provided perspective on the lack of legislative action: "No question about it, in my thirty-six years [in the House] I've never seen anything like it."[33] Senator David Boren (D., Okla.) echoed that sentiment, saying of the 102nd Congress: "This is the worst I've seen it. It's a total gridlock session."[34] In the first session of the 103rd Congress (1993–1994), members even went so far as to create a Joint Committee on the Organization of Congress specifically to examine possible changes in House and Senate rules, procedures, and committee structures. (See Chapter 5 for more details.)

Obviously, the dissatisfaction of members and citizens with legislative gridlock can be an artifact of certain periods, such as the mid-1940s, the late 1970s, and the early 1990s.[35] By the end of the first hundred days of the 104th Congress (1995–1996), by contrast, most dissatisfaction expressed by citizens centered around the rapid handling of the "Contract With America" in the House. However, the 104th Congress seems to have been an anomaly because it brought together newly elected Republican majorities in both chambers for the first time in a generation.[36] A slower and more deliberative pattern of decision making characterized the 105th Congress (1997–1998).[37] Only 60 roll call votes were cast in its first hundred days, compared to more than 300 such votes over the same time period in the 104th Congress.[38]

Although it is vital to understand similarities and differences in the House and Senate, it is also important to consider whether bicameralism impedes effectiveness in contemporary times. Is Congress functioning efficiently and governing effectively, given that it is a deliberative institution in a rapidly changing postindustrial society? That subsidiary question is addressed at several points throughout the book.

Subsequent chapters contain both data and description aimed at increasing understanding of the U.S. Congress. Throughout the book, we strive to combine theory and fact, occasionally offering anecdotes that convey the richness of life on the Hill. A comment from a former representative provides a fitting end to a chapter on bicameralism. In response to the observation that partisanship structures operations on the Hill, former Representative Al Swift (D., Wash.) observed that "the Republicans are [only] the opposition . . . the Senate is the enemy."[39]

NOTES

1. *Congressional Record,* January 6, 1987, H6.

2. "Jefferson's Manual" was prepared by Thomas Jefferson between 1797 and 1801 to guide him in his role as president of the Senate. In 1837, the House adopted all provisions of the manual that were consistent with its existing rules and orders. See *Constitution, Jefferson's Manual, Rules of the House of Representatives,* 96th Congress (Washington, D.C.: Government Printing Office, 1979), 109.

3. Ibid., 162.

4. William F. Buckley, "House Attacks Art of Euphemism by Ignoring the Other Body," *Bangor Daily News,* January 22, 1987, 13.

5. Ross K. Baker, *House and Senate,* 2d ed. (New York: Norton, 1989), 24–28.

6. Several excellent works exist on divided party government, such as Morris Fiorina, *Divided Government,* 2d ed. (Boston: Allyn & Bacon, 1996); Charles O. Jones, *The Presidency in a Separated System* (Washington, D.C.: Brookings Institution, 1994); and David R. Mayhew, *Divided We Govern* (New Haven, Conn.: Yale University Press, 1991).

7. James G. Gimpel, *Legislating the Revolution* (Boston: Allyn & Bacon, 1996).

8. "Contract Score Card," *Congressional Quarterly Weekly Report,* December 9, 1995, 3713; an excellent discussion of bicameral differences in budget issues may be found in Barbara Sinclair, *Unorthodox Lawmaking* (Washington, D.C.: CQ Press, 1997), 175–216.

9. Jackie Koszczuk, "With Tone, Tenor of First Session, It Seemed Like Old Times," *Congressional Quarterly Weekly Report,* December 6, 1997, 2975-3025.

10. Lawrence D. Longley and Walter J. Oleszek, *Bicameral Politics* (New Haven, Conn.: Yale University Press, 1989), 21.

11. *Congressional Record,* May 31, 1989, H2239, H2248.

12. Daniel Wirls, "Evaluating Bicameralism: The Gap Between Theory and Evidence," paper presented at the Annual Meeting of the American Political Science Association, Chicago, September 3–6, 1992.

13. Baker, *House and Senate,* 7.

14. See respectively, Barbara Hinckley, *Stability and Change in Congress,* 4th ed. (New York: Harper & Row, 1988); Roger H. Davidson and Walter J. Oleszek, *Congress and Its Members,* 6th ed. (Washington, D.C.: CQ Press, 1998); and Burdett A. Loomis, *The Contemporary Congress,* 2d ed. (New York: St. Martin's Press, 1998).

15. Baron de Montesquieu, *The Spirit of Laws,* Vol. 1, trans. Thomas Nugent (New York: Colonial Press, 1899), 155.

16. Alexander Hamilton, John Jay, and James Madison, *The Federalist,* intro. Edward Mead Earle (New York: Modern Library, 1937), 313.

17. *Origins and Development of Congress* (Washington, D.C.: Congressional Quarterly, 1976), 24.

18. Suzy Platt, ed., *Respectfully Quoted* (Washington, D.C.: Congressional Quarterly, 1992), 60.

19. Christopher Collier and James Lincoln Collier, *Decision in Philadelphia* (New York: Ballantine Books, 1986), 74–75.

20. *Origins and Development of Congress,* 33.

21. Collier and Collier, *Decision in Philadelphia,* 144.

22. Hamilton, Jay, and Madison, *The Federalist,* 338.

23. Ibid., 332.

24. Ibid., 322–323.

25. Norman J. Ornstein, "The House and Senate in a New Congress," in *The New Congress,* ed. Thomas E. Mann and Norman J. Ornstein (Washington, D.C.: AEI, 1981), 363–371; Baker, *House and Senate,* 175–176; Edward G. Carmines and Lawrence C. Dodd, "Bicameralism in Congress: The Changing Partnership," in *Congress Reconsidered,* 3d ed., ed. Lawrence C. Dodd and Bruce I. Oppenheimer (Washington, D.C.: Congressional Quarterly, 1985), 426–427.

26. David C. Kozak, "House–Senate Differences: A Test Among Interview Data," in *Congress and Public Policy,* 2d ed., ed. David C. Kozak and John D. Macartney (Chicago: Dorsey Press, 1987), 80. For a statistical assessment that confirms bicameral differences, see Gary J. Miller, Thomas H. Hammond, and Charles Kile, "Bicameralism and the Core: An Experimental Test," *Legislative Studies Quarterly* (February 1996): 83–103.

27. Ibid., 84.

28. Hamilton, Jay, and Madison, *The Federalist,* 402.

29. For a comprehensive review of the term limits issue prior to the Supreme

Court's ruling against such limits (in *U.S. Term Limits* v. *Thornton,* 131 L. Ed. 2d 881 [1995]), see Gerald Benjamin and Michael J. Malbin, eds., *Limiting Legislative Terms* (Washington, D.C.: Congressional Quarterly, 1992). For a subsequent analysis, see Gary W. Copeland, "Are Term Limits Still Needed? The Rationale for Term Limits After the 104th Congress," paper delivered at the Annual Meeting of the American Political Science Association, San Francisco, September 1996.

30. For background on the amendment and its wording, see Laura Michaelis, "1789 Pay Raise Amendment Returns to Haunt Congress," *Congressional Quarterly Weekly Report,* May 9, 1992, 1230–1231.

31. Jeffrey L. Katz, "Record Rate of Retirements Suggests Major Shake-Up," *Congressional Quarterly Weekly Report,* April 4, 1992, 851–855.

32. Rhodes Cook, "Rudman Bows Out; Eyes on Gregg," *Congressional Quarterly Weekly Report,* March 28, 1992, 828.

33. Associated Press, "Members Chide Congress for Inability to Enact Laws." Reprinted in the *Washington Times,* June 1, 1992, 3.

34. Ibid.

35. In the 1948 presidential election, incumbent Harry Truman waged a campaign against a "do-nothing" Congress. On the 1970s, see Joseph Cooper and William West, "The Congressional Career in the 1970s," in *Congress Reconsidered,* 2d ed., ed. Lawrence C. Dodd and Bruce I. Oppenheimer (Washington, D.C.: Congressional Quarterly, 1981), 83–106.

36. Ronald D. Elving, "Fireworks of 104th Now a Faint Glow," *Congressional Quarterly Weekly Report,* March 8, 1997, 606.

37. Koszczuk, "With Tone, Tenor of First Session, It Seemed Like Old Times," 2975.

38. John McCaslin, "Inside the Beltway," *Washington Times,* Weekly Edition, April 27, 1997, 6.

39. C. Lawrence Evans and Walter J. Oleszek, *Congress Under Fire* (Boston: Houghton Mifflin, 1997), 68.

2

Congress and the Constitution

The Declaration of Independence, written by Thomas Jefferson in 1776, is
a sweeping statement of individual rights, liberty, and equality. It is also a
pointed attack on executive rule. Colonists had suffered at the hands of
King George III and his royal governors for many years, and Jefferson penned a
document listing specific acts that colonists found objectionable. Many of the
complaints involved King George's control over representative assemblies—that
he forced colonial legislatures to adopt his policies, dissolved any legislatures that
objected, and refused to allow the timely replacement of legislatures that he dissolved. Jefferson mentioned those acts as partial justification for dissolving "all
political connection" with Great Britain.

Predictably, the delegates to the Constitutional Convention vested considerable power in the "people's branch" of government. They protected against arbitrary exercise of legislative power by creating two distinctive chambers, along
with a system of checks and balances.

The power of the U.S. Congress is particularly evident in a comparative context. Most democracies use a *parliamentary system* of government.[1] Within that
system, the executive and legislative functions are combined; the party (or coalition of parties) that controls parliament chooses the prime minister and the cabinet—the nation's top executive officials—out of the pool of majority-party
members. The majority-party legislators who are not part of the upper echelon
are called "back-benchers," denoting both their individual insignificance and
their actual physical location behind the leadership whenever parliament is in

session. Their obligation is to follow the party line faithfully, providing votes to implement policies and to keep the government in power. Their counterparts in the minority party (or parties) are quite marginal, because the ruling party governs until such time as it is displaced at the polls. Parliamentary systems are relatively predictable, because the allegiance of individual legislators to their party is virtually unshakeable. Majority-party dominance is routine.

Our system presents a stark contrast. The legislative and executive branches are separated by provisions in the Constitution, and a person's service in one branch precludes service in another. In addition, individual legislators have much more autonomy than their parliamentary counterparts. The electoral fate of members is not necessarily tied to the fortunes of their political party, but rather is determined by swing voters in a district or state. These factors make Congress more independent, unpredictable, and complicated than most parliaments.[2]

Congress also differs by virtue of its broad constitutional authority. Congress was created at a time when powerful representative assemblies were beginning to develop worldwide, and it emerged as one of the most powerful. According to one source: "No other legislature in the world has such a strong constitutional foundation of policy-making powers [as the Congress]."[3] This chapter examines both the extent and the limitations of congressional power, and it discusses the broad functions of Congress.

ENUMERATED AND IMPLIED POWERS OF CONGRESS

The major constitutional powers of Congress are listed in Article I. It is no accident that the very first article focuses on the legislature, nor that this article is nearly as long as the entire rest of the original (unamended) Constitution. The placement and length conveyed the delegates' priorities. The most significant powers bestowed on Congress are known as the *enumerated powers*. They are specified in Article 1, Section 8.

Table 2.1 shows the wide-ranging authority that Congress is given, including the power to declare war, appropriate money, and levy taxes. These prerogatives of the "sword and purse" are the principal powers exercised by any government. They are augmented by other powers that may sound marginal but that are very important. Consider the power to regulate interstate commerce, for instance. This allows Congress to regulate everything from trains, planes, and automobiles to civil rights, cable television, and the World Wide Web, because all of those things involve a person or product crossing state lines. Another example is Congress's authority to borrow money. This power enables Congress to spend more than it collects in revenue each year, with money borrowed from private investors making up the difference. By 1997, Congress had pushed the total national debt past the $4 trillion mark. President Bill Clinton's proposed 1998 budget estimated that $366 billion would be needed simply to pay the interest on the debt.[4]

At the end of Article I, Section 8 is the *implied powers clause,* which allows Congress "to make all laws which shall be necessary and proper" for carrying out its enumerated powers and "all other powers vested by this Constitution in the

Table 2.1   The Enumerated Powers of Congress

Financial	Procedural
tax	establish bankruptcy procedures
spend money	establish lower court systems
borrow money	establish a process for naturalizing citizens
coin money	
regulate commerce	**Miscellaneous**
punish counterfeiters	create a post office
	govern the District of Columbia
Defense-Related	issue patents
declare war	punish pirates
raise armies	
maintain navy	

SOURCE: Compiled by author.

government of the United States, or any department or office thereof." The implied powers clause (also known as the *necessary and proper* or the *elastic clause*) represents a broad grant of constitutional authority. It gives Congress the authority to create federal agencies judged to be essential to the process of governing even though they are not specifically mentioned in the Constitution. In conjunction with its power to regulate interstate commerce, for instance, Congress has created the Department of Commerce, Federal Aviation Administration (FAA), and Federal Communications Commission (FCC).

The Supreme Court laid the groundwork for broad congressional authority by giving an expansive interpretation to the implied powers clause in *McCulloch* v. *Maryland* (1819). In that case, the Court upheld the right of Congress to create a Bank of the United States. Although no such bank was mentioned in the Constitution the Court ruled that Congress's powers to tax, to borrow money, to regulate commerce, and to declare and conduct war implied the authority to create a Bank of the United States. Chief Justice John Marshall wrote for the Court: "Let the end be legitimate, let it be within the scope of the Constitution, and all means which are appropriate, which are plainly adapted to the end . . . are constitutional."[5] The sweeping language fixed a broad definition of implied powers for Congress, which it has used to create most of the agencies and programs of the federal government.

In addition to its enumerated and implied powers, Congress has virtual autonomy over its own operations. Both chambers are allowed to choose their own officers, to determine the winner of contested elections, and to punish members for misconduct. Both chambers are allowed to develop their own rules and proceedings. In addition, although required by the Constitution to keep a record of their deliberations, both chambers permit individual members to tailor their comments and to add extraneous material to the permanent record through the process of "revising and extending" remarks made during debate. Critics claim that this process creates an inaccurate account of congressional proceedings, but it also encourages individual members to submit information and opinions on key issues without consuming the institution's limited time. Finally, members have the right to set their salaries, within the parameters of the Twenty-Seventh Amendment (requiring an intervening election).

Members have other rights that they often take for granted but that are crucial to doing their job. The *speech and debate clause* (Article I, Section 6) protects members from the consequences of comments they make on the House or Senate floor. Imagine if every remark a representative or senator uttered could result in a lawsuit! A member who attacked the unethical behavior of administration officials or who maligned polluters for besmirching the environment might have a real problem. The Supreme Court has realized the importance of the "speech and debate" clause and has protected it from any serious challenge.[6] Another crucial right enables members to travel freely to congressional sessions. Unless a member is charged with treason, a felony, or breach of the peace, he or she is guaranteed unimpeded travel to and from Congress. The provision may seem superfluous, but it protects members against harassment or arrest by their political opponents.

CONGRESS AND OTHER BRANCHES

The powers given to Congress under the Constitution exceed those already mentioned. Congress also has authority relative to the other branches of government.

With respect to the executive branch, Congress may dictate the structure of the bureaucracy. It is free to create or close agencies or programs, increase or decrease agency jurisdiction, and determine agency budgets. Congress also has power relative to the president, such as the right to override a presidential veto of legislation by a two-thirds vote in each chamber. Furthermore, Congress may *impeach* and even remove a president from office for "treason, bribery, or other high crimes and misdemeanors." In the case of impeachment, Congress uses this bicameral division of labor: The House passes articles of impeachment, and the Senate decides whether to convict and remove a president from office. The impeachment process may sound purely mechanical, but it is an important political weapon, because the conduct of a president may be circumscribed by the existence of the impeachment process. For example, President Richard Nixon resigned after the House Judiciary Committee passed three articles of impeachment for his role in the Watergate scandal.[7] Finally, the Senate has *advice-and-consent powers* (lacked by the House), such as treaty approval, as well as the power to confirm the appointment of top executive branch officials, ambassadors, and federal judges. These latter powers serve as a check on the executive branch and are a major reason the Senate is considered the more prestigious chamber.

Congressional power over the courts includes the right to determine the size of the Supreme Court, to establish a system of "inferior" federal courts (meaning those below the Supreme Court), and to impeach and remove federal judges

---

BOX 2.1 Showdown Over the Legislative Veto

Time magazine called the Supreme Court's ruling in *Immigration and Naturalization Service* v. *Chadha* (1983) an "epic court decision."[1] In one ruling, the Supreme Court struck down a part, if not all, of more than 200 laws in force.

The fate of an individual was at stake—stereo salesperson Jagdish Chadha, who was trying to avoid deportation by the Immigration and Naturalization Service (INS) after his student visa had expired. The much larger issue in the case, though, was the constitutionality of the so-called legislative veto. The veto is simply language written into a law by Congress that allows either chamber to overturn (or veto) executive branch decisions. In the case of Chadha, the INS decided that he could stay in the country—a decision that the House overturned with the legislative veto language it had inserted in the 1952 Immigration Act.

Congress first used the legislative veto in 1932, when it permitted President Herbert Hoover to reorganize the structure of the executive branch, subject to congressional approval. Hoover appreciated the latitude he was given by Congress, which had the right under the Constitution to organize the executive branch as it saw fit. In turn, Congress appreciated Hoover's willingness to work out an arrangement and then subject it to congressional approval. In recognition of this mutually beneficial arrangement, Congress and the executive branch both accepted insertion of legislative veto language in more than 200 laws from 1932 to 1983, including major laws such as the War Powers Act of 1973 and the Congressional Budget Impoundment and Control Act of 1974. Presidents would have preferred the grants of authority being given to them by Congress without any strings attached, of course, but they accepted the legislative veto as a practical compromise.

That arrangement did not work well for Jagdish Chadha, who challenged the legislative veto when the House used it to deport him. He argued that the legislative veto violated the Constitution's "bicameralism" and "presentation" provisions, which require that laws be passed by both houses of Congress and then presented to the president for his signature or veto. Chadha argued that Congress was violating the Constitution when it simply inserted one-house legislative veto language into bills and then applied it in specific cases years later. Congress flatly disagreed, arguing that the legislative veto was merely a natural extension of its comprehensive lawmaking authority. In fact, the attorney for the House of Representatives, Eugene Gressman, asked the Supreme Court simply to dismiss the case rather than rule on it. In the absence of dismissal, Gressman said, the Court was obliged to side with Congress, in acknowledgment of the broad "implied powers" established in *McCulloch* v. *Maryland* (1819).[2]

(thirteen judges have been impeached for reasons ranging from their decisions to their own personal conduct, with six actually removed from the bench).[8] Congress may also reverse or restrict court decisions. Congress has overturned Supreme Court decisions on four separate occasions, with the help of the states, by passing a constitutional amendment. In addition, Congress regularly writes laws that narrow judicial decisions.[9] That practice dates back to Congress's reversal of the Supreme Court's decision in *Pennsylvania* v. *Wheeling and Belmont Bridge Company* (1851).[10] The guiding principle in such legislative actions is that Congress take the Court's objections to a previous law into account when it passes a new law.

Finally, Congress may restrict the appellate jurisdiction of the Supreme Court; that is, it can prevent the Court from hearing certain types of cases on appeal. Precedent exists for that tactic. In *Ex Parte McCardle* (1869), the Supreme

BOX 2.1 continued

By a 7–2 margin, the Supreme Court flatly rejected that position, siding with Chadha. It declared the section of the 1952 Immigration Act—containing the legislative veto language—unconstitutional on the grounds that it violated the "bicameralism" and "presentation" requirements of the Constitution. The Supreme Court stopped short of proclaiming the entire Immigration Act of 1952 unconstitutional, saying only that the provision embedded within it violated the Constitution. The sweeping language of the Court's decision, however, seemed to indicate that even two-house legislative vetoes (which obviously did not violate the bicameralism requirement), as well as entire congressional statutes, did not pass constitutional muster. The legislative veto seemed to be wiped off the books.

Yet, the reality is much more complicated. In some cases, Congress has discarded legislative veto provisions; in other cases, it has rewritten them; and in still other cases, in spite of the Supreme Court's ruling, it has continued to insert legislative veto language into bills.[3] It does so simply because the device serves the needs of Congress and of executive branch agencies.

Why does Congress "thumb its nose" at the Court? And how does it get away with it? The answer is that Congress has never fully accepted the Court's decision, particularly as it involved two-house legislative vetoes, and that agencies are reluctant to bring suit over the issue. They might win the battle, getting the courts to strike down legislative veto provisions, but they might lose the war in the process. Any executive agency that challenges Congress, which holds authority over its annual appropriations and even its very existence, assumes a grave risk. Executive branch agencies are usually willing to look the other way when they are affected by a legislative veto, and Congress still feels free to insert them from time to time. The Supreme Court cannot rule on cases unless they are brought forward, and the Court often is reluctant to directly challenge Congress even when cases are marshaled. The result is a formal stand on principle by the various branches of the federal government, with an informal understanding between them to leave alone what seems to work. Its reflects the genius of the system within the confines of the Constitution.

1. Kurt Anderson, "An Epic Court Decision," *Time*, July 4, 1983, 12.
2. "Arguments Before the Court: Constitutional Law," *United States Law Week* 51(23) (December 14, 1982), 51 LW 3453–3455.
3. An extensive and excellent discussion in the aftermath of the *INS* v. *Chadha* decision may be found in Louis Fisher, *The Politics of Shared Power*, 2d ed. (Washington, D.C.: CQ Press, 1987), 94–104.

Court ruled that it was powerless to hear the case of a man who was arrested for publishing "incendiary" articles about the Union's military occupation of Mississippi during the Civil War, on the grounds that Congress had passed legislation preventing the Court from hearing appeals on cases decided by military tribunals. The Court stated flatly that the "case must be dismissed for want of jurisdiction."[11] Keep in mind, however, that this case surfaced in the aftermath of a civil war, when feelings ran high. During more normal times, the constitutional prerogative of Congress to restrict the Court's jurisdiction is fairly meaningless, because Congress is not inclined to do so. Many members of Congress are lawyers by training, and they are reluctant to tamper with the Supreme Court's jurisdiction. Their viewpoint was summarized by Representative Robert Kastenmeier (D., Wis.) during hearings on "court-stripping" in 1981: "If

---

BOX 2.2   The Court Versus Congress in the 1990s

The Supreme Court is in the midst of a major reevaluation of Congress's legislative authority over the states. The reevaluation is being driven by a block of conservative justices determined to restore greater authority to the states.[1]

The trend first surfaced in *New York* v. *United States* (1992). In that case, the Supreme Court struck down a provision passed by Congress that required states to take possession of nuclear waste generated by commercial nuclear reactors.

The next pivotal case occurred several years later. In *Lopez* v. *United States* (1995), the Supreme Court was asked to weigh the constitutionality of the Gun-Free School Zone Act, approved by Congress in 1990. The legislation had passed in the aftermath of highly publicized shootings in public schools; it prohibited the possession of a firearm within 1000 feet of a school. By a narrow 5–4 margin, the Supreme Court struck down the law, rejecting the position that Congress had acted within its interstate commerce powers when it set limits on firearm possession.

The reevaluation of legislative authority continued with a second firearms case. In 1993, Congress passed the so-called Brady Bill. Named after former presidential advisor James Brady, who was shot during an assassination attempt on President Reagan, the bill had a provision requiring a five-day waiting period for anyone trying to purchase a handgun. The waiting period provided an opportunity for police to conduct a background check. In two related cases—*Mack* v. *United States* (1997) and *Printz* v. *United States* (1997)—the Supreme Court ruled by a 5–4 margin that Congress could not require state and local officials to conduct background checks while letting stand the five-day waiting period.[2]

Two days later, the Supreme Court handed down another major decision, striking down the Religious Freedom Restoration Act. That act, passed by Congress in 1993, required the government to show a "compelling interest" in any case in which it infringed on religious liberty. When a Catholic church in a Texas city was denied permission by the city government to expand because its building was located in a historic district, the church brought suit under the 1993 act. In *City of Boerne* v. *Flores* (1997), the Supreme Court ruled by a 6–3 margin that Congress had infringed on the Court's power and on states' rights when it passed the act.[3]

Will Congress strike back at the Supreme Court, trying to write laws that circumvent its rulings? Some liberals may wish to do so, but many conservatives on Capitol Hill support the idea of restoring power to the states. Yet, many conservatives expressed displeasure with the Court's decision on religious freedom. About the only certain development is that Congress and the Court will eye each other warily during this period of reevaluation of legislative authority over the states.

---

1. Dan Carney, "High Court Shows Inclination to Rein in Congress," *Congressional Quarterly Weekly Report,* January 25, 1997, 241–244.
2. Dan Carney, "Brady Decision Reflects Effort to Curb Congress' Authority," *Congressional Quarterly Weekly Report,* June 28, 1997, 1524–1525.
3. Dan Carney, "Religious Freedom Act Overturned, Curbing Congress' Power," *Congressional Quarterly Weekly Report,* June 28, 1997, 1526–1527.

Congress can decide willy-nilly that the Supreme Court and the federal appellate courts have no appellate jurisdiction [over an issue] by simple majority vote, then we have arrogated to ourselves considerable power."[12]

We should add that these interbranch relationships are a two-way street. By custom, the president is given the power to negotiate treaties for Senate approval, and by law, the president is given the right to veto acts of Congress. The president also may fill vacancies when Congress is out of session and may convene the legislature in extraordinary situations. The president may even adjourn Congress if it fails to agree on its own adjournment date, although that has never happened.

For its part, the Supreme Court may declare acts of Congress unconstitutional. The power of affirming or denying the constitutionality of legislative acts is known as *judicial review*. This judicial prerogative was mentioned in Federalist 78 by Alexander Hamilton, who argued that the courts are obliged "to declare all acts contrary to the manifest tenor of the Constitution void."[13] Yet, the framers of the Constitution did not expressly grant the Supreme Court that power. Instead, the Court quietly garnered it in *Marbury* v. *Madison* (1803); since that decision, the Court has struck down 137 federal and about 1,000 state statutes.[14] One of the most visible recent cases involved the Communications Decency Act of 1996 (PL 104-104). The Supreme Court struck down portions of that law in *Reno* v. *ACLU* (1997), ruling that attempts to regulate pornography on the Internet violated First Amendment rights of free speech.[15] The decision upheld lower court rulings.

LIMITS ON CONGRESSIONAL POWER

Although the architects of the Constitution wanted a strong Congress, they curbed legislative power with a system of checks and balances and with bicameralism. They also explicitly denied powers to Congress; these limits are listed in Article I, Section 9.

One of the important limits on congressional power is a ban on *ex post facto laws*. This ban means that Congress cannot enact retroactive criminal laws, subjecting a person to arrest for some action that was not illegal at the time it was performed. For example, assume that Congress outlawed the use of all tobacco products by citizens. The prohibition against ex post facto laws means that a person could not be prosecuted for having been a cigarette smoker before smoking was made illegal. Similarly, Congress cannot pass *bills of attainder*—that is, laws that punish an individual or specific group without a trial or conviction. Congress also cannot suspend *habeas corpus,* which is the right of citizens to know why they are under arrest. Finally, Congress cannot spend money except through lawful appropriation, nor can it selectively tax products exported from a particular state.

Two years after the original Constitution was ratified, the ten amendments known as the *Bill of Rights* were added. They further circumscribe congressional power. The First Amendment, for instance, states that "Congress shall make no law respecting an establishment of religion, or prohibiting the free exercise thereof; or abridging the freedom of speech, or of the press; or the right of the people peaceably to assemble, and to petition the government for a redress of grievances." Other amendments guarantee citizens the right to bear arms, to keep soldiers from being quartered in their homes, to receive a speedy and public trial, and to be protected from unreasonable searches. The Ninth Amendment states that people may have rights beyond those listed in the Constitution (such as privacy). And the Tenth Amendment reserves powers to the states that are not directly given to the federal government. These written guarantees protect the rights of individual citizens, limit congressional power, and literally define the essence of democratic government.

In the tradition of Aesop's fables, there is a simple moral to the story of congressional power: It is potent but difficult to wield. The Constitution provides extensive formal authority for Congress, but it then structures the institution so that it has difficulty exerting that power. Congress has the necessary tools to dominate the other branches of government. However, it often lacks the will because of partisan divisions and because two very different chambers operate with shared and separate powers.

Interestingly, the framers of the Constitution anticipated a difference in the true exercise of power by the House and Senate. They thought the House would be more assertive. For one thing, it had the exclusive right to introduce revenue bills, a power that seemed to dwarf the Senate's "advise and consent" powers. For another, representatives were elected directly by the people, rather than indirectly through the state legislatures, and direct election seemed to provide greater legitimacy. Furthermore, House members represented the population centers by virtue of the principle of proportional representation; the larger size of the House and its overrepresentation of the interests of the major cities seemed to provide leverage against the Senate. In Federalist 58, Publius explained the expected dominance of the House:

> Notwithstanding the equal authority which will subsist between the two houses on all legislative subjects, except the originating of money bills, it cannot be doubted that the House, composed of the greater number of members, when supported by the more powerful states, and speaking the known and determined sense of a majority of the people, will have no small advantage in a question depending on the comparative firmness of the two houses.[16]

Today these arguments are less relevant. Although the House has the exclusive right to originate revenue bills, for instance, the Senate easily circumvents the constitutional prohibition by simply substituting its revenue measure for the text of a minor House-passed bill. In addition, the House no longer possesses legitimacy derived from direct election, because senators are also directly elected. Finally, the notion that the House has leverage because it represents the population centers is less pertinent in a technological era, when both representatives and senators speak directly to large national audiences. The House and Senate remain different institutions, but they are similar relative to carrying out their constitutional mandate.

FUNCTIONS OF CONGRESS

Congress is expected to perform many different tasks because it has so many constitutional responsibilities. Its functions range from working with the president to formulate a budget to sending information to students working on term papers. It is difficult to actually describe all that Congress is supposed to do because its tasks are so varied. However, some of its central constitutional obligations are to legislate, to oversee implementation of laws by the bureaucracy, and to represent citizens.

Passing Laws

The principal responsibility of Congress is to legislate. Article I of the Constitution vests "all legislative powers in a Congress of the United States," and that function is probably the one that most citizens would identify as primary. The legislative function is paramount because our society is predicated on the rule of law. Former Senate Majority Leader George Mitchell (D., Maine) elegantly summarized the centrality of law in our society, in the context of a congressional investigation:

> The rule of law is critical in our society. It is the great equalizer. Because in America, everybody is equal before the law. We must never allow the end to justify the means, where the law is concerned, however important and noble an objective. And surely, democracy abroad is important and is noble. [Yet] it cannot be achieved at the expense of the rule of law in our country.[17]

The lawmaking responsibilities of Congress have dramatically increased over time. In 1790, when the first national census was conducted, 3.9 million people were living a mostly agrarian life in thirteen states; today, more than 250 million Americans live a fast-paced, mostly urban and suburban life in fifty states. Congress has passed more laws as society has become more complex and interdependent.[18] Table 2.2 reports the number of public bills enacted by Congress, in fifty-year increments, since the Constitution took effect in 1789.[19]

The table shows a steady rise in the number of public bills. In the first quartile (1789–1839), Congress passed 3,163 bills. In the second quartile (1840–1889), that number more than doubled to 7,279, and in the third quartile (1890–1939), it more than doubled again, to 15,372 bills. In the fourth quartile (1940–1989), the number rose another 20 percent over the preceding period, for a total of 18,381 bills. Put another way, of the 44,195 bills passed by Congress over 200 years, 41 percent of those were passed in the past 50 years. Although the table does not report annual variation, the larger pattern is clear: Congress has passed more and more bills over time.

Related to the increase in volume is an increase in complexity and scope. Steven Smith has shown that even as the number of enacted bills leveled off at 600–1,000 annually, the total number of pages of those bills more than tripled.[20] Other scholars have confirmed that finding, showing that the average length of a bill increased from 2.5 pages during the 80th Congress (1947–1948) to 19.1 pages in the 104th Congress (1995–1996).[21]

Another dimension in Congress's legislative responsibilities is its expanding jurisdiction during our nation's history. Not surprisingly, the 1st Congress (1789-1790) began very slowly, focusing mostly on organizational and procedural matters. Fifty-nine representatives and twenty-six senators devoted themselves mainly to constructing committees, establishing precedents for inviting the president to Capitol Hill, setting pay scales, and determining internal procedures for ratifying treaties.[22] Their legislative role was confined to authorizing a patent office, a census of inhabitants, and a provisional government for western territories.[23] They finished work during two brief sessions.

**Table 2.2   Number of Public Bills Passed by
Congress in Fifty-Year Increments, 1789–1989[a]**

Period	Number Passed
1789–1839	3,163
1840–1889	7,279
1890–1939	15,372
1940–1989	18,381
Total	44,195

[a]The total number of public bills passed from the 101st Congress
(1989–1990) through the 104th Congress (1995–1996) is 2,038.

SOURCE: Based on U.S. Department of Commerce, Bureau of the
Census, *Historical Statistics of the United States: Colonial Times to
1970* (Washington, D.C.: Government Printing Office, 1975); and
Norman J. Ornstein, Thomas E. Mann, and Michael J. Malbin, *Vital
Statistics on Congress 1997–1998* (Washington, D.C.: Congressional
Quarterly, 1998), 167.

The 2nd Congress (1791–1792) refined procedures and held the first formal
legislative investigation. Representative Hugh Williamson (N.C.) introduced a
resolution authorizing a House committee to investigate a military defeat in the
western lands by several Native American tribes.[24] That investigation set the stage
for many others. In a notable ten-year period (1816–1826), Congress undertook
twenty major investigations.[25]

Throughout the 1800s, congressional responsibilities kept expanding. As set-
tlers pushed westward, they demanded more protection and better roads.
Congress responded by appropriating money for military expeditions and for
internal improvements. As abolitionist sentiment grew in the North, Congress
became a focal point for the debate over the moral and economic consequences
of slavery. As immigrants started arriving in the United States in record numbers,
Congress was besieged by conflicting demands to stem the flow and to integrate
those who were allowed to enter. Those economic and moral issues created a
larger lawmaking role for Congress.

When the Industrial Revolution took root, capitalist barons began amassing
great wealth. Before long, citizens demanded that Congress break up the barons'
corporate monopolies. Their demands created a new task for Congress: regulating private industry. In 1887, Congress passed the Interstate Commerce Act,
which actively regulated railroads. Then, in 1890, Congress passed the Sherman
Anti-Trust Act, which prohibited industrial monopolies from engaging in any
"restraint of trade or commerce."[26] Congress thereby added regulation of business to its portfolio of tasks.

Congress's jurisdiction was further enlarged in the twentieth century.[27] The
Sixteenth Amendment, ratified in 1913, formally gave Congress the power to
levy income taxes; it used that prerogative to raise revenue and to redistribute the
wealth generated by the Industrial Revolution. During the Great Depression of
the 1930s, Congress acted on President Franklin Roosevelt's requests for legislation to combat unemployment and poverty, creating a "New Deal" in the process.
In the 1960s, President Lyndon Johnson pushed Congress to redouble its com-

BOX 2.3 The Golden Age of the Senate

In the period leading up to the Civil War, visitors thronged to the Senate chamber to watch the great debates between northern and southern senators. They heard some of the most eloquent words ever spoken in the chamber.

The first major debate started in the 21st Congress (1829–1830), when Senator Robert Hayne (S.C.) rose in opposition to a bill limiting the sale of Western lands. He called on westerners and southerners to unite against the Northeast, saying that its opposition to western expansion was an attempt to keep low-wage workers trapped in the industrial corridor. He attacked protective tariffs and consolidation of federal power.

The next day, Senator Daniel Webster (Mass.) challenged his colleague to a series of discussions about federal power. Senator Hayne eagerly accepted the challenge, and over the course of two days in January 1830, he delivered a brilliant justification of the states' rights position.

Senator Webster replied with an equally brilliant defense of federal power, which turned into a stirring defense of the Union. He captured the imagination of nationalistic westerners with his beautiful imagery: "When my eyes shall be turned to behold for the last time the sun in heaven, may I not see Him shining on the broken and dishonored fragments of a once glorious union . . . liberty *and* Union, now and forever, one and inseparable."[1]

Twenty years later, during the 31st Congress (1849–1850), Webster rose once again to challenge the arguments of a South Carolina senator. This time, his protagonist was John Calhoun, former vice-president of the United States and leading proponent of the southern cause in the Senate. Calhoun bitterly opposed a political compromise crafted by Senator Henry Clay (Ky.) to salvage the Union; Webster spoke elegantly on behalf of it, proclaiming that "I wish to speak today . . . not as a Massachusetts man, nor as a Northern man, but as an American. . . . I speak today for preservation of the Union. Hear my cause."[2] Clay's "Compromise of 1850" eventually passed, but it only delayed the coming Civil War. The period preceding the war—involving the Webster–Hayne and the Webster–Calhoun debates—is known as the Golden Age in Senate history.[3]

---

1. Quoted in Alvin M. Josephy, Jr., *On the Hill* (New York: Touchstone, 1979), 168.
2. Ibid., 196.
3. *Guide to Congress*, 2d ed. (Washington, D.C.: Congressional Quarterly, 1976), 77.

mitment to social welfare, through ambitious federal anti-poverty programs and through grants to the states.

Also in the 1960s, ethnic minorities and women began vigorously demanding equal political rights and a larger share of the nation's economic pie. A *conservative coalition* of southern Democrats and Republicans in Congress had stymied protective and remedial legislation for minority groups for years. However, under intense pressure from aggrieved groups and from many liberal politicians, Congress passed the Civil Rights Act of 1964, the Voting Rights Act of 1965, and the Open Housing Act of 1968. Those laws banned discrimination in the public realm on the basis of race, sex, religion, or national origin. Although many civil rights issues are ultimately decided in the courts, they occupy considerable time on the part of Congress.[28]

The lawmaking responsibilities of the contemporary Congress are daunting. Congress is expected to formulate an annual budget and to protect American interests around the world. Yet, it is also asked to provide health care, stop unfair trading practices, protect whales, and revamp public education, to name only a few responsibilities. Congress's agenda seems as full as at any time in its history.[29]

BOX 2.4 Civil Rights or Special Rights?

The issue of gay rights first burst onto the national scene in 1969, when hundreds of gay activists in New York City who felt they were being harassed fought with police. It gained additional attention in 1977, when television spokesperson Anita Bryant led a campaign to rescind a local Florida ordinance that extended civil rights protections to homosexuals.

At issue is the legal status of gays. Are they already protected by existing civil rights laws, and therefore constantly demanding "special rights," as their opponents claim, or are they a persecuted minority simply trying to establish their essential civil rights, as their proponents claim?

Generally, Congress remained aloof from those arguments and from local conflicts as the gay rights movement emerged, declining to consider measures that either advanced or restricted gay rights. In the 1980s, however, the dynamics began to change. Many states and communities began to pass ordinances banning discrimination on the basis of sexual orientation; other states retained their ordinances against practices such as sodomy.[1] In 1986, in a landmark gay rights case, a sharply divided Supreme Court ruled in *Bowers* v. *Hardwick* that a Georgia law prohibiting sodomy was constitutional. Many liberals and civil libertarians joined with gay rights activists to protest that decision, while many colleges and universities responded by enacting nondiscrimination provisions on campus.

In the 1992 presidential campaign, candidate Bill Clinton said that if he were elected president, he would repeal the existing prohibition against homosexuals serving in the U.S. military. When he tried to make good on that campaign promise, however, he encountered fierce opposition on Capitol Hill, led by Senate Armed Services Committee Chair Sam Nunn (D., Ga.). Throughout much of 1993, the president tried to reach a compromise with opponents in Congress. They eventually agreed to a policy of "don't ask, don't tell." This meant that the military services would not ask questions of prospective military recruits about their homosexuality, but that individuals seeking to enlist, or already serving in the military, could be discharged if they admitted to homosexuality.[2] The compromise became part of the fiscal year 1994 National Defense Authorization Act, which President Clinton signed into law on November 30, 1993.

As the issue of gays in the military was being fought out in the Capitol, states such as Oregon, Colorado, and Maine emerged as linchpins for anti–gay rights referenda. Probably the most celebrated case occurred in Colorado, where voters narrowly approved "Amendment 2" in 1992, which invalidated existing state laws protecting homosexuals from discrimination. (Both Oregon and Maine voted down their own versions of this referendum, although Maine reversed direction in 1998). Once the measure

Overseeing Implementation of Laws

A second major function of Congress is to oversee implementation of the laws it enacts. That job means supervising fourteen cabinet departments, along with hundreds of agencies, divisions, and bureaus, that together employ nearly 3 million people.[30] Although the Constitution does not mention legislative oversight per se, it does give Congress the power to appropriate funds, and it requires dissemination of a "regular statement and account of the receipts and expenditures of all public money from time to time." Implied in that constitutional requirement is Congress's power to ensure that public funds are being spent as intended.

When Congress creates a program, it charges the federal bureaucracy with implementing it. Most congressional oversight focuses on the quality of policy implementation. Congress checks to make sure that its mandates are being fol-

BOX 2.4 continued

passed, gay rights advocates sued to have it struck down. In *Romer* v. *Evans* (1996), another landmark gay rights case (with a very different outcome), the Supreme Court ruled that Amendment 2 effectively singled out gays and therefore discriminated against them. It struck down Amendment 2 as an unconstitutional violation of the "Equal Protection Clause" of the Fourteenth Amendment.

Back on Capitol Hill, Congress grappled with another dimension of gay rights—the legality of same-sex marriages. In 1991, several same-sex couples in Hawaii sued for the right to be legally married, eventually winning in the state Supreme Court. Facing the prospect of same-sex couples being married in Hawaii and then residing in other states where they would presumably be entitled to the same legal status because of the "full faith and credit clause" of the Constitution (requiring states to honor one another's contracts), several dozen state legislatures moved to forbid same-sex marriages.[3] Congress also did so, with unusual speed.

In spring 1996, Representatives Bob Barr (R., Ga.) and Steve Largent (R., Okla.) introduced a "Defense of Marriage Act"; a similar bill was introduced in the Senate by Don Nickles (R., Okla.) and Bob Dole (R., Kans.). It defined marriage as a legal union between one man and one woman, and it relieved any state from having to recognize a same-sex marriage performed in another state. Two months later, the House approved the measure without amendment by a 342–67 vote; in September, the Senate then approved the same measure passed by the House by an 85–14 vote.[4] President Clinton signed the measure into law on September 21, 1996.

Gay rights issues continue to reverberate on Capitol Hill. On the one hand, some members of Congress openly admit their homosexuality. Furthermore, Congress has passed bills making it easier for gay people to immigrate to the United States and requiring the Justice Department to publish data on "hate crimes" perpetrated against gay people. On the other hand, Congress has kept restrictions for gay people in the military and reinforced traditional heterosexual marriage. And Congress has yet to formulate clear policies on withholding or extending further protections.

1. James Button, Barbara Rienzo, and Kenneth D. Wald, "The Politics of Gay Rights in American Communities," paper delivered at the Annual Meeting of the American Political Science Association, New York, September 1–4, 1994; David C. Nice, "State Regulation of Intimate Behavior," *Social Science Quarterly* 69(1) (1988): 203–211.
2. David F. Burrelli, "Homosexuals and U.S. Military Personnel Policy: Current Issues," *CRS Issue Brief*, November 4, 1996, 2.
3. Mark Eddy, "Defense of Marriage Act," *CRS Report for Congress*, September 24, 1996, 2; see also Gina Marie Stevens, "Interstate Marriage Recognition and the Defense of Marriage Act," *CRS Report for Congress*, June 7, 1996.
4. Ibid.

lowed faithfully and that the bureaucracy is promulgating acceptable administrative rules in the absence of constant supervision by the legislative branch.

Both the House and the Senate regularly engage in oversight of the executive branch. In the House, the Government Reform and Oversight Committee continuously performs that role; its Senate counterpart is the Governmental Affairs Committee. In addition to those committees, most congressional committees have subcommittees that oversee programs in their policy areas. The House Commerce Committee, for instance, has a separate subcommittee on Oversight and Investigations, which has jurisdiction over the Department of Commerce and the Department of Energy. Committee and subcommittee work is augmented by the *General Accounting Office* (GAO), which audits executive branch expenditures (see Chapter 7).

Congressional oversight periodically involves high drama and extensive publicity. When the Watergate affair of the 1970s and the Iran–Contra affair of the 1980s produced allegations of misconduct, Congress created special committees to investigate.[31] When the space shuttle *Challenger* exploded in 1986, killing six astronauts and a schoolteacher, many congressional committees investigated the National Aeronautics and Space Administration (NASA). After Republicans seized control of the House in the 104th Congress (1995–1996), they tried to institutionalize oversight of the Clinton administration by requiring every committee to submit a comprehensive oversight plan at the start of each congressional session.[32] In the 105th Congress (1997–1998), Republicans focused a major investigation on Democratic Party fund-raising practices, with distinctly mixed results.[33]

Such dramatic examples notwithstanding, most congressional oversight is rather mundane. Unnoticed and unappreciated, it consists of periodic hearings on such issues as automobile emissions and farm price supports—activities that rarely catch the public eye.

Representing Citizens

A third major function of Congress, one that is tacitly assumed rather than explicitly stated in the Constitution, is representating citizens. The concept of representation dates back to the very origins of Western civilization; Aristotle recognized its necessity, given the impossibility of a nation's entire citizenry making decisions. In Federalist 52, however, Publius argued that ancient political philosophers imperfectly understood the concept of representation, because truly representative regimes did not exist until many centuries later.[34] The Founding Fathers spent considerable time explaining the concept and constructing an institution to carry it out.

In colonial times, House members represented about 30,000 constituents, and senators about 150,000; today, House members represent about 570,000 constituents, and senators anywhere from 450,000 to 26 million, depending on the size of the state. Representation is an enormous task in mere mathematical terms. Then, too, citizen expectations are different today. People expect members of Congress to respond to idiosyncratic complaints and requests. To cite an extreme example, a person wrote a letter asking a representative to pressure New York City officials into replacing a Mickey Mouse balloon with a Bullwinkle the Moose balloon in its Columbus Day parade. Others seek help getting loved ones released from jail or complain about the number of real peanuts in peanut butter.[35] The job of representing citizens mushrooms when high expectations, held by thousands of individuals, are combined with technological innovations making it easier for constituents to establish contact.

What does "representation" entail? Although it is difficult to summarize all of its facets, one of its principal components is *articulating citizen views*. Members are obliged to gain understanding of the views of the "folks back home" and then to convey those views to their colleagues, either informally or formally in debate. Anyone who has ever read or watched a debate in Congress knows that members often cite the views of their constituents as justification of their own stance or as evidence of the proper position. Members strive to learn those views by interacting with citizens on a regular basis.

A second component of representation is *educating citizens.* Members of Congress have some responsibility to disseminate information about the programs and policies of the federal government, and to explain complex issues. They educate their constituents through newsletters, interviews, and town meetings.

A third component of representation is *intervening with the bureaucracy.*[36] Citizens sometimes encounter problems with federal government agencies and require assistance. Perhaps a Social Security check was lost, or a relative was denied permission to immigrate. Whatever the circumstances, members of Congress are called on to assist constituents. In a pioneering study, one scholar found that members spent about 25 percent of their time aiding constituents.[37] Although legislative aides have gradually absorbed most of that work, the sheer volume of citizen–agency interaction guarantees that members remain engaged in problem solving.[38]

One of the difficulties facing members of Congress is balancing all of their responsibilities. Representing citizens is a multifaceted task requiring considerable skill, and it is only one aspect of the job. The situation becomes even more complicated because a member's responsibilities often conflict. Do I stay on Capitol Hill to cast a vote on a minor bill, a member muses, or do I keep my promise to attend the Chamber of Commerce luncheon back in my home state? Should I place my legislative obligations first, or my representational responsibilities? These tough choices arise precisely because the Constitution gives Congress so much power and because we ask individual members to do so much.

NOTES

1. Gary W. Copeland and Samuel C. Patterson, eds., *Parliaments in the Modern World: Changing Institutions* (Ann Arbor: University of Michigan Press, 1994).

2. Thomas M. Magstadt and Peter M. Schotten, *Understanding Politics,* 2d ed. (New York: St. Martin's Press, 1988), 102–105.

3. Gerhard Loewenberg and Samuel C. Patterson, *Comparing Legislatures* (Boston: Little, Brown, 1979), 49.

4. "Fiscal 1998 Budget by Function," *Congressional Quarterly Weekly Report,* February 8, 1997, 347.

5. 4 L.Ed 579 (1819).

6. See *Powell* v. *McCormack,* 395 US 486 (1969); *Gravel* v. *United States,* 92 S.Ct. 2614

(1972); *Doe* v. *McMillan,* 93 S.Ct. 2018 (1973).

7. An excellent book on congressional and presidential conflict that discusses impeachment is Louis Fisher, *Constitutional Conflicts Between Congress and the President,* 4th ed. (Lawrence: University Press of Kansas, 1997).

8. William H. Rehnquist, *Grand Inquests* (New York: Morrow, 1992), 119.

9. Joseph T. Keenan, *The Constitution of the United States,* 2d ed. (Chicago: Dorsey Press, 1988), 42–43, 80–81. The amendments overturning Supreme Court decisions are the Eleventh, Fourteenth, Sixteenth, and Twenty-Sixth.

10. For the Supreme Court's initial ruling, and the subsequent ruling after Congress

reversed its initial decision, see 54 US 518 (1851) and 59 US 460 (1856).

11. 19 L.Ed 264 (1869).

12. Nadine Cohodas, "Members Move to Reign in Supreme Court," *Congressional Quarterly Weekly Report,* May 30, 1981, 947.

13. Alexander Hamilton, John Jay, and James Madison, *The Federalist* (New York: Modern Library, 1937), 505.

14. For the Marbury case, see 1 Cranch 137, 2 L.Ed 60 (1803); for the use of judicial review, see Lee Epstein and Thomas G. Walker, *Constitutional Law for a Changing America* (Washington, D.C.: Congressional Quarterly, 1992), 53–54; for the number of laws declared unconstitutional, see Roger H. Davidson and Walter S. Oleszek, *Congress and Its Members,* 6th ed. (Washington, D.C.: CQ Press, 1998), 22, and Steffen W. Schmidt, Mack C. Shelley II, and Barbara A. Bardes, *American Government and Politics Today* (Boston: West/Wadsworth, 1998), 507.

15. Dan Carney, "Court Strikes Down Ban on Internet Indecency," *Congressional Quarterly Weekly Report,* June 28, 1997, 1519.

16. Hamilton, Jay, and Madison, *The Federalist,* 379.

17. "The Committee's Turn: Speeches to North," *New York Times,* July 14, 1987, 12.

18. For a discussion of the quality of laws passed by Congress, and the role of law in modern society, see Theodore J. Lowi, *The End of the Republican Era* (Norman: University of Oklahoma Press, 1996), 245–259.

19. The table excludes the number of "private bills" passed.

20. Steven S. Smith, "Taking It to the Floor," in *Congress Reconsidered,* 4th ed., ed. Lawrence C. Dodd and Bruce I. Oppenheimer (Washington, D.C.: CQ Press, 1989), 332–333.

21. Norman J. Ornstein, Thomas E. Mann, and Michael J. Malbin, *Vital Statistics on Congress 1997–1998* (Washington, D.C.: Congressional Quarterly, 1998), 167.

22. Alvin M. Josephy, Jr., *On the Hill* (New York: Touchstone, 1979), 41-54.

23. Ibid., 74.

24. Ibid., 81–82.

25. *Origins and Development of Congress*

(Washington, D.C.: Congressional Quarterly, 1976), 91.

26. Randall B. Ripley and Grace A. Franklin, *Congress, the Bureaucracy, and Public Policy,* 5th ed. (Pacific Grove, Calif.: Brooks/Cole, 1991), 104; Jay M. Shafritz, *Dictionary of American Government and Politics* (Chicago: Dorsey Press, 1988), 501.

27. Works providing varied perspectives on the growth of legislative power in the twentieth century include Lawrence C. Dodd and Richard L. Schott, *Congress and the Administrative State* (New York: Wiley, 1979); Theodore J. Lowi, *The End of Liberalism,* 2d ed. (New York: Norton, 1979); Kevin Phillips, *The Politics of Rich and Poor* (New York: HarperCollins, 1990); Donald F. Kettl, *Deficit Politics* (New York: Macmillan, 1992); and R. Kent Weaver, *Automatic Government* (Washington, D.C.: Brookings Institution, 1988).

28. Richard E. Morgan, *Disabling America: The Rights Industry in Our Time* (New York: Basic Books, 1984); Thomas Byrne Edsall and Mary D. Edsall, *Chain Reaction* (New York: Norton, 1991).

29. One bit of evidence is that Congress was in session for more hours in the 104th Congress (1995–1996) than at any time in the post–World War II period. See Ornstein, Mann, and Malbin, *Vital Statistics on Congress 1997–1998,* 161.

30. Schmidt, Shelley, and Bardes, *American Government and Politics Today,* 476–477.

31. One study of the composition of the Iran–Contra congressional committee is Bahman Baktiari and Matthew C. Moen, "American Foreign Policy and the Iran-Contra Hearings," *Comparative Strategy* 7 (1988): 427–438.

32. U.S. Congress, *Congressional Record,* January 4, 1995, H35.

33. Rebecca Carr, "With Reluctance, Thompson Brings Hearings to an Abrupt End," *Congressional Quarterly Weekly Report,* November 1, 1997, 2660–2661.

34. Hamilton, Jay and Madison, *The Federalist,* 343.

35. Based on observation by one of the authors while working in the U.S. House of Representatives.

36. Excellent studies of oversight include Morris S. Ogul, *Congress Oversees the Bureaucracy* (Pittsburgh: University of Pittsburgh Press, 1976); John R. Johannes, *To Serve the People* (Lincoln: University of Nebraska Press, 1984); and Joel D. Aberbach, *Keeping a Watchful Eye* (Washington, D.C.: Brookings Institution, 1990).

37. Roger H. Davidson, *The Role of the Congressman* (New York: Pegasus, 1979), 103.

38. Morris P. Fiorina, *Congress: Keystone of the Washington Establishment,* 2d ed. (New Haven, Conn.: Yale University Press, 1989).

3

Elections and Representation

Perhaps nowhere are the differences between the House and the Senate more pronounced than in the way their members are elected. In general, American elections are a diverse lot. Presidential elections dominate news coverage for months, attract nearly 100 million voters, typically are highly competitive, and cost candidates and their supporters around $250 million. At the other extreme, in some local elections, campaigns are virtually nonexistent, the number of candidates may be limited, outcomes are often one-sided, and voter turnout is sparse. It would be only a slight exaggeration to say that Senate races take on many of the characteristics of the high-profile presidential races while House races often look much like the lower-profile local campaigns. But, as we will see, it was not always so.

In this chapter, we examine the similarities and differences between House and Senate elections, focusing on such issues as eligibility, electoral rules, campaign regulations, and voter ignorance. Because of its increasing importance in the electoral process, we examine the role of money in the campaign process in detail. Finally, we consider what elections tell us about the representative character of Congress.

FORMAL DIFFERENCES BETWEEN
HOUSE AND SENATE ELECTIONS

The formal differences between House and Senate elections are due to two primary influences. First, in terms of representation, the bodies were intended to be different. Second, the particular structural differences often can be traced to the need to compromise or to protect various interests that might feel threatened by new arrangements.

The House of Representatives was designed to be the political institution that would be closest to and most responsive to the general public. During the colonial period, Americans had developed more confidence in the colonial legislatures than in their royal governors and judiciary. To ensure continued responsiveness, the Founding Fathers structured a House whose members would serve shorter terms from smaller districts. At the same time, many founders feared that the emotions of the public might carry the nation down dangerous paths. In Alexander Hamilton's words in Federalist 15, "the passions of men will not conform to the dictates of reason and justice without constraint."[1] More colorfully, he is reputed to have said, "your people, sir, are a great beast. . . ."

Having decided to make the House quite dependent on and in sympathy with this great beast of an American public, the founders next designed a body to balance that intimacy. Members of the Senate thus would serve comparatively long terms. Furthermore, they would be elected in thirds so that the passions of the moment could carry no more than one-third of the body at a time. Finally, they would be elected, not directly by the people, but rather indirectly by state legislatures.

Although there are many legitimate justifications for a bicameral legislature,[2] our particular bicameral system can be traced largely to the perceived need to protect the states, and especially the smaller states. Initially, the position of the states was enhanced by the legislatures' control of the selection of senators. However, even after enactment of the Seventeenth Amendment, which provided for the direct election of senators, the interests of states remained important to senators. Whereas House members represent a part of a state, senators represent the entire state. As such, they must win the support of a plurality of voters statewide. Because statewide electorates tend to be more diverse, Senate candidates must be more cognizant of the various interests of the state while campaigning.

Small states were, of course, protected by the provision for equal representation for all states, regardless of population. By tying the size of the Senate to the number of states rather than the number of people, the Founding Fathers guaranteed that senators would be more important than House members.

These various provisions and their underlying goals are reflected in congressional elections in a number of ways. Given the belief that the House would be responsive to the people and that the people would be easily swayed by the emotions of the moment, House elections were expected to be more volatile. Member turnover would be high because voters would have frequent opportunities to express shifting preferences. Furthermore, voters would know when to replace members because of their proximity to the voters. Finally, House campaigns would be relatively modest because they would conducted among friends and neighbors.

By contrast, the theory went, the Senate would be stable, evolving over a series of elections. Only when changes in the electorate had staying power would they be reflected in the makeup of the Senate. Moreover, with senators being selected by state legislatures, voter passions would be filtered through other elected elites. Finally, the system of indirect election would limit campaigning.

Little of this has turned out as planned, however. On the one hand, Senate elections are passionate and competitive, and battles for majority control of the Senate actually have been more volatile than in the House in recent years. On the other hand, House elections are often foregone conclusions, both individually and collectively. The remainder of this chapter explores the nature of Senate and House elections. We begin by looking at what the Constitution says about congressional elections.

CONGRESSIONAL ELECTIONS
AND THE CONSTITUTION

Term Lengths

In developing the framework for elections to their new legislature, the Founding Fathers had to wrestle with two important variables: term length and the selection process. On the first issue, by establishing terms of two years for the House of Representatives and six years for the Senate, the founders deviated substantially from the accepted practices of the day. Under the Articles of Confederation, by which the states governed themselves in their first years of independence, legislators were elected annually and could serve for only three years in any six-year period. Of the original thirteen states, Connecticut and Rhode Island held semiannual elections, nine states had annual elections, and South Carolina ran biennial elections. In Federalist 53, James Madison felt compelled to justify the long terms proposed for Congress. In fact, he opened that paper by acknowledging the widely held belief that "where annual elections end, tyranny begins."[3]

Although the authors of the Constitution believed that frequent and regular elections would provide the greatest assurance of popular control over the government, they obviously did not think one-year terms were necessary to preserve democracy. Madison, in fact, offered a number of reasons two-year terms are better than single-year terms for the House of Representatives. His most compelling argument was that the job would be more difficult at the national level than it was at the state level, and thus some on-the-job learning would be necessary. He further suggested that if the House did not have some experienced members, it would be in grave danger of being dominated by the Senate in the anticipated battle for power.

The preference for biennial terms also had a practical side. It might be difficult, some feared, to convince people to travel to the Capitol and to undertake the responsibilities of governance if service was only for a single year. Moreover, ill-intentioned individuals might challenge the election results of some members and delay seating them for so long that their term would be over before the issue was resolved.

The six-year term for the Senate was a wholly different matter. How could citizens accustomed to annual elections be convinced to seat a co-equal chamber of the legislative branch for six years? The first consideration was to stagger the terms of senators. The Senate does not operate on six-year cycles; it actually sits continuously, with one-third of the senators rotating every two years. But this justification for the six-year term is precisely what its critics might decry. Madison, in Federalist 63, countered that the Senate *should* act as an insulator from public sentiment because "there are particular moments in public affairs, when the people stimulated by some irregular passion, or some illicit advantage, or misled by the artful misrepresentations of interested men, may call for measures which they themselves will afterwards be the most ready to lament and condemn."[4] Although much of the government structure of the United States, including the bicameral nature of the Congress, can be traced to a determination to check the abuses of power, the Senate is designed to check the "abuses of liberty."

Contemporary research suggests that the Founding Fathers had the right idea about the consequences of term length. Impending elections do seem to affect the way legislators behave. For example, after comparing votes of the California State Legislature with popular referenda votes, James Kuklinski concluded that representatives reflect constituent opinion more closely than do senators, and senators reflect constituent opinion more closely during reelection years than in the off-years.[5] As the founders intended, then, the House is more responsive to the immediate will of the people, while the Senate provides for more independence and greater reflection. That pattern was evident as Congress tried to legislate the Contract With America in the 104th Congress (1995–1996).[6]

Selection Methods

The House of Representatives was designed in all ways to be the government institution that would be closest to the people. The direct election by the people of their representatives was intended to complement the relatively short term. The Founding Fathers hoped that the House would have an immediate dependence on the people and that the people would have substantial influence over its deliberations and actions. By contrast, the founders designed the Senate to cool the passions that they feared would emanate from the general public by combining indirect selection with longer terms. More significantly, just as selection by the people would make representatives dependent on them, selection of senators by state legislatures would give them an immediate dependency on the state.

Legislative studies often focus on principal–agent relationships. The principal is someone who grants authority to someone else to act on her or his behalf; the agent is the person entrusted with serving the principal. One concern, then, in

BOX 3.1   The Lincoln–Douglas Senate Campaign of 1858

The most famous congressional campaign in American history is probably the 1858 Senate race between Abraham Lincoln and Stephen A. Douglas in Illinois. Most of us learned the basic facts about the Lincoln–Douglas debates in that race from our history books. The debates were part of a Senate campaign that reflected the divisiveness of the slavery issue at that time. Douglas had sponsored the Kansas–Nebraska Act, which, along with the *Dred Scott* decision, appeared to be opening new territories for slavery. Setting the tone for the campaign, Lincoln gave his famous "House Divided" speech at the nominating convention. In it, he argued that "this government cannot endure, permanently half slave and half free." He said, "A house divided against itself cannot stand."

Our history books also provide a fuzzy evaluation suggesting that the debates made Lincoln widely popular and assured him of the Republican party nomination for president in 1860. We are told as well that he lost the Senate campaign because a majority of Democrats were elected to the Illinois legislature (aided by the fact that many remained because of staggered terms in the state Senate).

Because this campaign took place after candidates began to campaign for the Senate but before the enactment of the Seventeenth Amendment to the Constitution, it provides insight into the nature of Senate campaigns in the era. During this period, state legislative contests began to be overshadowed by Senate elections. Much the way voters in a parliamentary system focus on who will be prime minister rather than who will be their member of parliament, voters in this system often voted for a Republican or Democratic state legislator because of their preferred Senate candidate. In the case of the Lincoln–Douglas contest, Doug-

las was the incumbent seeking reelection. After Lincoln gained the Republican party nomination at its convention in June 1858, the two candidates began campaigning. But the winner would be the one who gained a majority in the state legislature.

Lincoln confronted a problem that would seem quite familiar to a contemporary Senate challenger—he had a difficult time getting people to notice him. Douglas had served in the Senate for over ten years and was highly regarded. As a ploy to gain attention, Lincoln began to follow Douglas around the state, making campaign appearances directly in his wake. When Douglas ridiculed Lincoln for this tactic, Lincoln responded with the challenge for a series of debates.

The famous Lincoln–Douglas debates consisted of seven debates held throughout the state. The first debate attracted 15,000 observers to the town of Freeport, which had a population of 5,000. The debates provided great entertainment, lasting for three hours at a time and extending through the summer and into the fall, and attracting national attention. They were also a major factor in crystalizing the differences between the two parties on how to resolve the slavery issue.

Lincoln and the Republicans gained the moral high ground, arguing that slavery should be abolished as a matter of principle. By contrast, the Democrats found themselves arguing that it should be a question of popular sovereignty; that is, voters in each state (and each newly admitted state) should be permitted to resolve the issue for themselves through the ballot box. Even that position alienated some of the Democratic party's southern support, helping Lincoln to gain the presidency and the Republicans to capture the Congress in 1860.

establishing a legislative body is who is principal over the representative. The Senate, as originally constructed, was designed to ensure that the states (through their legislatures) would have agency over that portion of the federal government. In Madison's words, the appointment process for the Senate had the advantage "of giving to the state governments such an agency in the formation of the federal government . . . [to] secure the authority of the former."[7]

We will see throughout this book, as Madison knew, that it is difficult for the principal to ensure that the agent is acting on behalf of the principal. In the case of the Senate selection system, the problem grew to extreme proportions. Very quickly, the "Senate cultivated strong bonds with the people and distanced itself from state legislatures."[8] Elaine Swift found that by the middle of the 1800s, state legislators had lost the capacity to instruct senators to vote in a certain way and to compel resignation if they did not. At the same time, senators began using state legislative campaigns as a tool to hold office. With the growth of political parties, senators found that they could secure their office by gaining a partisan majority in the state legislature. If that failed, they commonly resorted to bribery. In short, they turned the relationship on its head—the agent no longer served the principal.

The Seventeenth Amendment to the Constitution ultimately put an end to this relationship by providing for the direct election of senators. As early as 1826, an amendment to the Constitution was proposed to provide for direct election of the senators. However, because two-thirds of the senators themselves would have had to propose an amendment and three-fourths of the state legislatures (that elected senators) would have had to ratify it, changing the process did not come easily. But in the early twentieth century, as the progressive movement peaked and evidence of corruption mounted, the amendment finally passed. In 1914, for the first time in our history, citizens voted directly for senators.

Other Constitutional Provisions

The Constitution has little more to say about the selection of representatives and senators. Representatives must be at least 25 years old and residents of the state from which they are elected, and they must have been citizens of the United States for at least seven years. Senators must be at least 30 years old and residents of the state, and they must have been citizens for at least nine years. Article I, Section 4 allows states to legislate regarding the manner of holding elections, but it also allows Congress to make or alter those arrangements.

Article I, Section 5, provides that each chamber shall be the judge of election returns and the qualifications of its members. The latter point became relevant recently when some states tried to impose term limits on members of Congress elected from their state. In *U.S. Term Limits* v. *Thornton* (1996), the Supreme Court ruled that the state initiatives constituted an infringement on the powers of Congress. The Court interpreted term limit provisions as establishing a "qualification" of membership and ruled that only the Congress, not the states, can establish such a qualification.

TRENDS AND PATTERNS IN CONGRESSIONAL ELECTIONS

Just as the outcome of any specific election tells us about the politics of that district, the combined outcomes of many elections tell us about the politics of the nation and about trends over time. For example, one party or the other tends to be predominant for various periods of time, turnout is persistently low and declining, midterm elections differ from elections held in presidential election years, and congressional elections have become dramatically more expensive in recent decades and even in recent years.

Partisan Trends

We begin our exploration with partisan trends.[9] Knowing these trends tells us not only who governs but also what kinds of public policies might follow and in what directions the country will move. During the presidency of George Washington, a two-party system developed around differing views of the role of government in the new nation and, in part, around strong personalities. The Federalist party, led by Alexander Hamilton, advocated a strong national government, but the Jeffersonian Republicans gained dominance while supporting a more limited government. With the defeat in the early 1800s of the Federalists by the Jeffersonian Republicans (soon to be the Democratic party), the development of the nascent two-party system was delayed. The election of Andrew Jackson to the presidency in 1829, though, had a polarizing effect, and the two-party system was revived. In this case, the Democratic and the Whig parties were competitive at both the national and state levels.

With the gradual ascendence of the Republican party in the 1850s and its dominance of the election of 1860, the country entered a new era of two-party government. Although the roots of the new system were established with the election of Abraham Lincoln to the presidency, it was not until the end of the post–Civil War Reconstruction that it reached its full height. From that point, the Republican party increasingly stood for the growth of an industrial nation and became identified with business and financial interests. In the meantime, the Democratic party became firmly entrenched in the South and identified with rural interests and those who were not part of the new industrial juggernaut. The South was always a solid part of their base, which, at times, also included varied ethnic groups, workers, and agricultural interests.

These patterns were evident not solely in the outcome of presidential elections. In the election of 1860, the Republican party not only gained the White House for the first time but also won majorities in both houses of the Congress. As Table 3.1 shows, the Republican party, with its business interests, routinely maintained control of the Senate—often with huge majorities—until the New Deal of the 1930s. The House was more competitive during this period, but Republicans still held control about twice as often as the Democrats did.

The Great Depression, the election of Franklin Roosevelt, and the introduction of his New Deal led the way to a new party system. With few exceptions, the Democrats and their more activist government dominated Congress until the election of the Republican-controlled 104th Congress in 1994. Some observers think that we may be entering a new period of competition between the two parties. In fact, many have looked for signs of a new party system for decades. But history has shown, especially in the more insulated Senate, that the majority party tends to maintain its position over an extended period of time.

Table 3.1   Percentages of Party Membership in Congress, 1861–1997

Congress	SENATE			HOUSE OF REPRESENTATIVES		
	Democrats	Republicans	Other Parties/ Vacant	Democrats	Republicans	Other Parties/ Vacant
37th (1861)	22.0	62.0	16.0	23.6	59.6	16.8
38th (1863)	23.5	76.5	—	43.7	56.3	—
39th (1865)	19.2	80.8	—	24.1	75.9	—
40th (1867)	20.8	79.2	—	25.4	74.1	0.5
41st (1869)	14.9	82.4	2.7	30.0	70.0	—
42nd (1871)	23.0	77.0	—	42.8	57.2	—
43rd (1873)	25.7	73.0	1.3	30.0	69.3	0.7
44th (1875)	38.2	60.5	1.3	61.7	36.5	1.7
45th (1877)	47.4	51.3	1.3	53.2	46.8	—
46th (1879)	56.6	43.4	—	51.2	43.7	5.1
47th (1881)	48.7	48.7	2.6	44.4	51.9	3.7
48th (1883)	47.4	52.6	—	61.5	36.6	1.8
49th (1885)	44.7	53.9	1.3	56.0	43.1	0.9
50th (1887)	48.7	51.3	—	52.3	46.5	1.2
51st (1889)	44.0	56.0	—	47.3	52.4	0.3
52nd (1891)	44.3	53.4	2.3	69.4	26.4	4.2
53rd (1893)	50.0	43.2	6.8	61.8	35.4	2.8
54th (1895)	44.3	50.0	5.7	29.1	68.9	2.0
55th (1897)	37.8	51.1	11.1	37.5	57.7	4.8
56th (1899)	28.9	58.9	12.2	45.7	51.8	2.5
57th (1901)	32.2	62.2	5.6	42.9	55.5	1.7
58th (1903)	35.6	64.4	—	46.1	53.6	0.3
59th (1905)	35.6	64.4	—	35.2	64.8	—
60th (1907)	31.5	66.3	2.2	42.5	57.5	—
61st (1909)	34.8	64.1	1.1	44.0	56.0	—
62nd (1911)	45.7	53.2	1.1	58.3	41.4	0.3
63rd (1913)	53.1	45.8	1.0	66.7	29.2	4.1
64th (1915)	58.3	40.6	1.0	53.1	44.4	2.5
65th (1917	55.2	43.8	1.0	48.3	49.7	2.0
66th (1919)	49.0	50.0	1.0	43.9	54.5	1.6
67th (1921)	38.5	61.5	—	30.3	69.0	0.7
68th (1923)	44.8	53.1	2.1	47.6	51.7	0.7
69th (1925)	41.7	56.3	1.0	42.1	56.8	1.1
70th (1927)	49.0	50.0	1.0	44.8	54.5	0.7
71st (1929)	40.6	58.3	1.0	37.5	61.4	1.1
72nd (1931)	49.0	50.0	1.0	49.7	50.1	0.2
73rd (1933)	61.5	37.5	1.0	72.0	26.9	1.1
74th (1935)	71.9	26.0	2.1	74.0	23.7	2.3
75th (1937)	78.1	17.7	4.2	76.6	20.5	2.9

Continued on following page

Table 3.1 continued

Congress	SENATE			HOUSE OF REPRESENTATIVES		
	Democrats	Republicans	Other Parties/ Vacant	Democrats	Republicans	Other Parties/ Vacant
76th (1939)	71.9	24.0	4.1	60.2	38.9	0.9
77th (1941)	68.8	29.2	2.1	61.4	37.2	1.4
78th (1943)	59.4	39.6	1.0	51.0	48.0	0.9
79th (1945)	59.4	39.6	1.0	55.9	43.7	0.4
80th (1947)	46.9	53.1	—	43.2	56.6	0.2
81st (1949)	56.3	43.7	—	60.5	39.3	0.2
82nd (1951)	50.0	49.0	1.0	53.8	45.7	0.4
83rd (1953)	47.9	50.0	2.1	49.0	50.8	0.2
84th (1955)	50.0	49.0	1.0	53.3	46.7	—
85th (1957)	51.0	49.0	—	53.8	46.2	—
86th (1959)	65.3	34.7	—	64.9	35.1	—
87th (1961)	64.0	36.0	—	60.0	40.0	—
88th (1963)	67.0	33.0	—	59.3	40.5	0.2
89th (1965)	68.0	32.0	—	67.8	32.2	—
90th (1967)	64.0	36.0	—	57.0	43.0	—
91st (1969)	58.0	42.0	—	55.9	44.1	—
92nd (1971)	54.0	44.0	2.0	58.6	41.4	—
93rd (1973)	56.0	42.0	2.0	55.6	44.1	0.2
94th (1975)	61.0	37.0	2.0	66.9	33.1	—
95th (1977)	61.0	38.0	1.0	67.1	32.9	—
96th (1979)	58.0	41.0	1.0	63.7	36.3	—
97th (1981)	46.0	53.0	1.0	55.9	44.1	—
98th (1983)	46.0	54.0	—	61.6	38.4	—
99th (1985)	47.0	53.0	—	58.2	41.8	—
100th (1987)	55.0	45.0	—	59.3	40.7	—
101st (1989)	55.0	45.0	—	59.8	40.2	—
102nd (1991)	56.0	44.0	—	61.4	38.4	0.2
103rd (1993)	57.0	43.0	—	59.3	40.5	0.2
104th (1995)	47.0	53.0	—	46.9	52.9	0.2
105th (1997)	45.0	55.0	—	47.6	52.2	0.2

SOURCE: Norman J. Ornstein, Thomas E. Mann, and Michael J. Malbin, *Vital Statistics on Congress 1997–1998* (Washington, D.C.: Congressional Quarterly, 1998).

Voter Turnout

A second set of patterns relates to voter turnout in congressional elections. As Figure 3.1 clearly shows, voter turnout for congressional elections is always lower even than what is considered a low turnout for presidential elections. It is also lower than the turnout in most other major advanced democracies. Moreover,

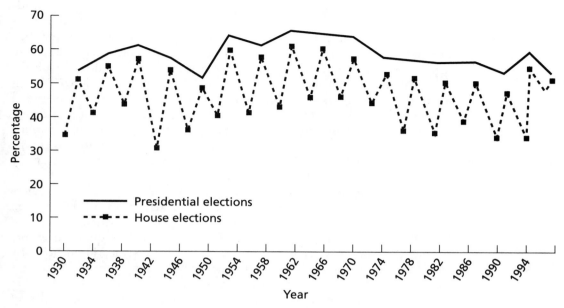

FIGURE 3.1   Turnout in Presidential and House Elections, 1930–1994

SOURCE: Norman J. Ornstein, Thomas E. Mann, and Michael J. Malbin, *Vital Statistics on Congress 1997–1998* (Washington, D.C.,: Congressional Quarterly, 1998).

despite some variation, the pattern has generally been one of declining turnout. Even in presidential election years, more people cast votes for a presidential candidate than for a congressional candidate, which means that some people who go to the polls do not even bother to vote in congressional races. In 1994, the percentage of the eligible electorate who actually voted in House races was 44.6.

The reasons people do not vote are many and varied.[10] Some explanations are structural. For example, it is harder to vote in the United States than in many other countries, for several reasons. States require registration and have residency requirements. Elections are held in midweek as opposed to on weekends or holidays. The United States also holds far more elections than other countries, leading to voter fatigue. Other explanations have to do more with the nature of congressional elections. Voters often believe that there is little difference between the candidates of the two parties. They may also perceive that the incumbent has so many advantages that there is no reason to vote. Or they may simply believe that it is too hard to find out information about the candidates. It may seem surprising that in races in which hundreds of thousands or even millions of dollars are spent, voters feel that they cannot figure out enough about the candidates to vote. But when congressional candidates are competing with presidential candidates, other congressional candidates, gubernatorial candidates, candidates for local offices, and so on, voters understandably may not be able to identify their senatorial or house candidates, get information about them, and make a decision.

Finally, individuals may not vote for personal reasons. Voters who have a harder time obtaining and processing information are less likely to vote. Some people do not vote because they are basically content and feel no urge to invest their time and effort into making a decision and going to the polls. But there are also many who do not vote because they are alienated from or unhappy with the political system and believe that they make no difference and that elected officials do not care about them. Not voting, for them, is a result of frustration or even a conscious protest. Many observers are unconcerned about low turnout except when it reflects dissatisfaction with the American political system. Although some argue that there is more widespread dissatisfaction than has been the case in the past, there is little evidence that low turnout is a serious threat to the legitimacy of the Congress at this time.

It is also interesting to examine why people *do* vote. Contrary to what some public-minded groups argue, one vote is highly unlikely to make a difference in any election, let alone a congressional election. In fact, some people have argued that voting is an irrational act. Citizens have to spend their time and energy studying the candidates, going to the polls, and perhaps waiting in line to cast a vote. What do they get in return? The best explanation for why people vote is because they believe. They believe in our representative democratic system and in the centrality of citizens in that system. Many voters simply want to be part of the process, to feel like they are part of the American political system.

Midterm Elections

Figure 3.1 shows one other important pattern: Turnout is higher for presidential or on-year elections than for midterm or off-year elections. The differences vary, but in recent years, turnout has been between 10 and 20 percent lower for midterm elections than for presidential elections. The reasons for that pattern are fairly obvious. The hoopla of presidential elections is more likely to catch voters' attention and encourage them to go to the polls. More importantly, voters are more motivated to vote in presidential elections than congressional elections.

Moreover, who votes may be different in presidential as opposed to midterm years.[11] Early voting studies suggested that the extra 15 percent or so who vote in presidential elections differ from the approximately 35 percent who vote in midterm elections. Those who vote in midterm elections tend to be more knowledgeable and informed and also to be more partisan. Those who vote only in presidential years are less committed to following either politics or a political party. Some evidence suggests that they vote because one of the presidential candidates appeals to them or because they are caught up in the frenzy of the presidential election, but when that election is over they again distance themselves from politics.[12]

This pattern has consequences for the outcome of congressional elections, especially those for the House of Representatives. The party of the newly elected president typically gains a few seats in the House in the year of the presidential election but then loses seats in the midterm election. Table 3.2 shows just how strong that pattern is. It is not at all surprising that the Republicans finally regained control of the Congress during a midterm election with a Democrat in

Table 3.2   President's Party Seat Change in Midterm Elections, 1862–1994

Year	Party Holding Presidency	President's Party Seat Gain/Loss in House	President's Party Seat Gain/Loss in Senate
1862	R	−3	8
1866	R	−2	0
1870	R	−31	−4
1874	R	−96	−8
1878	R	−9	−6
1882	R	−33	3
1886	D	−12	3
1890	R	−85	0
1894	D	−116	−5
1898	R	−21	7
1902	R	9	2
1906	R	−28	3
1910	R	−57	−10
1914	D	−59	5
1918	D	−19	−6
1922	R	−75	−8
1926	R	−10	−6
1930	R	−49	−8
1934	D	9	10
1938	D	−71	−6
1942	D	−55	−9
1946	D	−55	−12
1950	D	−29	−6
1954	R	−18	−1
1958	R	−48	−13
1962	D	−4	3
1966	D	−47	−4
1970	R	−12	2
1974	R	−48	−5
1978	D	−15	−3
1982	R	−26	1
1986	R	−5	−8
1990	R	−8	−1
1994	D	−52	−8

SOURCE: Norman J. Ornstein, Thomas E. Mann, and Michael J. Malbin, *Vital Statistics on Congress 1997–1998* (Washington, D.C.: Congressional Quarterly, 1998).

the White House. The Senate shows largely the same pattern, but it is muted somewhat due to some of the differences between House and Senate elections, which will be discussed in the next section.

Several factors influence the extent of this midterm effect, which is sometimes called *surge and decline*.[13] A prominent influence on the aggregate vote swing is the state of the national economy at the time of the election. Voters seem particularly prone to "punishing" congressional candidates of the president's party when the state of the economy is not good.[14] Those candidates also suffer more if public approval of the president is lower.[15] Research by Gary Jacobson and Samuel Kernell indicates that this effect is, at least in part, something of a self-fulfilling prophecy.[16] They argue that political elites act strategically, anticipating voter reaction to a weak economy or presidential popularity. Potentially good candidates will not run and potential campaign contributors will not donate money if they expect to be rejected because of national events or their affiliation with the president's party. Therefore, if good candidates of the president's party do not run and if those who do run are poorly financed, it is not surprising that candidates in the president's party fare poorly.

The other major trend in congressional elections is the tremendous growth in the amounts of money devoted to House and Senate campaigns, as well as changes in the sources of that money. We will address this trend later in the chapter.

AN OVERVIEW OF
CONGRESSIONAL ELECTIONS

House and Senate elections differ in many ways—some obvious, some less so. Previously, we considered some of the formal differences. In this section, we review some of the informal differences and consider the consequences of those differences. A key to understanding the differences between House and Senate campaigns is the role information plays in the two types of elections. Voters can reach a voting decision in many ways, but the role of information ultimately is pivotal.[17]

A very early voting study suggested that political campaigns can be used by candidates to *reinforce, convert,* and *activate* voters.[18] First, they can reinforce the predispositions of voters favorably inclined to vote for the candidate. In a given campaign, individual voters have predispositions based on party identification, on previous experience with a candidate, or on any number of other factors. A goal of a campaign, then, is to reinforce those predispositions so that the opponent's campaign is not successful in its efforts to convert those voters to the other side. Clearly, efforts to reinforce predispositions will usually be more successful than efforts to convert, because conversion requires convincing a voter who might be inclined to support the opposition to switch allegiance. Third, and perhaps most importantly, candidates seek to activate voters—that is, to convince latent supporters to take the time to go to the polls and actually vote. In low-turnout races like congressional elections—especially midterm elections—activating voters can make a critical difference in electoral outcomes.

BOX 3.2 Shoo-in Shuster

Bud Shuster (R., Pa.) lives the life most candidates for the House of Representatives dream about. Yet, his political career also reflects many of the realities of the life of a representative. First elected to the House in 1972, Shuster represents a heavily Republican area in south central Pennsylvania, where he has a very safe seat.

In Washington, Shuster has devoted much of his career to transportation issues. As a member of the minority party for most of his career, he had to develop his legislative skills to have an impact on policy. As a result, when the Republican party gained the majority in the House in 1995, he was ready. He was named chair of the Transportation and Infrastructure Committee, and he also serves on the Select Intelligence Committee.

Many House incumbents are safe, but few are safer than Bud Shuster. As he knows from experience, the best way to assure reelection is to be unopposed; he was granted that free ride in every election from 1986 to 1996. In 1984, the Democrats must have thought they had a strong opponent. Nancy Kulp (Miss Jane Hathaway on the original *Beverly Hillbillies* television show) had retired to a farm in Pennsylvania, but she ran a campaign attacking Shuster's inattention to his constituents, spending about $85,000. Shuster, though, countered by spending nearly a half million dollars and

running campaign ads featuring Buddy Ebsen (Jed Clampett on *The Beverly Hillbillies*), who called Kulp too liberal. Shuster won by a two-to-one margin, sending a message to potential opponents not to waste their time and money.

In 1996, the Democrats finally put forth another candidate, journalist Monte Kemmler, but Kemmler never had a chance. He was outspent by a more than ten-to-one margin and lost by a three-to-one margin.

Much of the Shuster story is typical of House elections, but perhaps to an exaggerated extent. Still, one more part of his story needs to be told. Shuster has encountered a series of allegations of ethical misconduct and has been ridiculed for pork barrel projects he obtained for his district. Like many in his position, if he becomes vulnerable, it will likely be because voters in his district believe the ethics charges and take them seriously. Even under those circumstances, he may be most vulnerable within a party primary. In 1998, he was subject to criticism, especially from fiscal conservatives within his own party, for the transportation bill he pushed through the House, which many saw as nothing more than a laundry list of pork barrel projects. Should he weather the ethics challenges, though, he is likely to continue outspending any candidates who dare to challenge him and then easily out-poll them on election day.

Voter Decision Making

Thinking about campaigns in this way helps explain the importance of information in campaigns. First, voters tend to start with a predisposition. Of course, not everyone is predisposed toward one candidate or the other, but few individuals enter a campaign season without some predisposition end up voting. So, where do these predispositions come from? Some are very sophisticated; others, much less so. We can point to a relatively limited number of factors that influence voters' preferences. One is political party. In fact, in most cases, party is the most important determinant of congressional election outcomes. Although political party identification is not a perfect predictor of either the views of voters or the characteristics of candidates, party is the best summary judgment regarding political preferences. When a voter and a candidate share the same party label, the voter is likely to be predisposed to support that candidate.[19] Votes follow more reliably from this factor than any other.

BOX 3.3   Kerry Ekes By

Senator John Kerry (D., Mass.), like most senators, may not have expected an easy reelection contest in 1996, but surely he must have thought life was treating him unfairly with the hand he was dealt. Kerry had been elected to his second term in 1990 with 57 percent of the vote. Moreover, he had developed a strong reputation in Washington as an independent voice and a hard worker. His general liberalism also served him well in the state of Massachusetts. He must have wondered, then, how he managed to be confronted by an opponent who had gained 71 percent of the votes in a statewide election just two years earlier.

Kerry's opponent was highly regarded Governor William F. Weld, who was eager to exchange the governorship for a seat in the Senate. With his proven vote-getting ability, Weld may actually have been the favorite entering the campaign. Weld, in fact, outspent Kerry by a substantial amount—almost $11 million versus just over $8 million. In this campaign, Kerry had little of what might be considered the advantages of an incumbent.

The challenge for these candidates was compounded by the fact that they were much alike in many ways—both politically and personally. Both were relatively liberal, and both were wealthy men with similar backgrounds. The campaign was quite clean and positive by contemporary standards. Kerry worked hard to connect Weld with House Speaker Newt Gingrich, but Weld had that $11-million war chest to make sure voters knew the difference.

In the end, though, incumbency may have been the difference. Two factors are widely cited as contributing to Kerry's narrow victory. First, voters may have decided that by reelecting Kerry, they could keep both men in office, because Weld would remain as governor (which he did until he resigned in 1997 while trying to convince the Senate to confirm him as ambassador to Mexico). Second, by most accounts, Kerry won a series of debates between the two candidates and gained momentum as the election approached. His experience in Washington and his understanding of national issues helped differentiate him from Weld.

The case of the Kerry reelection is typical of what confronts a senator, but perhaps to a slightly exaggerated extent. Senators rarely expect or get a free ride when it comes to reelection. Routinely, they expect to face a reputable challenger who will be able to raise enough money to run an effective campaign. They know that they can lose because they have seen it happen to their colleagues—even to respected colleagues. In Kerry's case, he survived to serve another six-year term, but he knows that he might have to do it all over again in 2002.

A second set of factors is the evaluation of the candidate's character.[20] This broad set of factors might include experience (including incumbency status), background, morality, race, and gender. Voters tend to put a lot of confidence in their judgment of what type of person a candidate is. Judgments such as "He's a good guy," or "She's just like us," or "He's a weasel" may be largely intuitive, but voters often rely on them. Furthermore, in an era in which the slightest hint of scandal results in intense media scrutiny, voters' judgments about a candidate's character and values are important. Finally, though slightly different from other character variables, incumbency is a factor in the evaluation of candidates. Voters who do not know much about the candidates may know which one is the incumbent and often have general impressions of him or her. In fact, the impressions generally are more positive than negative, so incumbency works to the advantage of candidates in terms of both name recognition and voter evaluation.

A third type of influence on voter decision making is issue preferences.[21] Issues can have an influence in three major ways. First, voters can judge a candidate's overall ideology and, based on a summary judgment of compatibility, develop a voting preference. Second, some voters are single-issue voters. That is, based solely on a candidate's position on an issue deemed critical to the voter, such as gun control or abortion, the voter might develop a voting preference. Third, some voters engage in sophisticated calculations comparing their positions on a range of issues to the positions of the candidates. Such a decision-making process requires identifying one's own position and the positions of both candidates, determining the relative gaps between stances, and combining them using some system based on the relative importance of each issue.

Additionally, some issues are what are called *valence issues*—issues on which essentially everyone agrees. Obviously, most voters and candidates prefer peace to war and a strong economy to runaway inflation or high unemployment. In fact, many of our most important issues are valence issues. But, rather than simply decide who is closest to their position, voters must somehow decide which candidate is most likely to deliver the desired outcome. The ways voters do this vary. Some rely on past history. Some voters, for example, might consider the Democrats to be the party of prosperity or the Republicans to be the party of peace and vote accordingly. Or they might conclude that the economy is weak and opt to vote against the incumbent party, in what is referred to as *retrospective voting*. Retrospective voting may be as simple as voters observing the world around them and rewarding or punishing the party in power. It may, however, involve a more complex calculation in which the past is used as a guide to what the future might hold.[22] Pure prospective voting is more difficult because it requires voters to analyze competing policy proposals and to judge which set is most likely to deliver the desired outcome (for example, whether a capital gains tax cut will provide economic growth). Another way voters handle valence issues is by relying on other evaluations of the candidate (specifically, party and character) to help predict whether the candidate will succeed in this regard. In reality, few voters rely heavily on issues, and those who do probably use some combination of these ideal types to determine whom they prefer.

Achieving Campaign Goals

The goal of a campaign is to win an election. As indicated, depending on the context in which candidates are operating, they will need to reinforce, convert, or activate voters to varying degrees. Campaigns achieve those goals by providing information to voters. This information might be designed to change the importance of the three factors in voter decision making—party, character, and issues—discussed previously. For example, a Democratic candidate in a largely Republican area might run a campaign designed in part to convince voters not to rely on party identification when voting. Campaigns also aim at influencing the way voters evaluate the candidates in critical areas. That is, campaigns are designed to convince voters that one candidate has better character than his or her opponent or that he or she is closer to the voters on critical issues.

How campaigns accomplish these goals is a complicated and sophisticated business. Most congressional candidates employ a number of professional staff including campaign managers, media consultants, media buyers, and fund-raisers. The campaign message and the delivery of that message are two major campaign components. Television has become a major force in congressional campaigns, helping both to drive up the cost and to increase the impact of campaigning. The messages delivered in campaigns, contrary to what many believe, tend to be fairly informative, providing information about the candidates and their backgrounds and beliefs. Of course, the information is meant to be not altruistic, but rather persuasive. Campaign messages embody the various techniques of propaganda that have become familiar in other types of advertising. Therefore, voters must work through the persuasive appeals to dispassionately analyze the candidates.

Increasingly, campaigns also rely on negative techniques to achieve their goals. *Negative campaigning* is a term that carries unfavorable connotations, but it simply refers to a technique in which one campaign provides information about the other candidate. Needless to say, that information is designed to help the campaign that originates the message, so it usually carries negative messages about the opponent. Some negative ads are blatantly scurrilous attacks on the candidate, while others rely on innuendo. Because the temptation to cross the line is great and the potential electoral reward is even greater, many negative ads cross the vague and undefined line of decency. African American Congressman J. C. Watts (R., Okla.), for example, in his first campaign had to contend with ads that carried negative racial overtones. One such ad featured a poor-quality black-and-white photograph of Watts as a college student sporting a bushy, Afro-style haircut.

The Role of Information in Campaigns

Negative or positive, any effort at persuasion takes place in a campaign context in which only a few voters have much information going into a campaign or actively seek it during the campaign. Of course, a relatively small percentage of citizens will vote, but more citizens will vote than might be considered knowledgeable. We often judge knowledge based on the ability to answer simple factual questions correctly. By those standards, observers often lament the ignorance of the typical American voter. Relatively few citizens can name their representatives, although more will recognize their names.[23] Many will not know which party controls the Congress. Few will be able to name anything Congress did in the last session, and, indeed, very few will be able to identify how their representative or senator voted on *any* issue.

If many voters are not very knowledgeable about these kinds of basic facts, then they likely are voting with very little information. In fact, that judgment has routinely been confirmed for House races, although it might be changing somewhat with more heavily financed campaigns. It is less true in Senate races—a comparison we will make more explicitly later in this chapter. The recognition that many campaigns are low-information campaigns raises the following question: What kind of information will voters have? One thing they will have is the political party identification of each candidate, because it is listed right on the ballot. Party identification is critical, therefore, when voter information is low. Party may have an impact as voters simply opt to vote for the candidate of their own party, but it might also come into play in the form of retrospective voting.

Incumbency also becomes very important when voter information is low. Voters often can recognize the name of the incumbent on a ballot (or use party to help identify the incumbent). Because voters tend to have a generally favorable view of the incumbent, incumbents have a distinct advantage when voter information is low.

Many elections, especially House elections, are low-information affairs in which party and incumbency dominate the decision-making process. In low-information elections, strong pro-incumbent biases are built into the process. To state it plainly, it is very difficult for a House incumbent to lose a low-information race. Incumbency and party—because the incumbent is likely a member of the majority party in the district—work to the incumbent's advantage. But that bias can be lessened when voters have more information. Information can come from a variety of sources; campaigns are very effective sources because they provide information that is directly useful to voters. Evaluations of candidate character and issues both play important roles in the outcome of Senate elections, but so, too, do party and incumbency.

Two specific differences are notable between House and Senate races. First, reelection rates for House incumbents are far higher than those for the Senate. Second, the amount of money spent in pursuit of Senate seats is far higher than for House seats. As Table 3.3 shows, in terms of reelection rates, House members seem to be quite secure. In the 1960s, the incumbent reelection rate for House members was over 90 percent. (Reelection rates are slightly lower in the years ending in the number two because they follow decennial redistricting and periodically lead to members running in substantially altered districts—even with two incumbents sometimes seeking election in the same district.) Moreover, careful examination shows that losing incumbents tend to have been implicated in a scandal or behaved in an inappropriate manner. Rarely do we see an incumbent lose because he or she is inept or is not aligned with his or her district on issues.[24]

As Table 3.3 shows, however, senators are more vulnerable. Analysis of both individual races and aggregate outcomes demonstrates that Senate incumbents can be beaten. The reelection rate for senators dipped to 55 percent in 1980, but it currently hovers around 80–90 percent. Moreover, one can look around the Senate and see the faces of people who were not expected to be there, candidates who somehow overcame obstacles that might have been insurmountable for House challengers. The experience of Senator Bill Frist (R., Tenn.) illustrates the dynamic nature of Senate elections. Frist's predecessor, three-term Democrat Jim Sasser, was first elected in 1976 after running a campaign quite similar to presidential candidate Jimmy Carter's, against a highly regarded Republican incumbent, William Brock III. When the campaign began, most considered Brock to be a safe candi-

Table 3.3 Reelection Rates as a Percentage of Those Seeking Reelection, 1946–1996

Year	Senate Incumbents	House Incumbents
1946	56.7	82.4
1948	60.0	79.3
1950	68.8	90.5
1952	64.5	91.0
1954	75.0	93.1
1956	86.2	94.6
1958	64.3	89.9
1960	96.6	92.6
1962	82.9	91.5
1964	84.8	86.6
1966	87.5	88.1
1968	71.4	96.8
1970	77.4	94.5
1972	74.1	93.6
1974	85.2	87.7
1976	64.0	95.8
1978	60.0	93.7
1980	55.2	90.7
1982	93.3	90.1
1984	89.6	95.4
1986	75.0	97.7
1988	85.2	98.3
1990	96.9	96.0
1992	82.1	88.3
1994	92.3	90.2
1996	90.5	94.0

SOURCE: Norman J. Ornstein, Thomas E. Mann, and Michael J. Malbin, *Vital Statistics on Congress 1997–1998* (Washington, D.C.: Congressional Quarterly, 1998).

date for reelection, but surprisingly, the Carter model worked, and Sasser won relatively easily. Republicans were not discouraged and ran a strong candidate in 1982. Sasser, however, was easily reelected. In 1988, Republicans fielded a relatively unknown candidate, and Sasser was reelected again, by a nearly two-to-one margin. Heading into the 1994 election, Sasser seemed securely positioned to become a major player within the Washington beltway, but political neophyte Frist ran away with the election. This is an illustration of why it is reasonable to conclude that there is no such thing as a safe seat in the Senate even though reelection rates have begun to increase again in recent years.

CAMPAIGN FINANCES

Recent Trends in Spending

The prominence and smaller size of the Senate help account for the differences in House and Senate elections. A particularly strong manifestation of those differences is the amount of money spent on campaigns. Before looking at differences, it should be noted that very large sums of money are spent on congressional elections and that those funds have increased substantially since 1974, when the Federal Elections Commission was first given the responsibility for collecting and disclosing contribution and expenditure data for federal elections.

In the 1995–1996 election cycle (that is, for the 1996 election), congressional candidates raised $790.5 million and spent $765.3 million. The parties spent another $35 million in coordinated expenditures, a legal designation indicating that the money was spent to build the party rather than to promote individual candidates. As we think about the high costs of congressional campaigns, it might be worth putting them in some context. For example, a thirty-second commercial during the 1998 Super Bowl cost advertisers $1.3 million; the U.S. advertising budget for Procter and Gamble is about $2.7 billion. Over a two-year period, then, Procter and Gamble outspent congressional candidates by almost seven to one.

Still, the amount of money is large. Typical members of the House are raising an average of nearly $1,000 a day, each and every day of their two-year terms. As Figure 3.2 shows, campaign spending in 1996 was 171 percent of what it was in 1990 and 224 percent of what it was in 1982. Overall, the chart shows a persistent increase in the cost of congressional campaigns.

House elections, taken together, are more costly than Senate elections. As Figure 3.3 shows, in 1996, contributions to House elections were double what they were for the Senate. (We will see, of course, that the pattern is quite different when we consider the cost of individual races.) The amount of money going into House races reflects a consistent trend over the last five elections. In each campaign, candidates raised more money than the preceding one, usually by a substantial amount. In Senate races, though, the pattern is not as neat because of the small number of Senate races. In fact, there is a substantial drop in the totals from 1994 to 1996.

The drop in receipts for Senate campaigns from 1994 to 1996 gives insight into the nature of both Senate elections and the institution itself. The Senate is a very individualistic body, with each seat in it being very valuable. What happened in 1994 to drive receipts up almost $100 million from the previous election? We can begin our search for an answer by looking at California. In 1994, Democrat Dianne Feinstein was up for reelection, having served two years of an uncompleted term. She spent nearly $15 million to retain that seat—a figure that actually seems small considering that her opponent, Michael Huffington, spent nearly $30 million of his own money trying to wrest the seat from her. Oliver North spent over $20 million trying to unseat Democrat Charles Robb in Virginia, who spent only $5.5 million. Another $18 million was spent in each of the contests

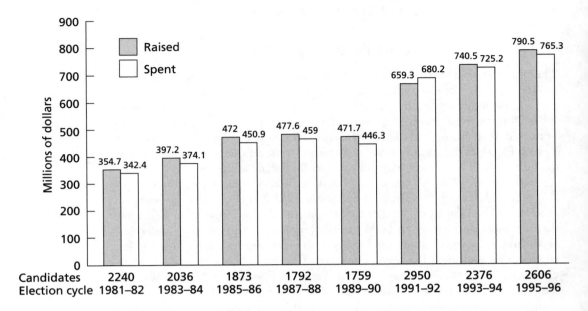

FIGURE 3.2   Congressional Campaign Financial Activity, All Candidates, 1981–1996

SOURCE: Federal Election Commission.

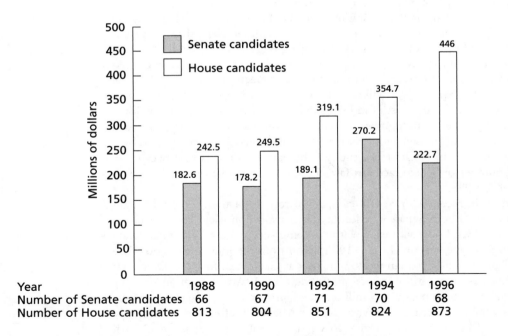

FIGURE 3.3   Campaign Receipts for Congressional Candidates, 1988–1996

SOURCE: Federal Election Commission.

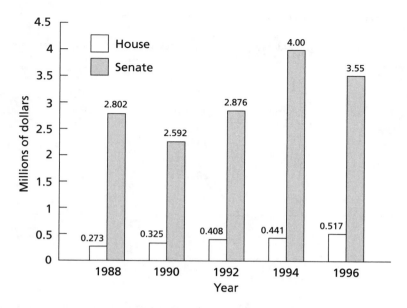

FIGURE 3.4   Average Congressional Campaign Expenditures, 1988–1996

SOURCE: Norman J. Ornstein, Thomas E. Mann, and Michael J. Malbin, *Vital Statistics on Congress 1997–1998* (Washington, D.C.: Congressional Quarterly, 1998).

that resulted in the reelection of Senators Edward Kennedy (D., Mass.) and Kay Bailey Hutchinson (R., Tex.). The Frist and Sasser contest in Tennessee mentioned previously was a nearly $15-million campaign. At least $12 million was spent in each state of Ohio, Pennsylvania, and New Jersey. The wealthy Herbert Kohl (D., Wis.) was willing to spend over $7 million, mostly his own money, to retain his Senate seat. What these figures suggest is that the amount spent pursuing Senate seats might differ considerably from one election to the next—even while there is a general trend toward costlier elections. The data also provide a stark reminder that many people consider Senate seats to be quite valuable and are willing to pay a heavy price to obtain one.

Given the value of a Senate seat and the cost of running a statewide campaign, as opposed to one in a House district, it is not surprising that the per candidate costs of campaigns present a different picture from the aggregate costs. Figure 3.4 shows what the average general election candidates spend in House and Senate races. Senate candidates spend six to eight times what House candidates do. Although there is great variation from state to state, Senate candidates spend an average of $3 to 4 million each while the average for House candidates is about $0.5 million.

The half-million-dollar figure for House candidates masks tremendous differences from campaign to campaign. Speaker Newt Gingrich (R., Ga.) raised over $6 million for his 1996 race, and several other candidates raised over $3 million, while a number of challengers raised under $20,000. In fact, spending varies

Table 3.4   Financial Activity of House Candidates, 1996

	Number of Candidates	Median Receipts	Median Disbursements
Democrats			
Incumbents	170	$523,020	$471,566
Challengers	211	112,694	112,343
Open seats	53	609,190	604,865
Republicans			
Incumbents	213	$700,220	$610,166
Challengers	172	80,754	77,887
Open seats	51	609,524	591,536

SOURCE: Federal Election Commission.

quite predictably in House races. More money, for example, is spent in races that are expected to be competitive. As Table 3.4 shows, much more money is spent by incumbents than by challengers, but the most expensive races are for open seats, for which both candidates tend to expend large sums of money.

Spending Levels and Election Outcomes

These expenditure patterns actually lead to what initially appears to be a strange relationship between spending levels and election outcomes. In low-information House elections, the incumbent tends to do very well. Thus, incumbents are generally happy when the campaign is quiet and very happy when the challenger is poorly funded. But if the race looks potentially challenging, the incumbent will work hard to raise substantial sums of money and run an aggressive campaign to counter that challenge. Apparently, the more an incumbent spends, the worse he or she will do. Obviously, spending does not lower vote totals, but it represents a response to an electoral threat. When the threat is there, the incumbent will try to save her or his seat through an aggressive campaign.

For House challengers, the pattern is quite different. Most challengers are seriously underfinanced, and even if they are potentially competitive, they often lack the means to run a substantial campaign. If the challenger cannot raise the level of information available to voters through an aggressive campaign, then voters will be left to vote based on the low-information cues that favor the incumbent. So, challengers enter the race disadvantaged and can do little to overcome those disadvantages because they lack the resources to run an effective campaign. The average level of spending for challengers is around $100,000, which is not enough to make a dent in the incumbent's vote total. Periodically, though, a challenger either has personal resources to spend or is perceived to be a credible candidate and is able to raise large amounts of campaign funds. In this case, the race has the *potential* to be threatening to the incumbent. The odds will almost always still favor the incumbent, but at some point, the incumbent does become vulnerable.

In the Senate, the pattern is quite different because in most cases, challengers can raise enough money to cross the threshold that makes them viable contenders. To put it another way, Senate seats are usually contested aggressively enough that the election becomes a high-information rather than a low-information one. The incumbents will win not by default, but rather because they are considered by voters to be the more suitable candidates. Incumbents still tend to outspend challengers, but most Senate challengers are capable of raising enough money to make their voices heard during the campaign. In fact, not surprisingly, in 1994, the average Republican challenger outspent the average Democratic incumbent.

Does this mean that money buys elections? The answer to that question is no. There is not, after all, a Senator Huffington or a Senator North in the U.S. Senate. What money buys is the opportunity to communicate with voters. Absent communication, the low-information cues discussed previously dominate voting decisions—a pattern that greatly favors incumbents. Campaigns do allow candidates to make their cases to voters and allow voters to make more informed decisions, rather than unconsciously accepting the status quo. Campaigns, then, are critical to competitive elections, and money is critical to campaigns.

Sources of Campaign Money

Political Action Committees (PACs) are widely discussed in the media as driving campaign finance. So, people are often surprised to find that most campaign money comes from individuals. As Figure 3.5 shows, in 1996, in both House and Senate races, the majority of funding came from individual contributors. But PACs were important in both types of contests, and especially in House races. For all House candidates, PAC contributions accounted for slightly less than 33 percent of the total. For winners, the percentage was somewhat greater—a little more than 38 percent. For all Senate candidates, PAC contributions made up 16 percent of the total contributions and a little under 25 percent of the contributions to winners. PAC contributions are obviously very important to congressional campaigns, but they are not as significant as individual contributions.

According to national surveys, over 10 percent of the public has made a political contribution. As you might expect, these individuals are atypical of the general population; that is, they are more likely to be college-educated, professional, and financially comfortable.[25]

Enough individuals make small contributions, usually defined as $200 or less, to make them very important to congressional campaigns. In fact, about 20 percent of the funds for congressional campaigns come from small donors.[26] Although federal law does not require the disclosure of information about small contributors, we can reasonably speculate that most of them see the donation as a way to participate in the system and to provide support for candidates with whom they identify.

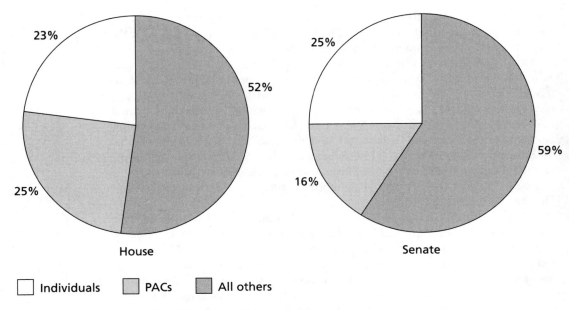

House   Senate

☐ Individuals   ☐ PACs   ☐ All others

FIGURE 3.5   **Congressional Campaign Contributions, 1996**

SOURCE: Norman J. Ornstein, Thomas E. Mann, and Michael J. Malbin, *Vital Statistics on Congress 1997–1998* (Washington, D.C.: Congressional Quarterly, 1998).

Donors of larger amounts of money are also critical to congressional campaigns. In fact, they are the single largest source of funds in Senate races. Approximately a quarter of a million people donate at least $1,000 to various political campaigns. These individuals seem more likely to participate because they have a specific interest in the outcome of the political process. They tend to be people who want their voices to be heard. Therefore, some pool contributions with like-minded individuals, while others donate enough to be able to participate in special forums or meetings with decision makers. In short, large contributors are more likely to see donations as an investment with an expected return.

Regulating Campaign Finance

The funding patterns just described can be traced to what campaign finance law allows and what it limits. Prior to the early 1970s, congressional campaigns were virtually unregulated. But a number of abuses (mostly in presidential campaigns) led to a series of laws designed to prevent many potential abuses. These laws, among other things, created the Federal Campaign Commission, which serves as both a clearinghouse for reporting and disclosing contributions and expenditures and the federal election watchdog, albeit not a very toothy watchdog.

Those laws and a subsequent court decision clarified the status of PACs. Previously, businesses could not make contributions to federal campaigns, but under present law, they can establish committees to collect donations from individuals and to make contributions to candidates. These PACs (or multicandidate committees as they are technically called) must have at least fifty different contributors and make contributions to at least five different federal candidates. Individuals may donate up to $5,000 annually to a PAC (with all contributions not to exceed $25,000 annually), and the PAC can contribute up to $5,000 per candidate per election (including primaries and runoffs).

Those amounts contrast with limits on individual contributions of $1,000 per candidate per election. Those limits are intended to prevent individuals from exerting too great an influence over electoral outcomes and to prevent candidates from becoming too beholden to individual contributors. But the Supreme Court in *Buckley* v. *Valeo* (1976) ruled that individuals have the right to make themselves heard during a campaign under the First Amendment's freedom of speech provision. Individuals must be allowed to express themselves during a campaign even if their ability to contribute to a campaign is limited. Therefore, anyone can make unlimited expenditures independent of a candidate's campaign committee, either on behalf of or against a candidate.

Campaign Finance Reform

Unlimited independent expenditures was only the first of many loopholes that developed over time and led to repeated attempts to modify congressional campaign financing. Two practices that distress some observers are bundling and the growth in soft money. *Bundling* refers to the practice whereby a group collects contributions from like-minded individuals and delivers them together (as a bundle) to a campaign so that the receiver does not miss the message—these like-minded individuals have made a substantial contribution. *Soft money* refers to unlimited amounts of money given to political parties for party-building activities. Parties can then spend this money essentially on behalf of congressional campaigns. The boundaries have been pushed in this direction over time, and the 1996 Supreme Court decision in *Colorado Republican Federal Campaign Committee* v. *Federal Election Commission* seems to have opened unlimited possibilities for party committees to support the efforts of congressional candidates.

Beyond these loopholes, the total amount of money being spent on congressional campaigns worries some observers. Primary among those concerns is the amount of time and effort that candidates (and members of Congress) must devote to raising money and the possibility that the victors will be obligated to the contributors. Furthermore, many observers are unhappy with the huge imbalance in the fund-raising capacity of incumbents versus challengers.

Volumes have been devoted to how to "fix" the campaign finance system, yet little gets accomplished for two reasons. First, campaign finance strikes at the heart of some key philosophical issues regarding freedom of association and expression. Second, the present system has biases (for example, toward incumbents and those with financial resources), and those who are favored by the current system will be directly involved in the decision making regarding reforms. Incumbents, in particular, are not likely to be receptive to changes that dramatically weaken the biases that currently favor them. If one includes the concern that any changes might carry partisan biases as well, the reform task becomes quite daunting.

Two dramatic changes—public financing and expenditure limits—have been widely discussed, but they are unlikely to be enacted. Public financing raises philosophical concerns about the role of elections and faces strong public opposition. Expenditure limits are problematic because of the Supreme Court's position that speech cannot be limited, so any limit must be "voluntary." Efforts to develop a voluntary system quickly become either too complicated or so coercive that they could hardly be judged voluntary.

Other reforms are more viable but still have proven elusive. The limits to campaign contributions, which have not changed since they were enacted in the early 1970s, might be raised. Increasing the cap on individual contributions would make it easier for candidates to raise money, and perhaps free them from that time-consuming task. But a concern is that total spending would simply increase proportionately, resulting in higher levels of spending, contributions, and obligations to contributors. Another proposed reform is to coerce television stations into providing some free time for candidates to air commercials or programs. Yet another proposal involves more efficacious disclosure by requiring candidates to file reports on contributions and expenditures on-line on a more regular basis to allow for more effective public and press scrutiny.

Many see campaign finance reform as one of our most intractable problems. Collectively, we cannot agree on a solution, and Congress is unable to provide leadership on the issue because it, too, is badly divided. The American public believes that the current system allows well-heeled contributors to gain special benefits from Congress, thereby undermining its institutional legitimacy. Coupled with the huge pro-incumbency biases in our current system, this has led to great frustration with Congress and a demand for term limits.

ELECTIONS AND REPRESENTATION

Elections are important in our democratic system because they determine who will govern and, indirectly, how we will be governed and what set of public policies we must live with. But equally important is the fact that elections are the linchpin of representative democracies. Dissatisfaction with the electoral process may, then, translate into dissatisfaction with the quality of representation provided by the Congress. In this section, we explore what we mean by representation and then evaluate it in the contemporary Congress.

What Is Representation?

If the question of the current nature of congressional representation is difficult, the question of what representation should entail is even more perplexing. Many contemporary critics of Congress, for example, object to a Congress that they see as a slave to constituents, providing every benefit requested and casting questionable votes because constituents seem to demand them. Other critics see a Congress out of touch with constituents, and instead owned by special interests, so that the average citizen has little chance to be heard, let alone have her or his interests reflected in the decisions of that body.

In fact, the question of how responsive elected officials should be to their constituents is as old as the notion of representative democracy. Some argue that our elected officials should act as our *delegates,* doing exactly what we want them to do. Recall that initially, senators were expected to be delegates of the states. They were often instructed by state legislatures to vote in specific ways and compelled to resign if they did not follow instructions.

Others argue, however, that acting as a delegate should not be part of the expectations in a representative democracy. The fact that citizens select representatives to act on their behalf has implications for both groups. Citizens no longer are compelled to become fully knowledgeable regarding each issue that comes before the government because they will not be required to make a decision on each. Representatives, though, are expected to become knowledgeable and to make informed decisions. That is, they can act as *trustees,* acting on our behalf even when we might not understand or approve of their actions. Moreover, some argue, they should be free to act on our behalf in a variety of ways. Trustees might judge, for example, that something is not in the short-term interests of their constituents, but rather in their long-term interests, and thus choose to act for the long-term good.

Additionally, it is common to identify the focus of representation. We tend to think of the focus in geographical terms. The question is whether elected officials see themselves as representing the district (or state) that selected them or as representing some broader interests, such as the nation as a whole or some demographic group. Put into its most stark terms, the question is whether representatives might vote against the interests of their constituents because it serves the national interest.

How Representative Is Congress?

To some, these are philosophical issues. But to our elected representatives, these are judgments that they must make daily—judgments that will be second-guessed. When elected officials stand for reelection, voters base their decisions to a large extent on their judgment regarding how well the officials have represented them. Even those who, philosophically, might agree that elected officials should act as trustees or should give preference to the well-being of the nation over their own district might express exasperation with the representation they received and vote against the incumbent. In any case, we see few of these ideal types of representational styles in Congress. Most representatives are what we call *politicos*—they make constant judgments about what they can get away with and still survive politically and gain reelection.

If we think of representation in terms of principal and agent, we might gain a handle on what members confront. According to that theory of representation, as constituents, we select agents to act on our behalf. But we do not, and cannot, be fully knowledgeable about what our agents are doing. Our agents have some discretion to pursue activities, issues, and positions that are priorities for them. In fact, Glenn Parker argues that members of Congress are discretion-maximizers.[27] They do what they need to do to satisfy their constituents, but at the same time they consciously seek ways to provide maximum flexibility to pursue personal goals. As one member explained in a confidential interview, "I can get away with anything I want as long as I don't vote for gun control." Understandably, the judgment he made was to vote against his conscience on gun control so that he could then pursue other issues that were important to him. (Incidentally, the day came when this member could not longer go against his conscience and voted for the Brady Bill; as he predicted, he was subsequently defeated for reelection.)

Parker's work also helps explain a phenomenon first explored by David Mayhew in two critical works on representation. Mayhew noticed that the number of what he called *marginal districts,* or districts won by a narrow margin, began to decline in the 1960s and 1970s.[28] These districts are important because they tend to be the ones in which incumbents are vulnerable. It is marginal districts that are most likely to change hands when the mood of the electorate changes. Without these districts, changes in sentiment in the electorate might not be reflected in changes in the sentiment of Congress. Further, the ability of constituents to control their elected official declines as the district becomes safer. In terms of the principal–agent relationship, the agents gain discretion.

The reasons for the decline of marginals have been widely explored. In a different work, Mayhew argued that members are simply "single-minded seekers of reelection" and are very good at it.[29] According to Mayhew, they gain advantages by claiming credit for popular outcomes, advertising themselves to their constituents, and taking positions that appeal to their district. Others pointed to pro-incumbent biases in redistricting. Parker suggests that because anything can happen during an election, members establish barriers to effective competition in a variety of ways, most notably by providing for pro-incumbent biases in campaign finance.

Morris Fiorina argues that members of Congress helped create an entire "Washington establishment" to protect their seats.[30] According to this viewpoint, Congress passes laws that create federal bureaucracies, which are then imposed on the lives of constituents. When distraught constituents seek relief, members of Congress can play the "white knight" and rescue them. The vagueness of many laws enables members to persuade bureaucrats to act on behalf of the aggrieved constituent. In a similar vein, Parker suggests that Congress may threaten an industry with a regulation or tax a target to encourage the flow of campaign dollars.[31]

Whatever the degree of intent one reads into these congressional activities, there is little doubt that they succeed. In fact, contrary to what the Founding Fathers expected, House members in recent decades have become reasonably insulated from public opinion. That is, they have much discretion and seem to exercise it with relative impunity. On the Senate side, though, there is greater vulnerability because senators have been unable to insulate themselves as effectively and Senate challengers are routinely able to raise enough money to make races competitive. As we saw in Table 3.3, incumbent senators are defeated in far greater percentages than are House members.

If members of Congress, both in the House and the Senate, do indeed have considerable discretion, one might conclude that there is an imperfect relationship between constituent opinion on policy matters and legislator voting patterns. In fact, though this conclusion is relatively accurate, we also often see congruence between constituent opinion and member voting behavior. As the preceding discussion suggests, members are more likely to reflect constituent opinion when an issue is salient to the public. If the public cares about it, members will feel less discretion and be more prone to follow the lead of their constituents. Representatives are also more likely to mirror their constituents when the district is homogeneous. This uniformity makes it easier for members to know district opinion and makes the consequences of going against it potentially more dangerous. Still, it is unwise to make too much of constituency control over legislators, because studies have routinely demonstrated that the general public lacks the information needed to exercise control. In fact, much of the congruence that we see likely can be traced to the simple fact that representatives tend to agree with their constituents on many important issues.

One additional notion of representation needs to be mentioned: Congress is not representative of the nation in a descriptive sense. Members are disproportionately male, white, well educated, and financially well-off. The importance of this notion of representation is much debated and will be discussed in some detail in Chapter 4.

Making Representation Work

One could easily be distressed about the lack of representation based on the preceding discussion. In fact, many observers are—especially in terms of descriptive representation, congruence between voter wishes and legislator behavior, or the capacity of either voters or elected officials to meet the requirements of the congruence model. But do these shortcomings automatically add up to ineffective representation?

In an important work on the topic, Hanna Pitkin argued that it is a mistake to consider representation based primarily on whether a legislature mirrors society or legislative votes reflect voter preferences. She suggested that representation is a process or an activity:

> Representing here means acting in the interest of the represented, in a manner responsive to them. The representative must act independently; his action must involve discretion and judgment; he must be the one who acts. The represented must also (be conceived of) as capable of independent action and judgment, not merely being taken care of. And, despite the resulting potential for conflict between representative and represented about what is to be done, that conflict must not normally take place. The representative must act in such a way that there is no conflict, or if it occurs an explanation is called for.[32]

Based on this conception of representation as an activity, Richard Fenno explored the constituency interactions of members of both the House and the

Senate.[33] Fenno traced a clear process of representation, but he argued that it seems harder for senators to avoid the conflict that Pitkin mentioned, which leads to greater frequency of electoral defeat. In his own words:

> Representation takes time. It is a process of continuous negotiation between politicians and citizens. And it is a process that involves both winning *and* fitting. In the short run, every campaign wants to win. But in the longer run, every candidate wants to negotiate a constituency *fit* that will sustain his or her representational relationship beyond election day.[34]

Effective elections, then, are critical for effective representation. If we cannot ultimately weigh or measure representation, then we must merely accept that it is an activity with obligations placed on both the representative and the represented. If Pitkin and Fenno are correct, then representation is effective to the extent that both legislators and constituents are comfortable with each other.

Pitkin, in fact, further argued that it is a mistake to think of representation primarily in terms of a dyadic relationship between legislators and constituents. Rather, we should focus on whether the overall process leads to the effective representation of citizens. "What makes it representation," she stated, "is not any single action by any one participant, but the overall structure and functioning of the system."[35] The question is whether the many people and groups operating within the context of our political institutions act in a manner responsive to and in the interests of the public.

The Founding Fathers consciously sought to make the House of Representatives more responsive to the people by providing for short terms, small districts, and direct elections. By contrast, the Senate was structured to put some distance between the passions of the people and public policy through indirect elections, longer terms, and smaller size. Over time, however, things have changed. Not only are senators now elected directly by voters, but Senate elections are more competitive than House elections, and House members are somewhat more insulated from the passions of the people. In fact, there is some evidence that the Senate reacts to changing public sentiment more than does the House.[36]

Except in extreme cases, House incumbents rarely lose after their first term or two. Many scholars suggest that incumbents want and have built a system designed to do just that. In any case, because elections are the linchpin of the representational process, issues such as the insulation of incumbents and the decline of marginal districts raise concerns about representation. Of course, the concept of representation is, itself, slippery. We can identify different styles of representation but must realize that most officials have a mix of styles. In the end, we may have representation to the extent that elected officials are responsive to their constituents and that both representatives and constituents are comfortable with the relationship.

NOTES

1. Alexander Hamilton, "The Federalist No. 15," in *The Federalist Papers by Alexander Hamilton, James Madison, and John Jay*, ed. Garry Wills (New York: Bantam Books, 1982), 72.

2. A recent summary is found in George Tsebelis and Jeanette Money, *Bicameralism* (New York: Cambridge University Press, 1997), esp. 13–70.

3. James Madison, "The Federalist No. 53," in *The Federalist Papers*, ed. Wills, 270.

4. James Madison, "The Federalist No. 63," in *The Federalist Papers*, ed. Wills, 320.

5. James Kuklinski, "Representatives and Election: A Policy Analysis," *American Political Science Review* 72 (March 1978): 165–177. See also Martin Thomas, "Electoral Proximity and Senate Roll Call Voting," *American Journal of Political Science* 29 (February 1985): 96–111.

6. See Jonathon D. Salant, "Senate Altering Its Course in Favor of 'Contract,'" *Congressional Quarterly Weekly Report*, April 29, 1995, 1151–1154.

7. James Madison, "The Federalist No. 62" in *The Federalist Papers*, ed. Wills, 313.

8. Elaine Swift, *The Making of an American Senate: Reconstitutive Change in Congress, 1787–1841* (Ann Arbor: University of Michigan Press, 1996), 140.

9. A vast amount of research explores these patterns. Classic works are V. O. Key, "A Theory of Critical Elections," *Journal of Politics* 17 (February 1955): 3–18; and Walter Dean Burnham, *Critical Elections and the Mainsprings of American Politics* (New York: Norton, 1970). A good comprehensive treatment for students is Everett Carll Ladd, Jr., *American Political Parties: Social Change and Political Response* (New York: Norton, 1970).

10. For overviews, see Raymond E. Wolfinger and Stephen J. Rosenstone, *Who Votes?* (New Haven, Conn.: Yale University Press, 1980); and Steven J. Rosenstone and John Mark Hansen, *Mobilization, Participation, and Democracy in American* (New York: Macmillan, 1993). See also Gregory A. Calderia, Samuel C. Patterson, and Gregory A. Markko, "The Mobilization of Voters in Congressional Elections," *Journal of Politics* 47 (May 1985): 490–509; and Jan E. Leighley and Jonathon Nagler, "Individual and Systemic Influences on Turnout: Who Votes?" *Journal of Politics* 54 (August 1992): 718–740.

11. Angus Campbell, "Surge and Decline: A Study of Electoral Change," *Political Opinion Quarterly* 24 (Fall 1960): 397–418.

12. Demographically, with the exception of age, the two electorates appear to be quite similar. See Raymond E. Wolfinger, Steven J. Rosenstone, and Richard A. McIntosh, "Presidential and Congressional Voters Compared," *American Politics Quarterly* (April 1981): 245–255.

13. Recent research suggests that this surge and decline is not so much due to different electorates, but rather to presidential coattails and other spillover effects. See James E. Campbell, *The Presidential Pulse of Congressional Elections* (Lexington: University of Kentucky Press, 1993). See also Campbell's "The Presidential Surge and Its Midterm Decline in Congressional Elections, 1868–1988," *Journal of Politics* 53 (May 1991): 477–487.

14. Howard S. Bloom and H. Douglas Price, "Voter Response to Short-Run Economic Conditions: The Asymmetric Effect of Prosperity and Recession," *American Political Science Review* 69 (December 1975): 1240–1254.

15. Edward R. Tufte, "Determinants of the Outcomes of Midterm Congressional Elections," *American Political Science Review* 69 (September 1975): 812–826.

16. Gary C. Jacobson and Samuel Kernell, *Strategy and Choice in Congressional Elections*, 2d ed. (New Haven, Conn.: Yale University Press, 1983).

17. The best overview of the importance of information remains Barbara Hinckley, *Congressional Elections* (Washington, D.C.: CQ Press, 1981).

18. Paul F. Lazarsfeld, Bernard Berelson, and Hazel Gaudet, *The People's Choice: How the Voter Makes Up His Mind in a Presidential Campaign* (New York: Columbia University Press, 1944).

19. Robert D. Brown and James A Woods, "Toward a Model of Congressional Elec-

tions," *Journal of Politics* 53 (May 1991): 454–473.

20. Donald Philip Green and Jonathon S. Krasno, "Salvation for the Spendthrift Incumbent: Reestimating the Effects of Campaign Spending in House Elections," *American Journal of Political Science* 32 (November 1988): 884–907.

21. Brown and Woods, "Toward a Model of Congressional Elections"; and Robert S. Erikson and Gerald C. Wright, "Voters, Candidate, and Issues in Congressional Elections," in *Congress Reconsidered,* 6th ed., ed. Lawrence C. Dodd and Bruce I. Oppenheimer (Washington, D.C.: CQ Press, 1997), 132–161.

22. Morris P. Fiorina, *Retrospective Voting in American National Elections* (New Haven, Conn.: Yale University Press, 1981).

23. Gary C. Jacobson, *The Politics of Congressional Elections,* 4th ed. (New York: Longman, 1997), esp. 92–97.

24. Monica Bauer and John R. Hibbing, "Which Incumbents Lose House Elections: A Response to Jacobson's 'The Marginals Never Vanished,'" *American Journal of Political Science* 33 (February 1989): 262–271.

25. Frank J. Sorauf, *Inside Campaign Finance: Myths and Realities* (New Haven, Conn.: Yale University Press, 1992), 29–59.

26. The data in these two paragraphs are drawn from a study completed by the Center for Responsive Politics, "The Big Picture: Money Follows Power Shift on Capitol Hill" (Washington, D.C., 1997). The report is available on the Internet at www. crp.org/crpdocs/bigpicture/default.htm.

27. Glenn R. Parker, *Institutional Change, Discretion, and the Making of Modern Congress* (Ann Arbor: University of Michigan Press, 1992).

28. David R. Mayhew, "Congressional Elections: The Case of the Vanishing Marginal," *Polity* 6 (Spring 1974): 295–317.

29. David R. Mayhew, *Congress: The Electoral Connection* (New Haven, Conn.: Yale University Press, 1974).

30. Morris P. Fiorina, *Congress: Keystone of the Washington Establishment,* 2d ed. (New Haven, Conn.: Yale University Press, 1989).

31. Glenn R. Parker, *Congress and the Rent-Seeking Society* (Ann Arbor: University of Michigan Press, 1996).

32. Hanna Fenichel Pitkin, *The Concept of Representation* (Berkeley: University of California Press, 1967), 209.

33. Richard F. Fenno, Jr., *Home Style: House Members in Their Districts* (Boston: Little, Brown: 1978), and *Senators on the Campaign Trail: The Politics of Representation* (Norman: University of Oklahoma Press, 1996).

34. Fenno, *Senators on the Campaign Trail,* 238. All italics in the original.

35. Pitkin, *The Concept of Representation,* 221.

36. Sara Brandes Crook and John R. Hibbing, "A Not-So-Distant Mirror: The 17th Amendment and Institutional Change," *American Political Science Review* 91 (December 1997): 845–854.

4

Membership:
Characteristics and Character

Bella Abzug (D., N.Y.) was the most outspoken feminist in the House of Representatives during the 1970s. In spite of the fact that she served only three terms (1971–1977), she left an indelible impression as a critic of the exclusive composition of the Congress. One widely publicized remark summarized her views: "Congress is a very unrepresentative institution. Not only from an economic class point of view, but from every point of view—sex, race, age, vocation."[1] She added that Congress was incapable of addressing the problems of ordinary working people because it had none.[2]

Abzug's claim that Congress was "unrepresentative" because its membership lacked specific personal characteristics in the same proportion as the general population is accurate, but it is also incomplete; representation involves many dimensions, only one of which is sharing ascriptive characteristics such as race, gender, or socioeconomic status.[3] Yet, Congress's atypical membership may cause disjuncture between the representative and the represented. Members are drawn disproportionately from higher social classes, with potential consequences for public policy.

This chapter focuses on the people who serve in Congress. It examines their collective characteristics, tenure in office, and norms of behavior within the institution. It also examines their ethical standards and conduct outside of the institution.

MEMBER CHARACTERISTICS

Theoretically, membership in Congress is open to many millions of Americans. The major stipulations in Article I of the Constitution for service in the House are that a person be twenty-five years old, a citizen for seven years, and an inhabitant of the state in which the office is sought; a senator must be thirty years old, a citizen for nine years, and an inhabitant of the state. The other requirement is that a person cannot hold any other federal office while serving in Congress. The Fourteenth Amendment, ratified in the aftermath of the Civil War, added one other stipulation: A person may not be "engaged in insurrection or rebellion" against the government of the United States. That provision kept Confederates out of Congress as southern states were readmitted to the Union.

Although membership in Congress is wide open in theory, it is highly restricted in practice. Some people have limited interest in politics, while others lack the ambition to run for Congress.[4] Most people lack the funding to launch an effective campaign, while many lack the rhetorical skills necessary to convince thousands of people to vote for them. It is not enough to meet the age, citizenship, and residency requirements; people who wish to serve in Congress must also possess the interest, resources, and skills needed to win election.

Then, too, keep in mind that certain groups historically have been excluded from politics by law and thus kept out of the pool of potential members. Many African Americans, for instance, lacked citizenship before the Civil War. Moreover, they were kept from active participation in politics even after they became full citizens through devices such as literacy tests, poll taxes, and "grandfather clauses."[5] Women received voting rights only after ratification of the Nineteenth Amendment in 1920, and only one woman served in Congress before then. Even though legal obstacles have been removed, minorities and women may still face antiquated attitudes among voters, which makes it difficult for them to win election. Such barriers restrict the potential pool of members, creating a situation in which a disproportionate share of the seats in Congress traditionally have been held by white males. A detailed examination of the correlates of membership provides information on the specific historical patterns.

Race

The first African American elected to Congress, Representative Joseph Rainey (R., S.C.), was born in 1832. He worked as a barber until the Civil War, when the Confederates put him to work on fortifications in Charleston. He escaped and fled to the West Indies, where he waited out the war. Subsequently, he returned to South Carolina and won election to the state senate. In 1870, he won election to the U.S. House of Representatives after it declared the seat of a white South Carolinian vacant. Rainey served nine years in the House, leaving to become a successful banker before he passed away in 1886.

Rainey ushered in the first of three distinguishable eras of African American membership in Congress. Figure 4.1 documents the party affiliation and the aggregate number of seats held by African Americans in the House since 1870.

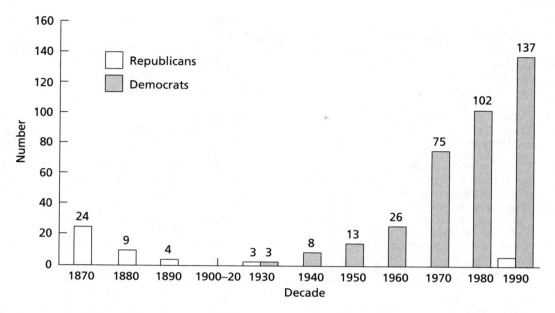

FIGURE 4.1   Number of Seats Held by African Americans in the House, 1970–1998

SOURCE: Based on "Minorities in Congress," *Congressional Quarterly Weekly Report,* November 10, 1990, 3836; Carol M. Swain, "Changing Patterns of African-American Representation in Congress," in *The Atomistic Congress,* ed. Allen D. Hertzke and Ronald M. Peters, Jr. (Armonk, N.Y.: Sharpe, 1992), 110, 119; and Norman J. Ornstein, Thomas E. Mann, and Michael J. Malbin, *Vital Statistics on Congress 1997–1998* (Washington, D.C.: Congressional Quarterly, 1998), 38.

The first era of African American representation extended from 1870 through 1900 (the 41st–56th Congresses). During that period, African Americans typically occupied from one to seven House seats, for a total of thirty-seven seats over the course of three decades; in contrast, they held only two Senate seats over the same period. That bicameral difference stems from the fact that it was much easier for ethnic minorities to win election in smaller House districts, where they might be a majority, than in statewide Senate races. The distinguishing feature of this period was the singular commitment of African Americans to the Republican party, which under the direction of President Lincoln had emancipated the slaves in 1862. A secondary feature was a drop in the number of African American representatives over the period as white southerners reestablished full control over state politics.

The second era ran from 1901 to 1928 (the 57th–70th Congresses), during which time no African Americans were elected to Congress. What accounts for the change? Basically, the relationship between African American and white Republicans disintegrated, offering Democrats the opportunity to win seats previously held by African Americans in southern states.[6] Republicans ceased to be competitive throughout the South. African American representatives did not return to Congress until the late 1920s, when majority African American districts were carved out in the Midwest.[7]

The third era began in 1929 and extends to the present (the 71st–105th Congresses). Its distinguishing feature is the shift in affiliation by African

---

BOX 4.1   Race, Taxes, and Partisan Politics on the Hill

Congressional caucuses are voluntary associations of members that seek to influence public policy. They work outside of the formal structure of the House and Senate; they are not permitted to bring legislation to the floor, nor are they recognized under the rules. Yet, caucuses wield influence by organizing members to promote policy objectives.

The first caucus was the Democratic Study Group, created in 1959 to advance the agenda of liberal Democrats. In the 1960s, a group of moderate Republicans banded together as the "Wednesday Group" because of the day of the week they met. During the 1970s and 1980s, the number of caucuses skyrocketed. Caucuses coalesced around the arts, women, copper, human rights, steel, automobiles, footwear, tourism, and soybeans, to name just a few. By 1991, at least 108 caucuses existed.[1]

Some of the caucuses organized along racial lines, with the Black Caucus and the Hispanic Caucus being the two most salient and powerful in the House. Each caucus consists of members representing their ethnic heritage; both caucuses deny membership to those outside of the ethnic group, claiming a need to preserve distinctiveness. The members of the Black Caucus and the Hispanic Caucus are overwhelmingly Democratic. The combination of racial exclusivity and Democratic affiliation caused Republicans to look askance at those caucuses. A third caucus, composed of Asian Americans, never received much attention because it was so informal as to be nonexistent.[2]

When Republicans seized majority power in the 104th Congress (1995–1996), they scrutinized its budget, looking for ways to cut government costs and to uproot forty years of Democratic control of the House. The Legislative Service Organizations (LSOs)—a small subset of caucuses with office space on Capitol Hill and funding from member's personal office expense accounts—caught their eye. Why allow taxpayer money to be given to members to LSOs, Republicans asked, when they are not a part of the formal congressional structure? Why not simply defund the LSOs, particularly in light of an audit showing some bookkeeping irregularities?[3] As part of the Contract With America, Republicans announced their intention to defund the LSOs on opening day of the 104th Congress.

The announcement created a firestorm. The practical effect of defunding the caucuses would be to eradicate established funding patterns for some voluntary groups of members,

---

Americans to the Democratic party. African Americans have held a total of 372 House seats since 1929, and 364 of them have been Democrats. What explains the shift to the Democratic party? At the risk of oversimplifying matters, the Democratic party became more oriented toward redistributive economic policies and civil rights than did the Republican party.

Another obvious trend is the gradual rise in the number of African American representatives. House membership has risen from 26 seats in the 1960s, to 75 seats in the 1970s, to 102 seats in the 1980s, to 137 seats in the 1990s (as of the 105th Congress). What explains the general pattern? Again at the risk of oversimplification, the steep rise in seats in the 1970s probably reflects passage of civil rights legislation in the 1960s. The more gradual rise in recent years may be the result of more minority districts, more diversity in the general population, and more racial tolerance. The total number of African Americans in Congress is open to interpretation. Some see remarkable progress over time, while others see insufficient progress, because even with increases in representation, only about 9 per-

---

BOX 4.1 continued

including the Black Caucus and Hispanic Caucus. Mild critics of the Republican initiative claimed that defunding the caucuses was an attempt to stifle dissenting viewpoints, while harsh critics claimed it was racist. They also claimed that defunding the LSOs singled out Democrats, whose Democratic Study Group (DSG) was the largest and most powerful caucus in the House. Republicans replied that they were simply trying to prevent taxpayer money from going into the pockets of informal caucuses. They noted that defunding the LSOs affected their party members, too.

On opening day, the Republicans delivered on their promise, ending financial support for the LSOs with a highly partisan 227–201 vote. Afterwards, the Republicans claimed the change would save taxpayers about $5 million annually. They also suggested that it might be possible to sell one of the House office buildings because the LSOs no longer required space.[4]

What happened to the LSOs and other caucuses once they were defunded? A few of them disbanded. Some kept their fundamental structure and mission in place and began seeking outside funding for their operations. Others converted to the status of Congressional Member Organization (CMO), a new hybrid that allows members to donate official resources out of their personal office toward a caucus cause.[5] Members of the Black Caucus, for example, may collectively donate part of a staff member's time toward the caucus, so that three members donating one-third of a staff position could effectively give the Black Caucus a full-time person. All CMOs must register with the Government Reform and Oversight Committee, in an effort to keep closer tabs on their operations. Several years after LSOs were abolished, amidst discussion over race and taxes, they still exist in different form.

---

1. Dean Covey, "Diverse Interests Split Capitol Hill Caucuses," Scripps-Howard wire service story reprinted in the *Washington Times,* August 19, 1991.
2. Brad Wong, "An Informal Caucus," *Congressional Quarterly Weekly Report,* January 2, 1993, 11.
3. David S. Cloud, "GOP's House-Cleaning Sweep Changes Rules, Cuts Groups," *Congressional Quarterly Weekly Report,* December 10, 1994, 3488.
4. Susan Webb Hammond, "Congressional Caucuses in the 104th Congress," in *Congress Reconsidered,* 6th ed., ed. Lawrence C. Dodd and Bruce I. Oppenheimer (Washington D.C.: Congressional Quarterly, 1997), 277.
5. Ibid., 284.

---

cent of House seats were occupied by African Americans in the 105th Congress (1997–1998).

The Senate presents a very different picture, with only two African Americans elected in this entire century. Edward Brooke (R., Mass.) served from 1966 to 1978; Carol Moseley-Braun (D., Ill.) currently serves in the Senate, having been elected in 1992; she is also the only African American woman ever elected to the Senate. The lack of African American senators seems to be driven by the more difficult situation they face running in statewide races and by the smaller pool of candidates with the political credentials to successfully contest a Senate seat.

Despite their comparatively modest numbers, though, African Americans have wielded substantial political power in the House in recent times. The apogee of their clout was probably the 101st Congress (1989–1990): William Gray (D., Penn.) served as majority whip, the third-ranking Democratic leadership position; Augustus Hawkins (D., Calif.), John Conyers (D., Mich.), Ronald Dellums (D., Calif.), and Julian Dixon (D., Calif.) headed standing committees; and Harold

Ford (D., Tenn.), Mickey Leland (D., Tex.), and Charlie Rangel (D., N.Y.) headed select committees. The retirement of Gray and Hawkins and the death of Leland emasculated that clout in the 102nd Congress (1991–1992). By the 103rd Congress (1993–1994), however, the power was partly restored, with election of thirteen more African American representatives and the ascendancy of Kweisi Mfume (D., Md.) to the chairship of the Congressional Black Caucus. Mfume forged enough solidarity among the caucus members to make it a critical swing bloc within the House Democrats, thereby making it a potent force in legislative negotiations.[8]

The political clout of African Americans plummeted with the Republican resurgence in the 104th and 105th Congresses (1995–1998). The demotion to minority-party status of Democrats in the House resulted in the loss of three committee and seventeen subcommittee chairships for African Americans.[9] Moreover, the District of Columbia Committee, which had served as a platform for the concerns of African Americans, was abolished entirely. Ironically, a principal beneficiary of Republican party dominance in the 105th Congress was J. C. Watts (R., Okla.), an outspoken, conservative African American who delivered the Republican response to President Clinton's 1997 State of the Union address.

African American members still wield clout through their high public profile on particular issues and through solidarity on roll call votes. They also now hail from a broader range of states. In the 102nd Congress, nearly one-half of African Americans came from California, New York, and Illinois; in the 105th Congress, less than a third came from those states, signaling an expanded electoral constituency. Even with record numbers, though, African Americans in Congress still constitute only about three-fourths of their proportion in the general population.

Other ethnic minorities are similarly underrepresented in relation to their numbers in the general population. In the 105th Congress, a total of eighteen Hispanics served in the House, which is about 4 percent of its total membership and only about one-half of the proportion of Hispanics in the general population. Asian American and Pacific Islanders are similarly situated. California and Hawaii send some members of those ethnic heritages, but the numbers are less than one-half of the proportion of Asian/Pacific Islanders in the population. Despite inroads by ethnic minorities over time, Congress still is dominated by Caucasians, with roots in a wide range of European nationalities.

Gender

In 1916, four years before enactment of the Nineteenth Amendment gave women the right to vote, Montana elected Republican Jeannette Rankin to the House. Voters in other states did not follow suit. Only 1–12 women won election in any given Congress until the 84th Congress (1955–1956), when 17 women won House seats. The total number of women representatives fluctuated thereafter, averaging 12 per Congress in the 1960s, 16 in the 1970s, 22 in the 1980s, and 44 in the 1990s. From Jeanette Rankin's election through the 105th Congress, women won only 597 of 17,835 (3.3 percent) possible House seats. Women are the most underrepresented group in Congress relative to their proportion of the population.

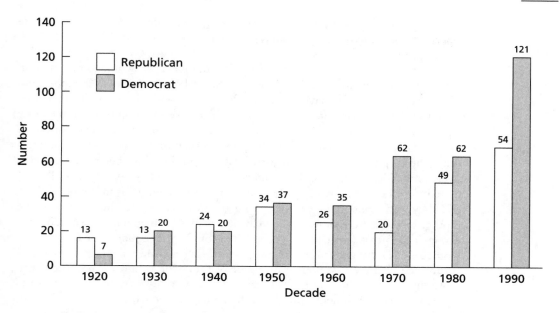

FIGURE 4.2   Number of Seats Held by Women in the House, 1920–1998

SOURCE: Norman J. Ornstein, Thomas E. Mann, and Michael J. Malbin, *Vital Statistics on Congress 1997–1998* (Washington, D.C.: Congressional Quarterly, 1998), 40.

Historically, women have fared even less well in the Senate. The first woman served in the 1920s; no more than two women ever served until the 103rd Congress, when six held Senate seats. (Their election was part of a global focus on the status of women, with 1992 having been declared by the United Nations as "The Year of the Woman"). The number of women senators has inched up since then, to nine in the 105th Congress; Maine and California, with two women senators each, lead the way. But given these numbers, not surprisingly, the Senate is pejoratively called a "gentlemen's club."

Why the lack of women in Congress? There are many possible explanations, all of which may have some merit. Perhaps voters actually resist sending women to Congress to perform work historically done by men. Or perhaps female candidates, on average, are less qualified for public service than their male counterparts because they have had fewer opportunities to serve in positions that are a ticket to Congress, such as governorships and state legislative seats.[10] Then, too, recall that incumbents are hard to dislodge; because most incumbents are men, replacing them with anyone (including women) is a slow process.

Yet, signs exist that these historical patterns are changing. The number of women state legislators is growing, creating a larger pool of candidates with the qualifications and experience necessary to win a seat in Congress.[11] To accompany the nine women senators of the 105th Congress, a record-setting fifty-one women served in the House. A large number of voluntary retirements in the early 1990s (discussed later in this chapter) paved the way for additional gains by dislodging many long-standing incumbents from their safe seats. Even with those developments, of course, change in the gender composition of Congress proceeds slowly, as Figure 4.2 suggests.

A striking affinity exists between the numbers of women and African American representatives in recent decades. Since 1975, a total of 339 women and 290 African Americans have served in the House, with the disparity that does exist mostly occurring in the last few election cycles. Despite their relatively equal numbers, though, the institutional fit is very different. African American members were well positioned in the power structure relative to their numbers (until the Republicans gained majority status), and they have been almost exclusively embedded within the Democratic party; women have not been well integrated into the hierarchy of the House, even with recent gains in membership,[12] and they have split more evenly among the two parties. In the history of the House, Democratic women have held 364 seats and Republican women have occupied 233 seats, a 61 to 39 percent division. No Republican or Democratic women currently serve in leadership posts in either chamber, and none serve as committee chairs. As women gain seniority, they will ascend to more powerful positions, but they have not yet done so. Their visibility may be high on issues such as sexual harassment and abortion,[13] but women's numbers and clout in Congress remain low.

Religion, Occupation, and Wealth

Virtually every religious denomination known to Christianity—from African Methodist to United Church of Christ—has some adherents in Congress. About two-thirds of House members claim a Protestant affiliation, with higher socioeconomic denominations like Episcopalian, Presbyterian, and Methodist particularly well represented. Southern Baptists also serve in large numbers. Although the number of Roman Catholics has risen steadily over time, less than one-third of House members claim that faith. The remaining members (about 7 percent) are mostly Jews; very few Buddhists, Hindus, Muslims, or atheists serve. Those proportions translate into 275 Protestants, 122 Catholics, 33 Jews, and 5 who declined to specify a religion in the 105th Congress.[14] In the Senate, the ratios are fairly similar. Religious affiliations are important to the degree that they structure members' actions and views. Article VI of the Constitution bans any "religious tests" for actually holding office.

Because most members identify with an established religion, it is commonplace to see religious trappings displayed on the Hill. Each chamber begins its day with an opening prayer by a chaplain. Religious rhetoric routinely surfaces in debates on social issues. "Members only" prayer breakfasts thrive. Various denominations have tried to capitalize by sending lobbyists to Capitol Hill to push a variety of policy positions, but with only mixed success.[15]

The occupations of members before they served in Congress are as varied as their religious affiliations. Representative Tom DeLay (R., Tex.), third-ranking Republican leader in the House, ran a pest control business. Representative Carolyn McCarthy (D., N.Y.) was a nurse. Senator John Glenn (D., Ohio) was the first astronaut to orbit the earth. In addition, business owners, journalists, educators, and former congressional aides serve in Congress. The single largest group, however, is attorneys. Over the past forty years, between 171 and 250 (39–57 percent) of the House's 435 members have been lawyers; in the Senate, the proportion of lawyers has been even higher, ranging from 53 to 68 percent.[16]

The presence of so many lawyers has brought Congress approbation and criticism from the earliest days of the republic. Foreign observer Alexis de Tocqueville thought it was a splendid situation, because lawyers valued orderliness and rule of law; Thomas Jefferson described another side of the legal profession in this quip: "That one hundred and fifty lawyers [in Congress] should do business together ought not to be expected."[17] Regardless of desirability, the presence of so many lawyers is understandable. They combine an interest in the promulgation of law with the skills necessary to win elections. Their numbers have declined in Congress in the 1990s, but lawyers remain a highly represented occupation.

In contrast to religious affiliation and occupation, limited differences exist regarding wealth. Quite simply, compared to average Americans, members of Congress are wealthy. Their annual salary of $136,672 in 1998 is more than three times the average income for a family of four. The salary alone does not make members rich. They must maintain residences in Washington, D.C., and in their home state, and their salary is low compared to professional athletes, rock stars, and corporate executives. Yet, members are wealthy by the standard of the average American family, which is part of the reason for the outcry whenever congressional salaries rise.

A bicameral difference is evident regarding wealth. Although they receive the same salary, senators tend to be more wealthy on average than representatives. In fact, the Senate has a historical reputation as a "millionaire's club." In the 1990s, heirs to the Heinz ketchup fortune and to the Ralston-Purina empire both served. Current "club" members would certainly include Jay Rockefeller (D., W. Va.), an heir to Standard Oil, and Herb Kohl (D., Wisc.), former owner of grocery stores and the Milwaukee Bucks professional basketball team.

All members receive a generous pension at the end of their congressional careers. The pension is estimated at five times the national average for members elected before 1984; it is based on years of service and the three highest years' salary. All members elected since 1984 receive a much less generous set of benefits, with the option to participate in a stock investment plan.[18]

Membership and Representation

The typical member of Congress is a white male Protestant, who is trained in the law or business and financially secure. He is married and about fifty-five years old. The composite of that average member translates into a Congress that is atypical of the general population. The larger House is somewhat more diverse than the Senate.

Does it make a difference that Congress does not mirror the characteristics of the American people? Contemporary liberals usually answer yes, arguing that a lack of diversity deprives minorities of role models and causes issues that do not interest wealthy white men to be shunted aside. Their claim is that more women in Congress, for instance, would give rise to higher aspirations for women in the general population and might result in more attention to "women's" issues like breast cancer and abortion rights. Conservatives generally dispute this line of reasoning. They argue that it is inappropriate to pigeonhole people on the basis of ascriptive characteristics—inappropriate because people do not have to share personal characteristics to support a group's goals and because such thinking reduces individuals to how they look, rather than focusing on how they act. Liberals generally perceive problems for minorities and clamor for action, while conservatives concentrate more on the implications of rectifying problems in the way liberals prescribe. The two sides speak past each other.

Many variations exist on these themes, of course, and it is easy to oversimplify liberal and conservative views. Most people would agree that the demographic composition of Congress will be a major issue for years to come, because it lies at the heart of contemporary struggles over representation.

TURNOVER AND TENURE

Retirement of Members

Chapter 3 provided data showing that most incumbents who seek reelection win it, and this chapter has discussed selected personal characteristics that prevail in Congress. One might logically conclude that the membership of Congress rarely changes, but that is not the case. In addition to electoral turnover, many members retire voluntarily. Table 4.1 presents information on retirements since the 1950s.

First look at the figures for the House. A total of 815 (419 Democrats and 396 Republicans) members have retired since 1950, an average of 35 retirements per Congress. Put another way, about 8 percent of members on average voluntarily retire each session. Although the percentage may seem low, it contributes to a median length of service of only three to five terms.[19] (In the 104th and 105th Congresses, the median was three terms of service while the mean was five.)

The pattern of retirements across the political parties is somewhat surprising. Because Democrats occupied more seats in the House during this period, one might expect more retirements. Yet, the number is relatively comparable to Republican retirements. One possible explanation is that Democrats have held more "safe seats," so that they have felt less pressured to retire because of strong electoral opponents. Another possible explanation is that Democrats enjoy public service more than their Republican colleagues, who are more likely to come from and return to the private sector.[20]

Although Table 4.1 does not show it explicitly, another interesting finding is a surge in Democratic retirements over the last three election cycles. A total of 97 Democrats (compared to 65 Republicans) voluntarily retired from the House from 1992 to 1996. Democrats will face a significant problem in the future if their members continue to retire disproportionately to their minority-party numbers. The trend continued at the start of the 1998 election cycle, with slightly higher numbers of Democratic than Republican retirements.[21]

Table 4.1   Voluntary Retirements in Congress, 1950–1996

Years	HOUSE			SENATE		
	Democrats	Republicans	Total	Democrats	Republicans	Total
1950–1959	61	87	(148)	10	10	(20)
1960–1969	64	63	(127)	10	9	(19)
1970–1979	116	94	(210)	18	17	(35)
1980–1989	78	79	(157)	11	13	(24)
1990–1996	<u>100</u>	<u>73</u>	<u>(173)</u>	<u>18</u>	<u>14</u>	<u>(32)</u>
Total	419	396	(815)	67	63	(130)

SOURCE: Based on Norman J. Ornstein, Thomas E. Mann, and Michael J. Malbin, *Vital Statistics on Congress 1997–1998* (Washington, D.C.: CQ Press, 1998), 61.

The pattern of retirements by decade also provides important insights into the institution. The fewest number of retirements from the House in any decade (127) came in the 1960s. Why then? It is probably a combination of several factors. First, the "Great Society" programs of the Johnson administration and the civil rights movement created historic legislative struggles between liberals and conservatives that no one already serving wanted to miss. Second, the national unrest in the face of the assassinations of John Kennedy, Martin Luther King, Jr., and Robert Kennedy obliged and enticed members to keep serving in order to provide continuity during tumultuous times. And third, the executive and legislative branches were controlled by the same political party for almost the entire decade, making service for majority-party Democrats quite rewarding.

The modest number of retirements in the 1960s, in turn, set the stage for a steep rise in the 1970s, when 210 House members quit. It was time for those who had stayed around to retire. The Watergate scandal fed the trend, creating such strong public dissatisfaction with politicians that many of them left rather than face angry voters. The rise of single-issue groups, a growing workload, and a more stringent campaign finance system—all of which made service more burdensome in some way—dovetailed with strong financial incentives to retire.[22] Table 4.1 does not present this data, but the number of retirements rose every election cycle, from 29 in 1970, to 40 in 1972, to 43 in 1974, to 47 in 1976, to 49 in 1978.[23] Once large-scale turnover occurred, the number of retirements began to slacken in the 1980s. Careerism revived.

Now look at the figures for the Senate. Of course, the numbers differ, but the pattern is similar to that for the House. There is virtual parity between the parties, with 67 Democratic and 63 Republican retirements. The fewest retirements occurred in the 1960s, and the most in the 1970s, for the same basic reasons.

In the 1990s, the number of House and Senate retirements has already topped totals for most previous decades. A powerful combination of voter unrest early in the decade and a law that allowed senior members to convert leftover campaign funds to personal use if they retired before the start of the 103rd Congress contributed to numerous retirements in the early 1990s.[24] House Democrats, in particular, may retire near the end of the decade if they weary of minority-party status and see limited prospects for regaining a majority in the chamber.

Seniority of Members

Another way to examine membership turnover is in terms of average length of service. This indicator summarizes the number of voluntary retirements, electoral defeats, and deaths while in office. It also provides some sense of the proportion of junior to senior members on the Hill. Figure 4.3 summarizes the length of service in the House from 1960 to 1996.

The figure shows that 42 percent of representatives have served only 1-3 terms. Another 27 percent has served 4-6 terms; the proportion of members serving 7–9 terms (16 percent), or more than 10 terms (15 percent), is virtually indistinguishable. What do the numbers suggest? Considerable turnover occurs in the House, and many more junior than senior members serve. Contrary to expectations, based on incumbency reelection rates and collective ascriptive characteristics, House membership is not stagnant. Thinking about the proportion of members serving 1–3 terms in a different way, more than two out of every five representatives have served less than six years.

Figure 4.4 shows one other dimension of turnover: the number of first-term members of the House (senators are not graphed due to the small number of cases). The sharp rise in the graph in the early 1990s, which is its most striking feature, illustrates the massive membership turnover of the last several election cycles. In the 105th Congress, a majority of representatives were serving their first, second, or third term.

For the Senate, it is easy to summarize findings in narrative fashion. From 1960 to 1996, an average of 37 percent of all senators were serving their first term (1–6 years). Another 28 percent were in their second term (7–12 years), 18 percent in their third term (13–18 years), and 16 percent in or beyond their fourth term (19+ years).[25] The breakdown mirrors the percentages in the House for years (not terms) of service; one thing revealed indirectly is that senators generally serve about twice as long as representatives. Recall the finding that the median length of service in the House is 5–6 years; in the Senate, the median length is 9–12 years. The prestige of the "upper chamber" evidently combines with longer terms to keep senators serving for longer periods.

Membership turnover has important consequences for Congress. One is lost expertise. When members with knowledge and experience in a public policy area leave, the institution loses much of the "in-house" expertise that helps it to compete with the executive branch. Congress is compelled to rely more heavily on advice from staff and executive branch bureaucrats, none of whom are elected. Another consequence is some loss of legislative efficiency. When members leave Congress, they set in motion a series of changes in staff, office space, and committee rosters. These changes may prove beneficial in the long run, but they create inefficiency in the short term. In the 105th Congress, for instance, newly elected Senator Susan Collins (R., Maine) did not even have a permanent office on the Hill until staffing changes occurred.

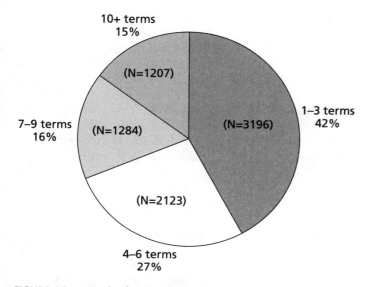

FIGURE 4.3   Length of Service in the House, 1960–1996

SOURCE: Norman J. Ornstein, Thomas E. Mann, and Michael J. Malbin, *Vital Statistics on Congress 1997–1998* (Washington, D.C.: Congressional Quarterly 1998), 19–20.

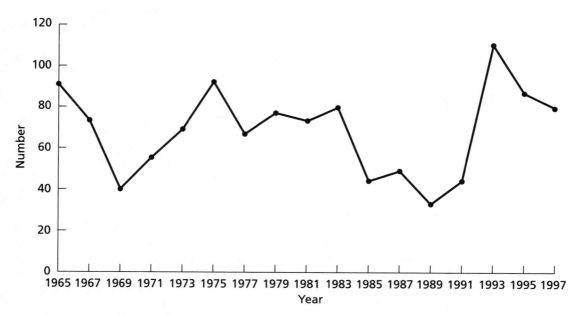

FIGURE 4.4   Number of Freshman Members in the House, 1965–1997

SOURCE: Norman J. Ornstein, Thomas E. Mann, and Michael J. Malbin, *Vital Statistics on Congress 1997–1998* (Washington, D.C.: Congressional Quarterly, 1998), 19–20.

Recent experience points up the dramatic effect of turnover. In 1974, in the wake of the Watergate scandal, many liberal Democrats won House seats. The so-called Watergate class instigated procedural changes that opened up the institution to more public scrutiny, and that weakened the power of committee chairs. Its impact on the workings of the House was so considerable that scholars churned out studies of it for years.[26] Similarly, the seventy-three Republican freshmen composing the Class of 1994 rewrote internal House rules and procedures and provided solid support for all facets of the Contract With America.[27] Thus, large-scale membership turnover can have dramatic institutional consequences. If nothing else, turnover forces the institution to assimilate and train newly elected members.

NORMS OF BEHAVIOR

Informal rules of conduct operate in many facets of life. The unwritten rule at the theater is that people stop talking once the movie starts; the unwritten rule in the classroom is that students raise their hands before vocalizing their thoughts. These norms of behavior are sometimes violated, but their purpose is to smooth everyday living. Pressure is placed on people to follow the norms, to conform to accepted patterns of behavior.

Congress has its own peculiar set of norms. Their existence seems especially important to an institution comprising members who are tossed together to serve a common purpose. Members do not pick their colleagues—voters do. How are new members supposed to learn their way around the institution? How are members supposed to act when they arrive? Informal norms provide an answer.

Political scientist Donald Matthews did the pioneering work in this area in the 1950s, discovering the presence of six norms in the Senate: apprenticeship, legislative work, specialization, courtesy, reciprocity, and institutional patriotism.[28] Subsequent studies found many of the same norms at work in the House.[29]

Apprenticeship is the idea that newly elected members of Congress will remain in the background. They are expected to accept a subordinate role, deferring to their senior colleagues on everything from office space to floor debate. In addition, they are expected to perform some of the mundane tasks of the institution, like presiding over "special orders," a time at the end of the legislative day when the chamber is deserted while individual members speak on any issue they wish. This norm assists the institution by minimizing the activities of the novice, making individual members learn their way around Congress before assuming more active roles. The downside is that it creates inequality among members, elevating some of the people's representatives above others. In any case, this norm has eroded considerably in recent times, due both to the refusal of newer members to accept it and to the crushing workload that pushes even freshman members into an active role.[30] Each member is expected to carry his or her share of the workload in the contemporary Congress.

A second norm, *legislative work,* encourages members to focus on the "nitty-gritty" of the legislative process, instead of parading before the television cameras.

BOX 4.2 Remaking a State Delegation

The state of Maine has a rich heritage on Capitol Hill. It has sent many well-known and highly regarded representatives and senators to the nation's capital. The quality of its delegation is credited to its tradition of participatory democracy, in which people hone the art of politics through the classic New England town meeting. Maine has always been a state of small towns, with its four largest cities composing only 13 percent of the population.[1] It enjoys one of the highest levels of political participation, with the highest voter turnout rate in the nation in 1996.

Back in the 1800s, the state sent notable figures such as James G. Blaine and Thomas Brackett Reed to the House of Representatives. Both men rose through Republican ranks to the position of Speaker. Reed was a particularly influential figure in the history of the House, developing a series of rules and practices that became widely known as "Reed's rules." Their essence was to make it more difficult for the minority party to delay business in the House. Application of those rules earned their author the nickname "Czar Reed."[2]

In the post–World War II period, Maine sent more members who rose to national prominence. Republican Margaret Chase Smith, one of the first women to serve in the Senate, won national acclaim for her "Declaration of Conscience" speech. She rebuked Senator Joseph McCarthy (R., Wis.) for his communist witch-hunt at a time when few public officials were willing to speak out. The small woman from Skowhegan, Maine, standing up to the powerful McCarthy emboldened others, and it eventually earned Senator Smith a place in history as the first woman to have her name placed into nomination for the presidency at a political party convention. In the 1960s, Democratic Senator Edmund Muskie was a towering national figure, winning the 1968 Demo-cratic party nomination for vice-president. He authored major environmental initiatives, such as the Clean Water Act and the Clean Air Act. He also played an instrumental role in the Congressional Budget Act of 1974, which re-asserted Congress's role in the budget process. He served as secretary of state under President Jimmy Carter.

More recently, Democrat George Mitchell rose to the position of majority leader of the Senate. He held the post for eight years (1986–1994), during which time he established a reputation as an adept leader. He recently served as a special envoy to Ireland. His colleague in the Senate, Republican Bill Cohen, first earned national attention in 1974 as a freshman representative on the House Judiciary Committee who voted to impeach President Richard Nixon. He established a reputation as an expert in defense issues and currently serves as secretary of defense for President Bill Clinton.

Despite its rich tradition of powerful members, the state of Maine now has one of the least powerful delegations on the Hill. The change began when George Mitchell decided to retire in 1994. His seat was won by Republican Congresswoman Olympia Snowe, who is now serving her first term in the Senate; Snowe's House seat was won by Democratic freshman John Baldacci. Baldacci is now serving a second term as a member of the minority party in the House. The First District narrowly elected conservative Republican James Longley in 1994 and then replaced him with liberal Democrat Tom Allen in 1996, giving the district freshmen in the last two elections. Finally, when Senator Cohen retired in 1996, he was replaced by Republican Susan Collins, who had never before held public office. In the 105th Congress, the Maine delegation was composed of three first-term and one second-term member. Only Senator Snowe has more than four years of experience on the Hill.

The Maine delegation is small in size and low in seniority. Like other state delegations in the 1990s that have experienced wholesale turnover, Maine is struggling to reestablish its former clout on Capitol Hill.

---

1. Matthew C. Moen and Kenneth T. Palmer, "Maine: Slow Growth in the Pine Tree State," in *God at the Grassroots, 1996,* ed. Mark J. Rozell and Clyde Wilcox (Lanham, MD: Rowman & Littlefield, 1997).
2. Roger H. Davidson and Walter J. Oleszek, *Congress Against Itself* (Bloomington: Indiana University Press, 1977), 24–26.

Those who are "work horses" rather than "show horses" earn the respect of their colleagues.[31] This norm assists the institution by distributing the workload among members; it also serves as a counterweight to the reelection quest, by rewarding members for activity other than campaigning.[32] Its drawback is that the institution of Congress is often upstaged by the president in a television age. Then, too, members who adhere to the norm risk electoral challenge because they are spending time on activities that may not receive recognition or approbation from constituents. On balance, the norm still exists, but the erosive pressure on it is steady.[33] No strong individual incentive to comply really exists.

A third norm, still very much in force, is *specialization*. Members are expected to develop expertise in a specific policy area, usually coinciding with their major committee assignment. Those who adhere to that unwritten rule are taken seriously when it's their turn to speak out, in contrast to those who claim to be "experts" on every issue. To cite just a few examples, Richard Lugar (R., Ind.) is well respected for his expertise in foreign relations; Representative John Dingell (D., Mich.) is legendary for his understanding of energy and commerce issues; and Senator Daniel Patrick Moynihan (D., N.Y.) is highly regarded for his knowledge of the tax code. Specialization assists the institution by focusing members' interests, providing a rational division of labor, and fostering policy expertise. It also gives individual members the opportunity to carve out a national reputation in a particular area. The downside of the norm of specialization is that members often become "captives" of the special interest groups and bureaucrats they intermingle with each day.

Reciprocity is the notion that members will support one another's projects. A hypothetical example is Senator Tom Daschle (D., S. Dak.) supporting a mass transit subsidy bill of Senator Alphonse D'Amato (R., N.Y.) in return for his support of a farm bill. This practice assists coalition building, although it elevates pragmatism over principle. This norm necessarily endures because mutual support among members is necessary to move things through a majoritarian congressional process. But it varies with the financial state of the federal government. When money is tight, members focus on alliances to protect cherished programs; when funds are more plentiful, they focus on supporting one another's projects.

The *courtesy* norm is one of the most interesting. Members are expected to refer to each other impersonally, as well as to be excessively formal and friendly. Thus, a member who wished to yield time during debate to Senator Dianne Feinstein (D., Calif.) would utter something like this: "I yield time to my good friend, the distinguished gentlewoman from California." This may sound overblown and even disingenuous, but such formality depersonalizes conflict in the midst of debate. Like any norm, it is violated periodically, when tempers flare. In the 1980s, for instance, an upset senator erroneously referred to Senator Jesse Helms (R., N.C.) as the "senator from South Carolina," and then "apologized" to the state of South Carolina for suggesting that it, and not the state of North Carolina, was Helms' home state. (The senator later apologized for his mock apology to South Carolina.) Allowing for those infrequent exceptions, the courtesy norm is one of the most enduring codes of conduct.

Finally, the norm of *institutional loyalty* requires members to show commitment to Congress and defend its reputation against critics. Like the courtesy norm, it may require a certain amount of disingenuousness from members at times, but it helps present the institution in the best possible light. As Richard Fenno has shown, however, this norm has disappeared in recent decades because it has become politically advantageous for members to criticize their own institution.[34] An extreme example is the case of the midwestern senator in the 1970s who voluntarily retired at the end of one term. In his waning days in office, he actually wore a lapel button that said, "Take this job and shove it," and he proudly mentioned his dismal attendance record, saying that those who stayed away from the Senate best served the American people! Few members slam Congress in that manner or to that degree—more typical is Bella Abzug's criticism of its exclusive composition. Yet, many current members do disparage the institution to some extent in order to tap into the anti-Washington sentiments of voters. Not surprisingly, Congress's reputation suffers when its own members disparage it. The self-inflicted wounds create perceptions of institutional ineffectiveness.

When work on legislative norms first appeared in the 1950s, observers agreed that those members who followed the norms were part of an elite "inner club" that wielded most of the power.[35] Such stalwart senators as Lyndon Johnson (D., Tex.) and Richard Russell (D., Ga.) dominated "the citadel."[36] Ralph Huitt's study of Senator William Proxmire (D., Wis.), however, showed that members outside of the inner club exerted power in their own right.[37] In the early 1970s, Herb Asher suggested that once-prevalent norms were virtually gone in the House, scarcely being transmitted to the new members.[38] In that context, it is hardly surprising that once-unthinkable ideas have taken hold, such as respecting members who show media savvy and express an interest in running for the presidency.[39]

Even so, members who openly flaunt the unwritten codes take risks. Senator Paul Wellstone (D., Minn.), first elected in 1990, is a case in point. He held a press conference in front of the Vietnam memorial to state his opposition to the war against Iraq, violated protocol in a receiving line by handing Vice-President Dan Quayle taped comments on that issue, and asked someone other than the senior senator from his state to be at his side during his swearing-in ceremony. Wellstone quickly alienated his colleagues. Even President George Bush expressed irritation at the swashbuckling newcomer, asking a member of the Minnesota congressional delegation, "Who is this chickenshit?"[40]

What dangers lurk for the member who follows Wellstone's path? The member may find that he or she is intentionally overlooked during floor debate or that formal rules are applied more rigorously in some cases.[41] It may also be difficult to find co-sponsors for legislation. Former Senator Wayne Morse (R., Oreg.), who supported the opposition party's presidential nominee in 1952, and Senator Phil Gramm (R., Tex.), who turned over sensitive budget information to the Republicans while serving as a House Democrat, learned a different lesson for violating established protocol: Both were bumped from prestigious committees.[42] (Gramm switched parties and is now serving his third term in the Senate.) No one sanction is devastating, but collectively, they may jeopardize a member's career. Voters sometimes punish those who are not seen as effective legislators.

Thus, sanctions exist for members who violate the established norms and accepted practices. Sanctions also exist for members whose conduct is unethical within or outside the institution.

CONGRESSIONAL ETHICS

Remember Joseph Rainey, the first African American elected to Congress? Remember that he took a seat that had been declared vacant by the House of Representatives? It was empty because its previous occupant, Benjamin Franklin Whittemore, was ousted for auctioning off congressional nominations to the U.S. military academy to the highest bidder. His removal opened the way for Rainey's election.

Interestingly, Whittemore's indiscretion was symptomatic of the times. In the Civil War era, congressional corruption reached historic proportions. Disciplinary actions were debated and voted on forty-six times during the 1860s and 1870s, compared to twenty-eight times during the preceding seventy years; and more representatives were charged with corruption during the 1870s than any other decade in the nation's history.[43] Alvin Josephy cited the lax morals of the post-Civil War era, in conjunction with the wealth created by the Industrial Revolution, as reasons for "widespread political and economic corruption."[44]

The most dramatic episode of the time, and one of the great scandals in congressional history, involved Credit Mobiliér. It was a "dummy" company, set up by officials of the Union Pacific railroad to hide excessive profits made by overcharging the government for costs incurred in building rail lines. Credit Mobiliér distributed millions of dollars in stock to members of Congress. What better way to head off potential problems than to give legislators a share of the proceeds? This scam was exposed in 1872, and the public outcry forced Congress to investigate. Yet, its inquiry was a whitewash. The Senate disciplined no one; the House censured Oakes Ames (R., Mass.) for his role in helping to distribute the stock and James Brooks (D., N.Y.) for having received more stock than anyone else. Even then, representatives privately apologized to the two men, saying that public opinion had forced them to support the condemnation.[45]

Crime and Punishment

The ethical conduct of members of Congress is rarely as much of an issue as it was in the 1870s. Scandals like Credit Mobiliér are the exception, not the norm. Most members serve honorably and honestly, compiling unblemished records of service. It is easy to lose sight of that fact when allegations of misconduct arise. The misdeeds of a few too often overshadow the exemplary behavior of the many.

When unethical conduct does occur, the Constitution gives Congress the authority to punish the perpetrators. Article I, Section 5 states: "Each house may determine the rules of its proceedings, punish its members for disorderly behavior, and with the concurrence of two-thirds, expel a member." That final clause describes the toughest sanction that Congress can impose on one of its own—expulsion from the institution.

Expulsion is a sanction that has been used sparingly. The House has voted to apply it less than thirty times in its 200+-year history, and it has actually removed only four members—John Clark (D., Mo.), Henry Burnett (D., Ky.), John Reid (D., Mo.), and Michael Myers (D., Pa.).[46] The first three were expelled in 1861 for supporting the Confederacy; Myers was expelled in 1980 for taking bribes during the ABSCAM undercover operation (discussed shortly).

The Senate has a very similar track record. It has debated expulsion on twenty-nine occasions, but it has actually expelled only William Blount (Ind., Tenn.) in 1797, for inciting Indian tribes to attack Spanish holdings in Florida and Louisiana.[47] (Like the House, the Senate expelled Confederates for political reasons.) Senators have faced expulsion for reasons ranging from Reed Smoot's (R., Utah) "Mormonism" to Robert LaFollette's (R., Wis.) "disloyalty" for opposing U.S. involvement in World War I. The common allegation, however, is financial misconduct.

Why are so few members considered for expulsion ultimately given that penalty? One explanation is that guilty members quit before they are expelled from office; in doing so, they avoid embarrassing proceedings and an inglorious place in congressional history. Another explanation is that other members are reluctant to apply the stiffest possible penalty. They dislike the idea of depriving voters in a state or district of their choice by evicting a member. It is easier and preferable to let the voters make that decision in the next election. The history of expulsion votes in the House since the Civil War confirms the fact that members are usually given the lesser penalty of censure.[48]

Censure is a formal resolution of disapproval that requires a simple majority vote in the chamber in which the member serves. Under the rules, the censured member must be present to hear the condemnation, but the person loses neither his or her seat nor any voting rights and privileges. The censured member could lose a committee or subcommittee chairmanship, an informal penalty that was instituted by House Democrats in 1980.

Twenty-two censure votes have been taken in the history of the House, and ten in the Senate.[49] In most cases, the censure has been approved. The reasons for censure vary: Representative John White (R., Ky.) was censured in 1882 for uttering offensive words; Representative Gerry Studds (D., Mass.) was censured in 1983 for soliciting sex from a teenager. In one of the most famous cases, Senator Joseph McCarthy (R., Wis.) was censured by the Senate ethics committee for suggesting that senators conspired to place communists in high government positions.[50] Both Oakes Ames and James Brooks of the Credit Mobilier scandal were censured.

More recently, a lesser punishment has been employed in the House. A *reprimand* is the same as a censure except that the member being reprimanded does not have to be present on the House floor during the proceedings. This penalty was first applied in 1968 to Robert Sikes (D., Fla.), who was accused of holding financial interests in defense companies related to his chairmanship of a defense subcommittee.[51] Barney Frank (D., Mass.) was reprimanded in 1990 for allowing a gay man to run a "call-boy service" out of his apartment.[52] The Senate has rarely used the reprimand, but it "denounced" Herman Talmadge (D., Ga.) in 1979 for keeping campaign contributions and David Durenberger (R., Minn.) in 1990 for circumventing legal limits on outside income.[53] These lesser penalties still serve as a deterrent.

One final punishment deserves brief mention. *Exclusion* results when the House or Senate refuses to seat an elected member at the start of a new Congress because of some past misdeed. The House used that prerogative to deny a seat to Adam Clayton Powell (D., N.Y.) at the outset of the 90th Congress (1967–1968), on the grounds that he had misused public funds in previous years while serving as chair of the Education and Labor Committee.[54] Among other things, Powell was charged with using committee funds to vacation and to pay his (mostly absentee) wife a large salary. He challenged his exclusion, suing the Speaker of the House. In *Powell* v. *McCormack* (1969), the Supreme Court ruled that Powell was entitled to his seat because he met the age, residency, and citizenship requirements of the Constitution.[55] The Court noted that Congress could censure or expel him, but it could not refuse to seat a duly elected representative. The issue dissipated when the House fined Powell for misusing funds and evaporated when he lost his next election. Yet, Powell left a legacy: He effectively ended the practice of exclusion.

The Enforcers

When allegations of member misconduct surface, the ethics committee of the appropriate chamber is usually the first stop. The committee will hear the allegations and the accused member's explanation in detail, and then decide whether a formal investigation is warranted. (An initial hearing typically is conducted behind closed doors to protect the accused.) Understandably, the policy of the Senate and House ethics committees is to "go slow." That policy protects members from false or exaggerated charges, and it gives those accused of misconduct an opportunity to rectify the situation or to resign.

The ethics committee normally proceeds with an inquiry only if strong evidence of misconduct exists. If it concludes that a member is guilty, it will recommend a punishment, but its suggestion is purely advisory. Remember the case of Gerry Studds, accused of soliciting a teenager? The ethics committee sought a reprimand, but the full House increased the penalty to censure.

The Senate created its ethics committee in 1964, five years before the House, after an inquiry into the financial situation of Bobby Baker. He worked as an aide to Senate Democratic leaders Lyndon Johnson (Texas) and Mike Mansfield (Montana) from 1955 to 1963, and he used his position to amass a fortune. His business dealings are too complicated to explain, but by the time he quit in October 1963, the $19,000-per-year employee was worth $2 million. The scandal dominated headlines for months because of its scope and because Lyndon Johnson was vice-president at the time that Baker resigned. In July 1964, the Senate voted 61–19 to establish a Select Committee on Standards and Conduct. Today it is known simply as the *Select Ethics Committee.*

The structure of the committee has remained the same over the years. It consists of three Republicans and three Democrats, with one of the three committee members from the majority party serving as chair. Often, the chair is a lawyer, because it is helpful to have someone familiar with the presentation and evaluation of evidence.

The House established an ethics committee in 1969, following public pressure to follow the Senate's lead. Called *Standards of Official Conduct,* it is composed of seven members of each party, with one of the majority-party members serving as chair.[56]

Historically, it has been very difficult to recruit members to serve on the ethics committees. Most members treat the appointment like a plague—as something to be avoided at all costs. And it is easy to see why. It is unpleasant judging colleagues; it can create powerful adversaries if someone in a leadership position is the person accused of misconduct; it is time-consuming; it provides no direct benefits to one's constituents; and it is fraught with peril because voters might hear a committee member's name in the context of scandal, without sorting out the specifics. Thus, congressional leaders often must promise rewards to get members to serve, such as a personal appearance in their district during election season.

The Ethics Record

The ethics committees have investigated many allegations over the years. Their work tends to be episodic—that is, periods of intense committee activity are followed by tranquil times, when members guard against even the appearance of impropriety. The only case that the Senate ethics committee pursued after the Bobby Baker scandal involved allegations that Thomas Dodd (D., Conn) billed the government twice for travel expenses. The Senate censured him in 1967. For its part, the House ethics committee never conducted a formal inquiry from its genesis in 1969 through 1975.

In 1976, the ethics situation changed. In addition to Representative Sikes' pecuniary relationship with defense contractors (mentioned previously), seventeen members admitted to receiving free trips from defense contractors. Senate minority leader Hugh Scott (R., Pa.) resigned amidst allegations that he accepted $100,000 in illegal campaign contributions from Gulf Oil. Andrew Hinshaw (R., Calif.) resigned from the House and was jailed for taking a bribe from the Tandy Corporation.[57] In a widely publicized scandal, Representative Wayne Hays (D., Ohio) quit the House following revelations that he kept a mistress on the payroll. Ostensibly a secretary, she dumbfounded reporters with this tidbit: "I can't type. I can't file. I can't even answer the phone."[58]

Few sanctions were applied to the members touched by scandal because most of them paid restitution and/or quit Congress. In 1977, though, three House members were reprimanded in conjuction with "Koreagate," an influence-peddling scheme in which lobbyist Tongsun Park contributed money to election campaigns in hopes of winning favorable U.S. policy toward South Korea. Together with the 1976 scandals, Koreagate pushed Congress to agree quickly on ethics legislation.

Congress passed two separate ethics codes.[59] The first one, adopted in 1977 by both chambers, laid out internal guidelines. It set limits on members' compensation for delivering speeches to outside groups, prohibited unofficial office accounts, tightened travel reimbursement procedures, and more stringently regulated the *franking privilege,* which lets members send first-class mail to their constituents at taxpayer expense. The second law, the Ethics in Government Act (1978), applied to many public officials. It required legislators, executive branch officials, and Supreme Court justices to disclose the parameters of their wealth each year. Both ethics codes have been amended over the years, but their essential provisions remain intact and in force. The codes encourage more open and honest government by requiring members to report their assets. Yet, the codes also make public service more burdensome, by implying the existence of misconduct and forcing members to familiarize themselves with dozens of pages of ethics provisions.

Ironically, ethics concerns were so widespread in the late 1970s that a major ethics controversy arose in the 96th Congress (1979–1980) where none would otherwise have existed. In an undercover operation known as ABSCAM, Federal Bureau of Investigation agents dressed up as Arab sheiks and offered bribes to senators and representatives. The FBI's handiwork created a stir because television networks broadcast leaked videotapes of some members stuffing cash into their pockets. ABSCAM outraged many members because it was a "fishing expedition," in which bait was cast merely to see who could be hooked. What right, members demanded, did the FBI have staging crimes to entrap legislators? Following intense public discussion, the House expelled Michael Myers (D., Pa.) for taking the cash offered; several other members quit or were defeated for reelection. The only senator implicated in ABSCAM, Harrison Williams (D., N.J.), resigned before an expulsion vote. Congressional ethics had become a major public issue, one that would only intensify.

The Era of Partisan Conflict

In 1989, allegations of financial misconduct in Congress splashed across the front pages of newspapers. Whip Tony Coelho (D., Calif.), third-ranking Democrat in the House, resigned his seat rather than face charges that he profited from an "insider" junk bond deal. House Speaker Jim Wright (D., Tex.) resigned two weeks later amidst allegations that he and his wife had profited from sweetheart deals with a businessman and that he had evaded limits on outside income by bulk sales of his book *Reflections of a Public Man*. His resignation came two months after the House ethics committee announced that Wright may have violated sixty-nine provisions;[60] it ended a long investigation that began when the public interest group Common Cause and Representative Newt Gingrich (R., Ga.) filed formal papers with the ethics committee seeking an inquiry. Wright was a particularly partisan Speaker, and politics seemed to drive the Republicans' initial interest in the investigation. Eventually, however, their demand for an inquiry was vindicated.

The Senate also had a difficult year. In 1989, Common Cause asked the ethics committee to investigate whether five senators had pressured federal regulators to overlook the operations of financier Charles Keating in return for campaign contributions. (Keating's defunct business, Lincoln Savings and Loan, eventually cost taxpayers about $2 billion.)[61] The so-called Keating Five claimed that they were simply interceding on behalf of a private citizen who was being harassed by federal regulators; the Senate ethics committee rejected their contention following a two-year investigation. Yet, its verdict was not harsh. It concluded that John McCain (R., Ariz.) and John Glenn (D., Ohio) had used poor judgment, that

Dennis DeConcini (D., Ariz.) and Don Riegle (D., Mich.) had used poor judgment and taken improper actions, and that Alan Cranston (D., Calif.) had engaged in improper behavior, a more serious charge that caused the Senate to reprimand him.

The adage that "when it rains it pours" was true for ethics in the 101st Congress (1989–1990). In addition to the financial scandals, the House was rocked by sex scandals. Barney Frank's (D., Mass.) relationship with a male prostitute was exposed. Donald Lukens (R., Ohio) was charged (and eventually convicted in court) of sexual contact with an underage girl. Gus Savage (D., Ill.) and Jim Bates (D., Calif.) had to write letters of apology to women following allegations of sexual harassment.

In 1992, scandal again rocked the House of Representatives. A "House bank" received most members' paychecks. Although it did not loan money or pay interest on deposits, the House bank cashed members' personal checks. The revelation that dozens of members overdrew their accounts, sometimes by thousands of dollars over many months, without any penalty, created a firestorm of public protest. Even though members were borrowing against one another's funds, and not against taxpayer dollars, they were slammed for "bouncing checks." Citizens viewed the issue in terms of a privileged elite living by different rules than everyone else.

House Republicans tried to milk the scandal for partisan advantage because it occurred with the Democrats in control and because it involved more of their party members. The scandal provided the opportunity to attack a second consecutive Democratic Speaker, Tom Foley (Wash.). Jim Nussle (R., Iowa) used a clever gimmick to turn the issue into a national obsession—he appeared in the well of the House with a paper bag over his head, stating that he was ashamed to be a part of the institution. Republicans pushed a bill through the House requiring the ethics committee to release the names of members who had overdrawn their accounts. The vote paved the way for members' confessions, explanations, and retirements.[62] Speaker Foley closed the bank after the vote. Although the hullabaloo subsided, it exacted a toll on individual members and on the institution. The record number of retirements in the 1992 election cycle was due mainly to the House bank scandal.

The partisan rancor over Speaker Wright and the House bank contributed to an atmosphere of charges and countercharges in the House by the mid-1990s. Representative Dan Rostenkowsi (D., Ill.), head of the powerful House Ways and Means Committee, was found guilty of trading in office postage stamps for cash at the House post office. He lost his chairmanship in the 103rd Congress (1993–1994) and then his seat. His high-profile case contributed to a deteriorating ethics environment, in which members from one political party accused those in the other party of a variety of misdeeds. By 1995, a scholar argued that Congress had moved from individual to institutional corruption; others believed that the process of lodging ethics allegations was simply out of control.[63] The ethics charges involving Speaker Newt Gingrich raised the levels of partisanship and animosity in the House to new heights in the 104th and 105th Congresses. Once the Gingrich case was settled, the House placed a moratorium on ethics complaints while it discussed alternative ways to handle disputes.

BOX 4.3   The Case of Speaker Gingrich

On January 21, 1997, only fourteen days after he was elected Speaker for the 105th Congress, Newt Gingrich was reprimanded and fined $300,000 for ethics violations. His punishment was approved by an overwhelming 395–28 vote in the House. Speaker Gingrich became only the second Speaker in history to face formal ethics penalties; ironically, the first was Jim Wright (D., Tex.), who resigned in 1989 amidst charges brought by a junior Republican from Georgia— Newt Gingrich.

The case against Gingrich began in September 1994, when Ben Jones (D., Ga.) filed a formal ethics complaint. He claimed that Gingrich inappropriately used money donated to a political action committee called GOPAC to underwrite the teaching of a college course. The allegations received attention because of Gingrich's ethics charges against Speaker Wright years earlier. The House Committee on Standards of Official Conduct discussed the allegations in October 1994. It questioned Gingrich's ties to GOPAC and the nature of the college course he taught, which seemed to focus on promoting Republican candidates. The ethics committee did not finish its investigation prior to adjournment of the 103rd Congress. When Republicans won control of the 104th Congress and elevated Gingrich to the speakership, the fierce ethics battle began.

House Democratic Whip David Bonior (Mich.) publicly called for a special counsel to investigate Speaker Gingrich. He also filed formal charges in the spring of 1995, claiming that Gingrich had violated House rules when he touted GOPAC in speeches delivered on the floor. In December 1995, the ethics committee ruled that Gingrich had indeed improperly promoted GOPAC and his college course in floor speeches; yet, it did not recommend any punishment.

Eight days later, Bonior filed an entirely new set of charges based on the public documents of GOPAC. He accused Gingrich of violating tax law by using a network of tax-exempt foundations to help fund the Republican takeover of Congress. Bonior's complaint triggered the appointment of a special counsel, former prosecutor James Cole, to investigate.

The situation worsened for Speaker Gingrich during 1996. In February, Bonior and other Democrats filed yet another set of charges, accusing the Speaker of intermingling the resources of his personal campaign, tax-free foundations, and PACs. (From the first complaint in 1994 through the formal reprimand in 1997, Democrats would lodge more than 100 complaints against the Speaker). In July 1996, the case took an odd twist. Jim McDermott (D., Wash.), a member of the ethics committee, said

---

In contrast to the House, the Senate tackled only one major ethics case in the mid–1990s. It started in 1992 with a story in the *Washington Post* that Senator Bob Packwood (R., Oreg.) had sexually harassed some women who worked for him. He admitted wrongdoing but noted that he had worked avidly for women's causes throughout his congressional career. As accusations became more public and as pressure on him increased, Packwood became more defensive. He resisted Senate instructions to turn over his personal diaries, which were an issue because Packwood cited them in defense of his version of events. The Senate voted 94–6 in 1993 to authorize the ethics committee to subpeona the diaries. Months later, it voted to pursue legal action on behalf of the ethics committee because Packwood declined to turn over the diaries. As the bitter fight continued, Packwood publicly positioned himself as the victim of a witch-hunt.[64] In 1995, however, he voluntarily resigned his seat, thus averting possible expulsion proceedings.

BOX 4.3 continued

on the House floor that the committee was deadlocked; Republicans were furious that McDermott had disclosed information about a pending investigation. Two months later, the case took another twist. The Ethics Committee announced that it was expanding its inquiry to include the accuracy of material supplied by Speaker Gingrich.

In December 1996, Speaker Gingrich publicly admitted to two ethics violations: (1) He had used funds from tax-exempt foundations for political purposes, and (2) he had given "inaccurate, incomplete, and unreliable" information to the ethics committee.[1] The first admission would earn him the formal reprimand, while the second would earn him the $300,000 fine. (He was asked to help defray the cost of the ethics investigation, which was extended because of the inaccurate information he provided the ethics committee.)

Democrats and some Republicans called on Gingrich to step down before a January 1997 vote for Speaker of the 105th Congress. Gingrich declined. House Republicans stuck behind him, reelecting Gingrich to the speakership despite the fact that the special counsel had not finished his investigation. Republicans received a break the week before the reprimand vote when McDermott admitted wrongdoing. He had obtained a tape of a confidential cellular phone conversation between Gingrich and Republican operatives and then leaked it to the press. Although the conversation portrayed Gingrich in a bad light, the public reacted more strenuously to a leak of a private phone conversation. McDermott stepped aside during the final phase of the ethics inquiry.[2]

The ethics committee convened to recommend a punishment to the full House. It listened to the public testimony of special counsel Cole, who sharply criticized Speaker Gingrich for "disregard and lack of respect for the standards of conduct."[3] The ethics committee recommended the reprimand and fine; while Gingrich continued to serve as Speaker, he became the first and only sitting Speaker in history to be formally reprimanded.

---

1. Rebecca Carr, "Subcommittee Lays Out Details of Gingrich Ethics Violations," *Congressional Quarterly Weekly Report,* January 4, 1997, 13–15.
2. Jonathan Weisman, "Alleged McDermott Offense Not 'Serious,'" *Congressional Quarterly Weekly Report,* January 18, 1997, 158.
3. Jackie Koszczuk and Rebecca Carr, "Committee Votes for Reprimand, $300,000 Fine for Gingrich," *Congressional Quarterly Weekly Report,* January 18, 1997, 160–161.

Ethics Lessons and Prospects

Today many people seem to share the opinion of humorist Mark Twain, who once observed that "it could probably be shown by facts and figures that there is no distinctly native American criminal class except Congress."[65] The litany of recent cases contributes to popular cynicism.

Mindful of citizen perceptions and anxious to formulate new policies to lessen partisanship in ethics cases in the aftermath of the Gingrich affair, the House created a bipartisan task force to examine the ethics process at the outset of the 105th Congress. The task force recommended two structural changes, which were adopted by the House in September 1997. First, outside groups were no longer allowed to lodge complaints against members without co-sponsorship by a member of the House. That provision was designed to stop partisan ethics complaints filed by outside groups. Second, the chair and ranking member of the ethics committee were empowered to appoint investigative subcommittees, composed of members outside the ethics committee. That provision was designed to expedite ethics complaints and to give an accused member better due process rights. However, a proposal requiring dismissal of a complaint if the ethics committee deadlocked for six months was rejected; it sought to head off baseless ethics charges filed during election season. Republicans generally supported the task force recommendations, believing they improved the process; Democrats mostly opposed the recommendations, arguing that they insulated the House from public scrutiny.[66]

The prognosis for ethics controversies in the years ahead is uncertain. Stricter procedures for filing complaints in the House may decrease the overall number; on the other hand, past patterns of partisan ethics allegations will be difficult to break, even with new procedures.

One lesson we can cull from ethics issues, and indeed from this entire chapter, is that Congress is a dynamic institution. New members are added at regular intervals, resulting in a more diverse institution over time. New members bring with them a set of expectations about their roles that foster episodic challenges to prevailing institutional norms. Higher standards for personal and professional conduct abet new types of ethics controversies. Contrary to popular perception, the composition and character of Congress is constantly changing.

NOTES

1. Gorton Garruth and Eugene Ehrlich, *The Harper Book of American Quotations* (New York: Harper & Row, 1988), 150.

2. Clair Safran, "Impeachment?" *Redbook,* April 1974, 160.

3. Hannah Fenichel Pitkin, *The Concept of Representation* (Berkeley: University of California Press, 1967), 60–91.

4. On the issue of political ambition, see David T. Cannon, *Actors, Athletes, and Astronauts* (Chicago: University of Chicago Press, 1990); Louis Sandy Maisel, *From Obscurity to Oblivion: Running in the Congressional Primary* (Knoxville: University of Tennessee Press, 1982); Linda L. Fowler and Robert D. McClure, *Political Ambition: Who Decides to Run for Congress* (New Haven, Conn.: Yale University Press, 1989); and James A. Schlesinger, *Ambition and Politics: Political Careers in the United States* (Chicago: Rand McNally, 1966).

5. "Grandfather Clauses," which exempted whites from literacy tests if their grandfathers had voted prior to the Civil War,

were struck down by the Supreme Court in *Guinn* v. *United States,* 238 U.S. 347 (1915). Literacy tests were outlawed in the 1965 Civil Rights Act, poll taxes abolished by the Twenty-fourth Amendment, and both literacy tests and poll taxes further laid to rest by the Supreme Court in *Harper* v. *Virginia Board of Elections,* 383 U.S. 663 (1966).

6. Hanes Walton, Jr., *Black Republicans* (Metuchen, N.J.: Scarecrow, 1975).

7. Carol M. Swain, "Changing Patterns of African-American Representation in Congress," in *The Atomistic Congress,* ed. Allen D. Hertzke and Ronald M. Peters, Jr. (Armonk, N.Y.: Sharpe, 1992), 120–122.

8. Graeme Browing, "Flex Time," *National Journal,* July 31, 1993, 1921–25; Kitty Cunningham, "Black Caucus Flexes Its Muscles on Budget—And More," *Congressional Quarterly Weekly Report,* July 3, 1993, 1711–1715; Steven V. Roberts, "New Black Power on Capitol Hill," *U.S. News & World Report,* May 23, 1994, 36; on Kweise

Mfume, see Peter J. Boyer, "The Rise of Kweise Mfume," *The New Yorker,* August 1, 1994, 26–35.

9. Eleanor Clift, "The Black Power Outage," *Newsweek,* November 28, 1994, 32; for background information on how Republican control undercut growing African American clout in Congress, see Sally Friedman, "House Committee Assignments of Women and Minority Newcomers, 1965–1994," *Legislative Studies Quarterly* 21 (February 1996): 73–81.

10. Barbara C. Burrell, *A Woman's Place Is in the House* (Ann Arbor: University of Michigan Press, 1996). See also Robert Darcy, Susan Welch, and Janet Clark, *Women, Elections and Representation* (New York: Longman, 1987); Susan J. Carroll, *Women as Candidates in American Politics* (Bloomington: Indiana University Press, 1985); and Carol M. Swain, "Women and Blacks in Congress, 1870–1996," in *Congress Reconsidered,* 6th ed. (Washington, D.C.: Congressional Quarterly, 1997), 81–99.

11. Iva Ellen Deutchman, "Ungendered but Equal: Male Attitudes Toward Women in State Legislatures," *Polity* 24 (Spring 1992): 417–432. On related issues, see Emmy Wermer, "Women in Congress: 1917–1964," *Western Political Quarterly* 19 (March 1966): 16–30; Kristi Anderson and Stuart J. Thorson, "Congressional Turnover and the Election of Women," *Western Political Quarterly* 37 (March 1984): 143–156; and Susan Welsh, "Are Women More Liberal Than Men in the U.S. Congress?" *Legislative Studies Quarterly* 10 (February 1985): 125–134.

12. Janet Hook, "Women Remain on Periphery Despite Electoral Gains," *Congressional Quarterly Weekly Report,* October 9, 1993, 2707–2713.

13. Richard S. Dunham, "Mr. Smith Goes to Washington," *Business Week,* September 26, 1994, 96–98; on the degree of distinctiveness of women legislators, see Arturo Vega and Juanita M. Firestone, "The Effects of Gender on Congressional Behavior and the Substantive Representation of Women," *Legislative Studies Quarterly* 20 (May 1995): 213–222.

14. "Religious Affiliations," *Congressional Quarterly Weekly Report,* January 4, 1997,

29; an excellent study of religious beliefs in Congress is Peter C. Benson and Dorothy L. Williams, *Religion on Capitol Hill* (New York: Oxford University Press, 1986).

15. Matthew C. Moen, *The Christian Right and Congress* (Tuscaloosa: University of Alabama Press, 1989); Allen D. Hertzke, *Representing God in Washington* (Knoxville: University of Tennessee Press, 1988); Daniel Hofrenning, *In Washington but Not of It* (Philadelphia: Temple University Press, 1995).

16. Norman J. Ornstein, Thomas E. Mann, and Michael J. Malbin, *Vital Statistics on Congress 1997–1998* (Washington, D.C.: CQ Press, 1998), 22–33.

17. Alexis de Tocqueville, *Democracy in America,* trans. George Lawrence, ed. J. P. Mayer (Garden City, N.Y.: Anchor Books, 1969), 263–270; Garruth and Ehrlich, *The Harper Book of American Quotations,* 151.

18. Anick Jesdanun, "Congressional Pensions About Five Times Average," Associated Press wire story, reprinted in the *Bangor Daily News,* December 30, 1997, 1.

19. Ornstein, Mann, and Malbin, *Vital Statistics on Congress 1997–1998,* 19–20.

20. Alan Ehrenhalt, *The United States of Ambition* (New York: Random House), 1991.

21. "Departing the Hill," *Congressional Quarterly Weekly Report,* January 10, 1998, 95.

22. Joseph Cooper and William West, "The Congressional Career in the 1970s," in *Congress Reconsidered,* 2d ed., ed. Lawrence C. Dodd and Bruce I. Oppenheimer (Washington, D.C.: CQ Press, 1981), 83–106.

23. Harold W. Stanley and Richard G. Niemi, *Vital Statistics on American Politics,* 2d ed. (Washington, D.C.: CQ Press, 1990), 186; for an argument that the high number of retirements in the 1970s were an aberration, see Steven G. Livingston and Sally Friedman, "Reexamining Theories of Congressional Retirement: Evidence from the 1980s," *Legislative Studies Quarterly* 18 (May 1993): 231–253.

24. "Campaign-Cash Loophole Closed," *Congressional Quarterly Almanac 1989* 45 (Washington, D.C.: Congressional Quarterly, 1990), 55; for information on

what members do after they retire, see Rebekah Herrick and David L. Nixon, "Is There Life After Congress? Patterns and Determinants of Post-Congressional Careers," *Legislative Studies Quarterly* 21 (November 1996): 489–499.

25. Calculated from data provided in Ornstein, Mann, and Malbin, *Vital Statistics on Congress 1997–1998,* 21.

26. An excellent summary is Leroy Rieselbach, *Congressional Reform* (Washington, D.C.: CQ Press, 1986); for one of the major studies, see Burdett A. Loomis, "Congressional Careers and Party Leadership in the Contemporary House of Representatives," *American Journal of Political Science* 28 (February 1984): 180–202.

27. Matthew C. Moen, "The House Freshmen of the 104th Congress," paper presented at the Annual Meeting of the New England Political Science Association, Portland, Maine, May 5–6, 1995. For a published excerpt of the paper, see *Extensions* (University of Oklahoma: The Carl Albert Center, 1995): 3–6.

28. Donald R. Matthews, *U.S. Senators and Their World* (New York: Vintage Books, 1960), 92–117.

29. Clem Miller, *Member of the House* (New York: Scribner, 1962); Charles Clapp, *The Congressman: His Work As He Sees It* (New York: Doubleday, 1963); Donald Tacheran and Morris Udall, *The Job of the Congressman* (Indianapolis, Ind.: Bobbs-Merrill, 1966).

30. Norman J. Ornstein, Robert L. Peabody, and David W. Rohde, "Change in the Senate: Toward the 1990s," in *Congress Reconsidered,* 4th ed., ed. Lawrence C. Dodd and Bruce I. Oppenheimer (Washington, D.C.: CQ Press, 1989), 17–33.

31. Matthews, *U.S. Senators and Their World,* 94–95.

32. On the latter point, see David Mayhew, *Congress: The Electoral Connection* (New Haven, Conn.: Yale University Press, 1974).

33. See Samuel Kernell, *Going Public* (Washington, D.C.: Congressional Quarterly, 1986); Stephen Hess, *The Ultimate Insiders: U.S. Senators in the National Media* (Washington, D.C.: Brookings Institution, 1986).

34. Richard Fenno, *Home Style: House Members in Their Districts* (Boston: Little, Brown, 1978), 167–168.

35. Matthews, *U.S. Senators and Their World,* 114–117.

36. William S. White, *The Citadel: The Story of the United States Senate* (New York: Harper & Brothers, 1957).

37. Ralph K. Huitt, "The Outsider in the Senate: An Alternative Role," *American Political Science Review* 55 (September 1961): 566–575.

38. Herbert B. Asher, "The Learning of Legislative Norms," *American Political Science Review* 67 (June 1973): 499–513.

39. John R. Hibbing and Sue Thomas, "The Modern United States Senate: What Is Accorded Respect," *Journal of Politics* 52 (February 1990): 143.

40. Eleanor Clift, "Crashing the Capitol Club," *Newsweek,* January 14, 1991, 26.

41. Huitt, "The Outsider in the Senate: An Alternative Role," 567–569.

42. Ralph K. Huitt, "The Morse Committee Assignment Controversy: A Study in Senate Norms," *American Political Science Review* 51 (June 1957): 313–329; Ross K. Baker, "Party and Institutional Sanctions in the U.S. House: The Case of Congressman Gramm," *Legislative Studies Quarterly* 3 (August 1985): 315–337.

43. Calculated from data supplied in *Congress A to Z* (Washington, D.C.: Congressional Quarterly, 1988), 491–494; a record six House members were considered for expulsion on corruption charges in the 1870s.

44. Alvin M. Josephy, Jr., *On the Hill* (New York: Touchstone, 1979), 232.

45. Ibid., 239–240.

46. *Congress A to Z,* 491; *Congressional Ethics: History, Facts, and Controversy* (Washington, D.C.: Congressional Quarterly, 1992).

47. Ibid., 492.

48. Ibid., 491.

49. Ibid., 493–494.

50. The penalty was lessened to "denunciation" on the Senate floor.

51. *Congress A to Z,* 113.

52. For background, see Tom Morgenthow, "Barney Frank's Story," *Newsweek,* September 25, 1989, 14–16.

53. For background on the Durenberger case, see "Scandals Kept Ethics Panels Busy," *Congressional Quarterly Almanac* 45 (Washington, D.C.: Congressional Quarterly, 1990), 47–48.

54. Andy Jacobs, *The Powell Affair* (New York: Bobbs-Merrill, 1973), 4. The author sat on the House ethics committee that judged Powell and wrote a book about the affair.

55. *Powell v. McCormack,* 395 US 486 (1969).

56. Nearly one year into the 105th Congress, only Chair James Hansen (R., Utah) and Howard Berman (D., Calif.) served on the ethics committee, while the House awaited a task force report on reorganizing the ethics process. See Jackie Koszczuk, "Filing Complaints in the House: Now for Members Only?" *Congressional Quarterly Weekly Report,* September 20, 1997, 2199–2200.

57. "Congress 1976: Spotlight on Ethics," *Congressional Quarterly Almanac 1976* (Washington, D.C.: Congressional Quarterly, 1977), 32.

58. Josephy, *On the Hill,* 379.

59. For a historical overview of congressional ethics, see *Congressional Ethics,* 2d ed. (Washington, D.C.: Congressional Quarterly, 1980).

60. "Wright Becomes First Speaker to Resign," *Congressional Quarterly Almanac 1989* 45 (Washington, D.C.: Congressional Quarterly, 1990), 36–40.

61. Jill Abramson and David Rogers, "The Keating 535," *Wall Street Journal,* January 10, 1991, 1.

62. Beth Donovan, "A Slowly Spreading Scandal: Check-Kiters Retrench," *Congressional Quarterly Weekly Report,* March 31, 1992, 691–696. On the fallout of the House bank scandal, see Gary C. Jacobson and Michael A. Dimock, "Checking Out: The Effects of Bank Overdrafts on the 1992 Election," paper presented at the Annual Meeting of the Midwest Political Science Association, Chicago, April 1993; Charles Stewart III, "Let's Go Fly a Kite: Correlates of Involvement in the House Bank Scandal," *Legislative Studies Quarterly* 19 (November 1994): 521–535.

63. Dennis F. Thompson, *Ethics in Congress: From Individual to Institutional Corruption* (Washington, D.C.: Brookings Institution, 1995); Brent Thompson, "Ethics Overkill on the Hill?" *Washington Times,* December 4, 1995, 16.

64. Mark P. Moore, "Rhetorical Subterfuge and 'The Principle of Perfection': Bob Packwood's Response to Sexual Misconduct Charges," *Western Journal of Communication* 60 (1996): 1–20; Peter J. Boyer, "The Ogre's Tale," *The New Yorker,* April 4, 1994, 36+.

65. Suzy Platt, ed. *Respectfully Quoted* (Washington, D.C.: Congressional Quarterly, 1992), 57.

66. Koszczuk, "Filing Complaints in the House," 2199–2200.

5

Committees:
The Little Legislatures

I n 1884, a young political scientist was putting the final touches on a book manuscript. He argued that Congress had dominated the presidency in recent decades and that a major reason was its powerful committee structure. He summarized his thesis in a simple sentence: "Congressional government is committee government."[1] The statement seems somewhat ironic, coming as it did from an author who later became president of the United States. Woodrow Wilson realized at the time, however, that the committee system was the key organizing principle of Congress.

Congress uses committees for many reasons. First, they help it process legislation. Committees provide a rational, stable, and predictable means for channeling work; those characteristics are essential to an institution that tackles issues ranging from the availability of abortion to Zaire's zinc exports. Other than committees, how would 535 members of Congress divide and process work?

The role of committees in processing legislation may take a positive or negative dimension. Committee members enthused about a bill will schedule hearings, draft changes to improve a bill's quality and/or odds of passage, and report it out with a strong recommendation that the full chamber accept it. Alternatively, committee members may kill a bill by refusing to act on it. That outcome is common, for a variety of reasons. For example, the bill may be ill conceived or poorly drafted, it may be similar to a bill already being considered, or it may be badly timed.

The House Judiciary Committee is one example of a committee that often disposes of legislation. With jurisdiction over social issues, it receives proposals on controversial issues like abortion, school prayer, gun control, and gay rights. Many representatives seek to avoid votes on those "no-win" issues; those in the minority party often introduce bills on those subjects simply to score political points against the majority party. During the 1980s, for example, Democrats on the Judiciary Committee killed so many conservative proposals on social issues that Henry Hyde (R., Ill.) wryly compared its three top leaders to the three points of the Bermuda Triangle, which is famous for making things disappear.[2] With the Republicans now in control, the Judiciary Committee has become a burial ground for Democratic bills favoring gay rights, abortion services, and handgun control.

Second, Congress uses committees to produce quality legislation. The committee system allows members to specialize in particular policy areas and thereby to author informed bills. In conjunction with their committee assignments, members attend hearings on bills, listen to expert witnesses, ask questions, and rewrite legislation. They quickly develop expertise in a policy area if they lacked it prior to their committee assignment. This institutional division of labor gives those members with the most knowledge of a subject the greatest role in drafting legislation. The overall quality of drafted bills is usually high, even though their substance might be controversial. Poorly drafted bills are the exception to the rule.

The very idea of Congress producing quality legislation may sound peculiar in modern times. Critics write books with titles like *Parliament of Whores* that portray members as knaves and fools.[3] Citizens understandably get the impression that members are the principal obstacle to sound law, when the incredible complexity of policy-making is the more likely culprit. The sponsor of a high-quality "clean air" bill, for instance, must understand current environmental regulations, the major sources and the current levels of air pollution, the toxicity of certain substances, the costs to affected industries to comply with more stringent standards, and the prospects for enforcing new standards. He or she needs expertise on topics ranging from automobile emissions, to ozone depletion, to smokestack "scrubbers." The story is similar in other policy areas: Members require knowledge of existing statutes, scientific principles, causal relationships, budget implications, and so on. The practice of specialization is indispensable, making the committee system that facilitates it essential.

Third, Congress employs committees for oversight purposes. Recall from Chapter 2 that permanent oversight committees and subcommittees, as well as temporary investigatory committees, are used to monitor the operations of the executive branch. Congress also employs committees to oversee its internal operations. The House Oversight Committee and the Senate Rules and Administration Committee, both of which may be traced back to the 1st Congress (1789–1790), are responsible for "housekeeping." They track the work of congressional support agencies, and they serve as a liaison between the individual member and the institution. These committees traditionally have not been considered prestigious. They have gained new prominence in the era of

---

BOX 5.1   Fraud and Oversight in the 46th District?

Republican Robert Dornan represented the 46th District of California in the House for eighteen years, beginning in 1976. The district lies between Los Angeles and San Diego, spanning much of conservative Orange County. It is home to Disneyland, defense contractors, and the "positive thinking" ministry of Dr. Robert Schuller.

Dornan established a national reputation as a fiery conservative during his tenure in office. He lambasted liberal solutions to social problems, and he promoted the military in the strongest possible terms, earning himself the nickname "B-1 Bob." His rhetorical flourishes on the House floor were legendary. In January 1995, House Republicans rebuked him for accusing President Clinton of providing "aid and comfort to the enemy" during the Vietnam War. Dornan brushed aside the criticism, announcing his intention to run against Clinton for the presidency in 1996. His presidential campaign quickly fizzled during the Republican primary season, though, so Dornan returned to the 46th District to reclaim his House seat.

He failed to do so. Dornan actually won on election day by 233 votes, but when the absentee ballots were counted, he lost to Democrat Loretta Sanchez by 984 votes. A bitter fight ensued.

Dornan claimed widespread voter fraud, charging that hundreds of people in the 46th District voted illegally. His allegations quickly assumed racial overtones. Loretta Sanchez was a Latina, whose large margin of victory in the Hispanic sections of the district became a focal point of contention. Racial tensions were already high in California, because of a 1996 ballot measure dealing with affirmative action, and the claims and counterclaims of the two candidates inflamed feelings. Dornan said that Sanchez was an unqualified candidate who ran a dirty campaign; Sanchez claimed that Dornan was simply a poor loser.[1]

Sanchez attended orientation for the freshman class and was sworn into the 105th Congress (1997–1998). Dornan counterattacked with thirty-four subpoenas of citizens supporting his allegations of voter fraud. He demanded that state officials investigate. The California secretary of state discovered that 303 voters had been improperly registered by an immigration rights organization, giving credence to Dornan's claims. Although 303 votes were not

---

Republican control of Congress, however, as the vehicles to institute organizational changes and staffing cuts on the Hill. In anticipation of a more important role, Speaker Gingrich was given authority in the 104th Congress (1995–1996) to name the Republican members of the House Oversight Committee.

Fourth, Congress uses committees to help socialize members. This usage has both personal and professional dimensions. On the personal side, committees let members establish working relationships with subgroups of their colleagues. Such an opportunity is important for new members, and especially so for representatives, who have many colleagues. On the professional side, committees help train new members, giving them an opportunity to learn the rules and norms of the institution in a less formal setting. This training particularly aides members with no background in parliamentary procedures or the legislative process. They assimilate knowledge and hone their skills through committee work.

Although committees serve analogous functions for the House and Senate, their position within the chamber differs. The committee system is generally more important to the individual members and the institution of the House, as we shall see throughout this chapter.

BOX 5.1 continued

enough to overturn Sanchez's victory, the illegalities caused the House to investigate.

Consistent with its specified jurisdiction, the eight-member House Oversight Committee considered Dornan's allegations in the opening weeks of the 105th Congress. The committee retained the services of outside attorneys. It also appointed a three-member task force to delve deeper into the matter, composed of Vern Ehlers (R., Mich.), Bob Ney (R., Ohio), and Steny Hoyer (D., Md.). The task force held a contentious day of hearings in Washington, D.C., during which time Democrat Hoyer fought a losing battle against his two Republican colleagues to dismiss Dornan's case. He also lost a vote on field hearings. Ehlers and Ney agreed to hold a second day of hearings out in the 46th District, where they could listen to first-hand allegations of voter fraud. Sanchez supporters organized a counterdemonstration to coincide with the field hearings.[2]

The Dornan–Sanchez race raised delicate issues for the House Oversight Committee, and particularly for its Republican members, who are appointed by the Speaker. Should they sacrifice Dornan, thereby losing an outspoken conservative and a reliable vote in a House in which they held a narrow margin, or should they promote his claims and risk alienating a large ethnic voting bloc across the country? Democrats faced an easier task. They simply argued that the certified winner of the seat should keep it.

The House Oversight Committee moved cautiously in the early weeks of the 105th Congress. Republicans eventually concluded that 748 votes were cast illegally but noted that the margin was insufficient to overturn Sanchez's victory; Democrats contested the figures cited by Republicans. Both sides saw reason to close the case. On February 12, 1998, the House voted 378–33 to end the investigation, thus leaving Loretta Sanchez the duly elected representative of the 46th district of California.[3]

1. "Democrat on Brink of Victory Against Dornan in California," *Seattle Times,* November 13, 1996.
2. Nancy Cleeland, "O.C. Latinos Plan Protest of 46th District Hearing," *Los Angeles Times,* April 12, 1997.
3. "House Ends Investigation of Sanchez's Election," *Congressional Quarterly Weekly Report,* February 14, 1998, 376.

ORIGIN AND EVOLUTION
OF THE COMMITTEE SYSTEM

The normal routine in the House and Senate during the early years of the republic was to have the entire Congress address issues whenever feasible. What better way to achieve the ideals of representative government than to have all of the members participate in debate and decision making? The arrangement reinforced members' wishes to keep the institution egalitarian and participatory, and it reflected the reality of a small number of members addressing a limited range of issues. In fact, committees were formed only on an ad hoc basis; they were disbanded after they studied an issue and made recommendations to the full chamber.[4] But over time, a steadily expanding membership and more legislative complexity reconfigured the equation, and both chambers created permanent committees to receive and process bills. They became known as *standing committees* because they "stood" from one Congress to the next. (These and other types of committees will be discussed in more detail later in this chapter.)

The House experimented with standing committees prior to the Senate because of its larger size. A total of sixty-four representatives, as compared to twenty-six senators, served in the 1st Congress, a size differential that increased as the population grew. The House was forced to delegate responsibility to subsets of members because its agenda was too crowded and its process too cumbersome for the whole chamber to address each issue. Then, too, the House was a more dynamic institution early on, producing most of the major bills.[5] It needed a reliable and efficient method of drafting legislation to replace the convoluted process of forming and dissolving ad hoc committees. Representatives created standing committees such as Commerce and Manufactures (1795), Public Lands (1805), Post Office and Postal Roads (1808), and Pensions and Revolutionary Claims (1813), all predecessors of committees still in existence in the 1990s. The House also created a few standing committees that still exist today by the same titles, such as Ways and Means (1802) and Judiciary (1813).[6] Standing committees were institutionalized once members became adjusted to the idea of permanent committees and developed a personal stake in maintaining fixed areas of jurisdiction.[7]

Senators were reluctant, however, to follow the route of their House colleagues. Their small numbers made it less necessary to delegate responsibility, and they preferred to act second on legislation. In Chapter 1, we noted how bicameralism arose from a combination of Montesquieu's teachings and practical experiences with Parliament and colonial legislatures; we also noted the assumption that an "upper house" would judge the work of a "lower house." Senators believed that they should evaluate the work of the House, not compete with it to write legislation. Senators' reluctance to seize legislative initiative prevented a standing committee system from emerging in the Senate until 1816.

What finally caused the Senate to form standing committees? Several things coalesced: (1) an expansion of the membership, caused by the admission of five new states; (2) a recognition that parallel committee structures would facilitate bicameral coordination; and (3) an emerging desire to share the national limelight. Senators created twelve standing committees in 1816, nine of which still exist in some form. These new committees were not as important as their House counterparts initially, because they were not given as many legislative prerogatives. Yet, their creation paved the way for future expansion of the committee system.

Committee Rise and Retrenchment

The committee system became a central feature of Congress in the decades preceding the Civil War.[8] From 1820 to 1860, the U.S. population grew by a staggering 226 percent and its territory by 68 percent, fostering a larger role for government; Congress's membership grew by 18 percent, reinforcing the need to delegate responsibility.[9] The population explosion and territorial expansion coincided with internal procedural changes in Congress to expand the role of the standing committees. In the House, the Speaker began to systematically "stack" committees with his cronies to establish control over major legislation.[10] That practice made committees a tool of the leadership, which encouraged top leaders to institutionalize their use. Likewise, both chambers adjusted their rules to make it easier for committees to report bills to the floor, thereby placing them in the center of the legislative process.[11]

In the late 1800s, standing committees continued to flourish and proliferate, and new committees were regularly added. It became easier to expand the committee pie than to rearrange individual members' portions. The proliferation of standing committees in the House put the Speaker in an awkward position. So long as he controlled the committees, they were a fine surrogate to exercise power, but if the Speaker lost control of committees, they became counterveiling centers of power. Most of the Speakers in the post–Civil War era felt confident enough to encourage expansion of the committee system. The resulting escalation was symbolized by the need to construct a Rules Committee in 1880, under the auspices of Speaker Samuel Randall (D., Pa.), specifically to regulate the flow of legislation from standing committees to the floor of the House.[12] The Senate needed no such counterpart then, and it lacks one even today.

In the midst of this thriving committee structure, Woodrow Wilson penned his observations about "committee government" in Congress. He described a sacrosanct House committee structure:

> The leaders of the House are the chairmen of the principle standing committees. Indeed, to be exactly accurate, the House has as many leaders as there are subjects of legislation; for there are as many standing committees as there are leading classes of legislation, and in the consideration of every topic of business the House is guided by a special leader in the person of the chairman of the standing committee, charged with the superintendence of measures of the particular class to which that topic belongs.[13]

Wilson also observed that each committee worked at its own pace, unruffled by the progress and operations of others. Confusion often resulted. Members lacked certainty about the jurisdiction of particular committees and the timing of action on bills. Although the House had enshrined a standing committee system, evident in Wilson's pithy observation that "Congress in its committee rooms is Congress at work," it had constructed an increasingly chaotic and decentralized system.[14] An able and determined leader could seize the opportunity to impose order from the top down.

Thomas Brackett Reed (R., Maine) embarked on that course. He rose to the speakership in 1889 and served in that role for six of the next ten years. He reduced the autonomy of the standing committees first by appointing himself chair of the Rules Committee and then by using that post to rewrite a number of House procedures. The so-called *Reed Rules* enhanced the ability of the Speaker to expedite business, and they provided him with more leverage over the committees. The Reed Rules gave the full body the right to close off debate on bills under consideration, which actually positioned the Speaker to do so because of his powers as presiding officer.[15]

Beginning with the 58th Congress (1903–1904), Joseph Cannon (R., Ill.) pushed the Speaker's role to new heights. He elevated the practice of "stacking" committees with loyal subordinates to an art form, and he took advantage of the Speaker's referral powers to influence the outcome of many bills. Roger

BOX 5.2   The Twentieth-Century Committee Barons of the House

The advent of the seniority system institutionalized power for the standing committee chairs. Democratic control of the House for forty years following World War II meant that the "committee barons" rose from their ranks.

One of the most powerful committee barons was nicknamed the "Swamp Fox" for his parliamentary intrigue. Representative Carl Vinson (D., Ga.) served in the House for fifty years, which is the third-longest tenure of any representative. He served as chair of the Naval Affairs Committee for sixteen years, during which time he authored the bill that created a two-ocean navy; he later served as chair of the Armed Services Committee for fourteen years. Once described as the "first of the autocratic [Armed Services] chairs," Vinson promoted higher military spending and advised presidents on military issues.[1]

Howard Smith (D., Va.), chair of the House Rules Committee from 1955 to 1967, was a particularly audacious committee baron. He routinely killed bills dealing with civil rights and federal aid to education, often by refusing even to convene the Rules Committee. When Speaker Sam Rayburn (D., Tex.) was told that Smith could not come to the nation's Capitol to act on an important civil rights measure because his barn had burned down, Rayburn quipped that he knew Smith would resort to almost anything, but he hadn't figured on arson.

Wilbur Mills (D., Ark.) served as chair of the Ways and Means Committee from 1958 to 1975. He authored much of the tax and health care legislation of the period; he also wielded power within the Democratic Caucus because the Ways and Means Committee determined other members' committee assignments. But Mills fell fast and hard from his pedestal. First, the "Watergate Class" of 1974 revoked Ways and Means' committee assignment powers. Then Mills was caught cavorting publicly with stripper Fanne Foxe, popularly known as the "Tidal Basin Bombshell." Mills resigned as chair of the Ways and Means Committee and entered treatment for alcoholism.

Dan Rostenkowski (D., Ill.) also served as chair of Ways and Means, from 1981 to 1994. He was a Chicago ward politician, who went head to head with the Reagan administration over issues such as tax reform.[2] "Rosty" was one of the true wheeler-dealers in the House. He was an effective, politically courageous legislator, who bragged that his support for a congressional pay raise at a time when few members dared to support it was proof of his "titanium testicles." Like Wilbur Mills, however, Rostenkowski plunged quickly from power. Allegations of embezzlement pushed him out of the House and eventually landed him in a federal penitentiary in Oxford, Wisconsin. Having finished his "Oxford education," as he called it, Rosty began life anew in 1998.[3]

Perhaps the last committee baron of the twentieth century will be John Dingell (D., Mich.). While serving as chair of the Energy and Commerce Committee from 1981 to 1995, Dingell earned a reputation for rewarding supporters and punishing opponents. The vast jurisdiction of Energy and Commerce presented him the opportunity to legislate in areas such as health, fossil fuels, telecommunications, transportation, energy, and tourism. When Republicans gained a majority in the 104th Congress, however, they greatly narrowed the jurisdiction of the committee. Dingell fell to the position of ranking minority member on an eviscerated committee, a role he still occupied in the 105th Congress.

With a six-year limit imposed on standing committee chairs by the Republican party, the prospects for any "barons" rising within House ranks are slim. The days of the omnipotent committee chairs are gone for the foreseeable future.

1. *Congress A to Z*, 2d ed. (Washington, D.C.: Congressional Quarterly, 1993), 22.
2. See Jeffrey H. Birnbaum and Alan S. Murray, *Showdown at Gucci Gulch* (New York: Vintage Books, 1987).
3. Daniel Klaidman and Evan Thomas, "Rosty's Difficult Winter," *Newsweek*, January 12, 1998, 36–37.

Davidson and Walter Oleszek summarized Speaker Cannon's clout: "As beneficiary of the Reed Rules, he enjoyed such powers as appointing committees, designating chairmen, referring bills to committees, sitting as chairman of [the] Rules [Committee], and determining who would speak on the floor."[16] His dictatorial use of those powers led to the *Revolt of 1910–1911,* in which reform-minded Republicans and minority-party Democrats joined forces to curb the powers of the Speaker. This "rank and file" revolt against the leadership paved the way for a wholesale restructuring of the committee system.

The number of standing committees actually peaked right after Cannon's reign, in the 63rd Congress (1913–1914), with sixty-one committees in the House and seventy-four in the Senate.[17] Many of the committees were inactive. Over several congresses, senators pared down the number, and then they eliminated forty-one committees at once in the 66th Congress (1919–1920). The House similarly reduced its number of standing committees. It also turned the Appropriations, Rules, and Ways and Means Committees into *exclusive committees,* which gave them special status. A member serving on one of them was prohibited from serving on any other major committee. That change facilitated specialization on key committees and reduced the need for as many committees by restricting dozens of members to a single assignment.[18]

Members in both chambers not only streamlined the committee system but also moved to insulate it from leadership. They began following the *seniority rule* in committee assignments, automatically making the person with the most years of continuous service on a particular committee the chair. Seniority gave members strong incentive to serve on the same committees year after year, so that they could work toward a chairship. What better way to enhance expertise and to prevent leaders from stacking committees with their cronies than to create incentives and craft rules for continuity? Ironically, the major beneficiaries of the seniority system (committee chairs) soon exercised power in a manner reminiscent of "Cannonism."

The dramatic reduction in the number of standing committees has proved durable—only a few of the standing committees created in the early 1900s still exist today. The period from 1919 to 1946 involved a "consolidation" of the standing committee system,[19] with 1946 being a milestone in the evolution of committees.

Autonomous Committees

Congress ushered in a new era of committee development with the *Legislative Reorganization Act of 1946.* The act locked into place the essential elements of the modern committee system.[20]

The Legislative Reorganization Act of 1946 was supported by members for many reasons. First, the House and Senate had done some backsliding on committee consolidation, thereby creating a system of fuzzy and overlapping committee jurisdictions. The House, for instance, had separate committees on Flood Control and on Rivers and Harbors; the Senate had one committee on Public Lands and another on Public Buildings and Grounds. A hodgepodge of ill-defined committee jurisdictions fostered inefficiency. Second, the two chambers had difficulty coordinating their work because they possessed such different committee structures. The parallel structure evident in the early 1800s was obliterated by decades of political infighting, so that the committees in one chamber did not necessarily correspond to those in the other. Third, the executive branch grew so much during World War II that it was difficult for Congress to oversee it effectively. Thus, Congress needed a new committee structure to fulfill its responsibility. Fourth, the U.S. population again mushroomed, growing from 92 to 151 million between 1910 and 1950. (Congress grew little—only two states were added and the number of representatives was capped at 435 after the 1910 census.) A burgeoning population placed new demands on the institution. Congress responded with a major structural overhaul.

The Legislative Reorganization Act of 1946 cut the number of standing committees from 48 to 19 in the House, and from 33 to 15 in the Senate. These reductions were achieved by merging and abolishing committees; in one instance, eight standing committees were consolidated into one! Members also clarified jurisdictions once they reduced the total number of committees. The current committee system still specifies policy jurisdictions; Table 5.1 summarizes the current arrangement.

The clarification of committee jurisdictions was more than an organizational step. It was a major political development that facilitated cozy relationships between committee members and organized interests, who knew which members and what committees to lobby. Stable committee memberships predicated on seniority and fixed policy jurisdictions removed an element of uncertainty. Before long, interest groups were pleading for special treatment with sympathetic members on specific committees; in turn, members received campaign contributions. This quid pro quo actually blossomed in later years, but it germinated in the revamped committee system.

The clarification of standing committee jurisdictions also minimized the ability of the leadership to decide jurisdictional disputes. When many committees with fuzzy jurisdictions existed in the House, for example, a Speaker could justifiably send bills to the most loyal committees. But now, his discretion was limited by written rules. The committee chairs benefited from such codification, because their turf was outlined and protected.[21]

The Legislative Reorganization Act also specified committee size. The Senate created thirteen slots on each of its standing committees, except for Appropriations, which was given twenty-one seats because of its sweeping jurisdiction; the House put between nine and forty-three people on every committee, with Appropriations being its largest as well. Although the aggregate numbers have changed dramatically over time, the fundamental principles are still intact. The Appropriations Committee in each chamber remains large, and House committees vary more in size than Senate committees.

Passing the Legislative Reorganization Act was difficult despite the rationale for it. The proposed changes clipped the power of chairs whose committees were being abolished. Proponents of reorganization gained political support by attaching several provisions to sweeten the package, such as higher pay and a retirement plan for members. They also added provisions to make congressional service easi-

Table 5.1   Jurisdiction of House Standing Committees in the 105th Congress (1997–1998)

Committee	Major Areas of Jurisdiction
Agriculture	agriculture, forestry, animals
Appropriations	government spending
Banking and Financial Services	banking, securities, urban development, international finance
Budget	budget process
Commerce	interstate and foreign commerce, energy, health, tourism, nuclear waste
Education and Workforce	education, labor
Government Reform and Oversight	civil service, post office, District of Columbia, efficiency of government
House Oversight	House accounts, information systems, congressional support agencies, federal elections
International Relations	relations with other nations, exports, foreign loans, United Nations
Judiciary	civil and criminal law, immigration, judicial branch, bankruptcy, patents
National Security	defense establishment, merchant marine, intelligence, armed forces
Resources	public lands, fisheries, parks, mining, pollution
Rules	House order of business
Science	scientific research, space exploration, environmental research, civil aviation
Select Intelligence	Central Intelligence Agency, National Security Agency
Small Business	small business, paperwork reduction
Standards of Official Conduct	ethics
Transportation and Infrastructure	Coast Guard, flood control, roads, water, transportation, customs
Veterans' Affairs	veterans, cemeteries, pensions, hospitals
Ways and Means	revenue, charitable foundations, Social Security

er, such as funding to hire more staff.[22] Many members benefited from reorganization, of course, including the chairs of the committees still left, whose rivals were being stripped of authority. Even many members whose committees were being abolished ultimately gained from consolidation and codification by swapping several minor assignments for a major one. The legislation proved unstoppable.

The reorganization created stability in the committee system that lasted until the 1970s. The fact that during this era, Democrats controlled both chambers, except for the 80th (1947–1948) and 83rd (1953–1954) Congresses, contributed to the stability of the structure. Democrats organized the chambers as they pleased and left them that way. The seniority principle also played a role; because the same party controlled Congress, and members with the longest tenure rose to chairships, the same southern conservatives stayed in power. They had a vested interest in preserving the existing structure and in keeping junior members quiescent (the darker side of the apprenticeship norm discussed in Chapter 4). Committee chairs blended skill and finesse with an institutional base of authority. Their power was even conceded by House Speaker John McCormack (D., Mass.), who advised junior members: "Whenever you pass a committee chairman in the House, you bow from the waist. I do."[23] What a remarkable change from the days of Cannonism! Even the Speaker acted deferential to the committee barons, who effectively wielded power in the 1950s and 1960s. Yet, they faced formidable challenges in the 1970s, when it became clear that the chairs, as a group, were out of sync ideologically with rank-and-file Democrats.

Subcommittee Government

The first sign of restiveness by liberal Democrats with the conservative committee barons surfaced after the 1958 elections, when Democrats gained forty-eight House and twelve Senate seats. The new House members and the new senators were more liberal than their senior colleagues.[24] Liberal representatives promptly started up an informal organization known as the *Democratic Study Group* (DSG), which they designed as a counterweight to the conservative House hierarchy.[25] The junior members sought safety in numbers, and their collective efforts ultimately brought progressive change in civil rights, health, and education policy.[26] In 1964, another large cadre of liberal Democrats won office, padding the Democratic margin in both chambers and further augmenting reformist impulses. In 1965, liberal Democrats rallied behind the establishment of a *Joint Committee on the Organization of Congress,* whose designated purpose was to examine legislative organization and procedures. It proposed committee reforms that engendered fierce opposition from conservative Democrats holding committee chairships; during the mid-1960s, Southerners held 100 percent of the exclusive committee chairships in both the House and Senate, plus 50 percent (House) and 56 percent (Senate) of the total number of chairships.[27] It took liberal reformers five years to even partly overcome conservative opposition.

The *Legislative Reorganization Act of 1970* advanced the cause of reform-minded members by fundamentally restructuring the way committees did business and decentralizing political power. It revised chamber rules to ensure that committee sessions were open to the public and that committee bills were available for public scrutiny several days before they were considered on the floor. It required roll call votes in committee to be recorded, jeopardizing the practice of members quietly killing legislation in committee without a public record of it. All of those changes opened up Congress to greater scrutiny.

Besides the institutional reforms, each chamber adopted provisions specific to its needs. The Senate agreed to a rule restricting members to service on only one of the four most prestigious committees (Appropriations, Armed Services, Finance, and Foreign Relations) and adopted a policy that prevented any senator from heading more than one full committee. The House adopted provisions that lessened the discretion of the committee chairs. Committees were required to adopt a set of written rules, curbing arbitrary use of procedure by chairs.

Committees were allowed to meet on bills opposed by the chair. The Speaker was authorized to recognize any committee member to call up a bill on the floor, not just the chair.[28] The new provisions directly undercut the power of committee chairs and indirectly diminished the clout of southern conservatives. As Figure 5.1 shows, their share of committee chairships would drop precipitously by the end of the 1970s.

It may be a reflection on human nature, but once they tasted success, the reformers wanted more. Pressure for additional reform was particularly acute in the House, where by tradition the committee system was more enshrined. Reform-minded Democrats pushed for changes through their party caucus. Julia Butler Hansen (D., Wash.) was picked to lead the *Committee on Organization, Study, and Review* (known as the "Hansen Committee"). Its charge was to examine the untouched dimension of previous reform efforts—the sacrosanct seniority system. The Hansen Committee produced reform packages over the next several years.

The first set of reforms, called "Hansen I," were adopted in 1971. The reforms placed committee chairs on notice by creating a process that put all chairships to a caucus vote, one at a time. This new process was palpably different from the old system, in which the most senior member of each committee was automatically nominated and the entire slate was accepted en bloc. The "Hansen II" reforms, adopted in 1973, made it easier for rank-and-file Democrats to vote against a committee chair by providing for a secret ballot in cases in which 20 percent of the party caucus requested it. That mechanism for mutiny (or device for democracy, depending on how one looks at it) would be used two years later to topple several committee chairs. The Hansen II package also contained a *Subcommittee Bill of Rights,* which forced the committee chairs to refer legislation to subcommittee within two weeks and allowed subcommittee chairs to hire their own staff.[29] The "Hansen III" package, adopted in 1974, required almost all standing committees to have at least four subcommittees. That simple change prevented the committee chairs from centralizing power by refusing to use a subcommittee structure. The last package was accepted in lieu of a much more drastic proposal, crafted by Richard Bolling (D., Mo.), that would have restructured the committee system and redrawn the lines of jurisdiction.[30] The simple existence of the Bolling proposal signaled the intensity of reformist impulses in the 1970s. The reform movement crested in 1975, both tangibly and symbolically, when the Democratic Caucus wielded its secret ballot tool to depose three southern conservatives from committee chairships: W. R. Poage (D., Tex.) of Agriculture, Wright Patman (D., Tex.) of Banking, and F. Edward Hebert (D., La.) of Armed Services. But the reform movement lost its steam following this coup de grace, a victim of its own success. The House essentially tabled two other proposals to redraw the committee system.[31]

The effect of the Legislative Reorganization Act of 1970 on the Senate's committee system was very different, in part due to that chamber's own unique character. In contrast to newly elected Democrats in the House, who formed the DSG to promote their liberal agenda because they were poorly positioned in the committee structure, newly elected Democrats in the Senate were well situated and did not feel the same sense of helplessness.[32] The Senate was also more collegial, so

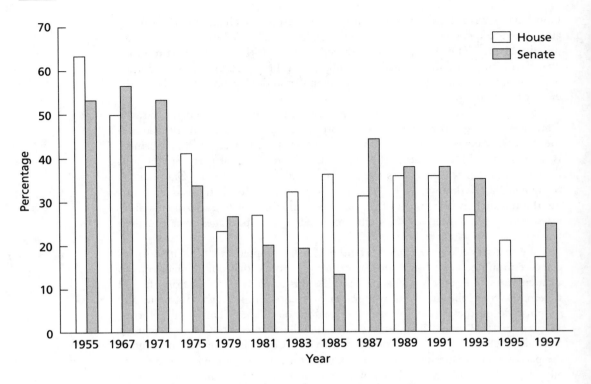

FIGURE 5.1   Percentage of Southern Standing Committee Chairships, 1955–1997

SOURCE: Norman J. Ornstein, Thomas E. Mann, and Michael J. Malbin, *Vital Statistics on Congress 1997–1998* (Washington, D.C.: Congressional Quarterly, 1998), 126.

the hierarchy of chairships mattered less. Disagreements could be worked out informally or redressed on the floor if necessary. Options existed other than toppling committee chairs. Equally important, the Senate faced a fundamentally different problem: Senators did not lack opportunities to participate in committee work because of unresponsive committee barons. Rather, they had too many assignments and too many obligations—they were expected to be everywhere at once. Senator Everett Dirksen (R., Ill.), the Senate Republican leader from 1959 to 1969, made that point in a lighthearted way with his observation that he needed roller skates to make it to all of his subcommittee meetings.[33]

The Legislative Reform Act of 1970 did nothing to curb either the number of subcommittees or the total number of assignments per senator. The Senate eventually revisited its committee system in 1976 through the *Temporary Select Committee to Study the Senate Committee System,* otherwise known as the "Stevenson Committee," after its chair, Adlai Stevenson (D., Ill.). The Stevenson Committee recommended reductions in the number of assignments per senator by abolishing selected committees and subcommittees. Its recommendation was accepted. A few standing committees and dozens of subcommittees were abolished, creating a dramatic drop in the total number of assignments per senator, from about eighteen to ten by the beginning of the 96th Congress (1979–1980).[34] The Senate also clarified referral of energy, science, and human resource bills. The Stevenson Committee provided the most comprehensive retooling of the Senate committee structure since the Legislative Reorganization Act of 1946. It proved to be the only major committee-related initiative in the Senate in the 1970s. Senators lacked the same ideological and regional tensions as representatives, and they restricted their focus to the issue of too many assignments.

In retrospect, the 1970s inaugurated fundamental changes in the committee system, as members of Congress tailored it to fit their goals. House Democrats altered the committee structure to give rank-and-file members a larger role and to force change in the collective ideology of chairs; senators consolidated the structure to ease the burden of too many committee assignments. Those changes were consistent with the history of committee reform packages in the bicameral legislature—the House usually undertakes reform to redistribute power, while the Senate usually tries to streamline its operations. The distinctive natures of the two chambers are evident in the paths traveled by committee reform.

Were the reforms of the 1970s a good thing? The answer is mixed. The democratization of power, particularly in the House, created a more egalitarian and responsive institution; yet, the very same changes made the House less coherent and predictable. Leroy Rieselbach described the trade-off as one of responsiveness (to rank-and-file members and to constituents) versus responsibility (to legislate effectively).[35] This was most evident in the House because of the far-reaching nature of reform.[36]

The decline in legislative efficiency, as members redesigned their institution, fed citizen perceptions of ineffectiveness.[37] What did people care about secret ballots for selecting committee chairs or for requirements that committees have subcommittees? Their interest was in public policy outcomes. The gridlock resulting from introspective reform contributed to harsh evaluations of job performance. A Gallup Poll taken at the end of the 1970s showed that only 19 percent of citizens approved of Congress's performance, in contrast to 61 percent who disapproved.[38]

Committees in the Postreform Era

Once reformers achieved their goals in the 1970s, the House entered a period of structural stability. The committee system, created and presided over by Democrats throughout the 1980s and early 1990s, remained virtually untouched. Only partisan adjustments were made in an effort to fend off a more conservative agenda following the 1980 election, when Republican Ronald Reagan was elected president and Republicans picked up thirty-three House seats and twelve Senate seats. Specifically, House Democrats stacked key committees with reliable liberals. Yet, that move reflected partisan manuevering rather than reformist impulses. If anything, House Democrats tried to avoid divisive internal reform during the 1980s. They needed unity against a Republican Senate (1981–1986) and successive Republican presidents.

The Senate committee structure was a prime target for reform after Republicans captured majority-party control in 1980 for the first time in a quarter century. However, little actual reform resulted. Republicans launched a *Temporary Select Committee to Study the Senate Committee System,* known as the "Quayle Committee," after its chair (and future vice-president) Dan Quayle (R., Ind.). It was asked to revisit the bipartisan problem of too many committee assignments per senator; yet, its modest recommendation that the Senate enforce its rules regarding committee assignments fell to expediency.[39] The Senate barely touched its standing committee structure in the 1980s and 1990s, other than to make changes in subcommittee titles to reflect partisan priorities. The lack of change is striking because the Senate was controlled first by Republicans (1981–1986) and then by Democrats (1987–1994), before reverting to Republican control (1995–1998). The lack of change highlights the collegial and participatory nature of the Senate.

The lack of reform to the committee structure well into the 1990s did not necessarily mean that it was not on members' minds. During the 103rd Congress (1993–1994), with Democrats in control of both chambers, a bicameral, bipartisan committee was established. Known as the *Joint Committee on the Organization of Congress,* it was charged with producing a comprehensive reform package that could carry Congress into the twenty-first century. It was headed by two senators, David Boren (D., Okla.) and Pete Domenici (R., N. Mex.), and two representatives, Lee Hamilton (D., Ind.) and David Dreier (R., Calif.); five other senators and representatives from the two parties also served, making it genuinely bicameral. The Joint Committee's mission was broad, and it considered reform in many different areas: reducing staff, moving to a biennial budget process, applying workplace laws to Congress, and reforming the Senate filibuster.[40] It also considered committee reform, with the usual issues resurfacing, such as abolishing committees, redrawing jurisdictional lines, and reducing the total number of assignments per member.[41]

Proposals to revamp the committee system encountered fierce opposition from existing House committee chairs, who tried to deflect jurisdictional reforms by focusing effort on reducing the size of committees. The Congressional Black Caucus opposed reform aimed at reducing the number of assignments per member, on the grounds that its members would be pushed off major committees at a critical time in their careers.[42] Perhaps the most serious obstacle at the time, however, was the opposition of top leaders in each chamber. Neither Speaker Tom Foley (D., Wash.) nor Senate Majority Leader George Mitchell (D., Maine) relished the prospect of presiding over internal reform, particularly at a time when a Democratic president, Bill Clinton, was in the White House. They preferred policy fights to jurisdictional squabbles, with Speaker Foley once saying that he would not recommend touching committee reform with a ten-foot pole.[43]

The constellation of forces arrayed against the Joint Committee's work proved too strong. Bipartisanship and bicameral cooperation steadily eroded. House Democrats declined to make concessions to minority-party Republicans, for instance, unless Senate Democrats were given greater latitude to stop minority-party filibusters in their chamber. Senators of both parties resented House intrusion into their own procedures and countered by unveiling their own proposal. House Republicans criticized the House Democrats for moving to the precipice of meaningful reform and then stepping back. Ultimately, the Joint Committee's proposals, known as the *Legislative Reorganization Act of 1994,* died quietly in the House Rules Committee and more noisily on the Senate floor near the end of the 103rd Congress. Interestingly, though, it set the stage for a massive overhaul of the committee system once the Republicans gained control of the House in the 1994 elections.

Committee Reform in the Republican Era

The Republican Contract With America pledged to reduce the overall number of House committees and to reduce the number of committee staff by one-third, without specifying where downsizing would occur. In the interregnum between the 1994 elections and the start of the 104th Congress (January 1995), David Dreier (R., Calif.) produced four plans to restructure the committee system. His work on the House Rules Committee and his service as vice-chair of the Joint Committee on the Organization of Congress over the previous two years had familiarized him with jurisdictional politics in the House.

Dreier's basic task was to redesign the committee system to increase its efficiency and to make it congruent with Republican policy objectives. His more elaborate plans to remake committees encountered stiff opposition from incoming chairs, who would hold those posts for the first time in their careers. Incoming Speaker Newt Gingrich, like his Democratic predecessor Tom Foley, also wished to avoid the imbroglio of substantial internal reform, so he advocated incremental change. (Speaker Gingrich wished to fulfill the Contract With America above all else, so he favored reform to the extent it delivered on those promises.) Despite Dreier's call for comprehensive reform, the Republican Conference agreed to the most incremental of the four proposals. Its major provisions were as follows:

1. Abolish the Merchant Marine and Fisheries Committee, placing most of its jurisdiction into a Resources Committee

2. Abolish the District of Columbia Committee, placing most of its jurisdiction into a Government Reform and Oversight Committee

3. Abolish the Post Office and Civil Service Committee, placing most of its jurisdiction into a Government Reform and Oversight Committee

4. Retitle the Energy and Commerce Committee as the Commerce Committee, and redistribute some of its jurisdiction

5. Retitle nine other standing committees to reflect Republican priorities

The jurisdictional changes resulted in fewer committees and less committee staff, just as Republicans promised in their Contract With America.

Fewer full committees also meant fewer subcommittees. Figure 5.2 summarizes the trend by showing the number of subcommittees in the House at the beginning of each new Congress since the 97th Congress (1981–1982). The graph shows that House Democrats used between 130 and 142 subcommittees

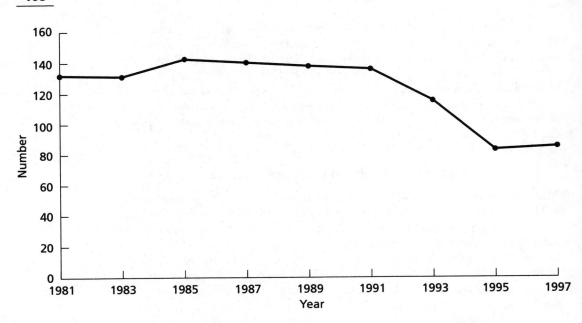

FIGURE 5.2   Number of House Subcommittees, 1981–1997

SOURCE: Norman J. Ornstein, Thomas E. Mann, and Michael J. Malbin, *Vital Statistics on Congress 1997–1998* (Washington, D.C.: Congressional Quarterly, 1998), 120.

throughout the 1980s but eventually cut the total number to 115 in the 103rd Congress. And once Republicans took control in the 104th Congress, they abolished 31 additional subcommittees, dropping the total number to 84. (It crept back up to 86 in the 105th Congress.) Clearly, House Republicans reduced the number of subcommittees as part of their committee reform plan.

In addition to jurisdictional changes, Republicans agreed to revamp long-standing committee practices. They instituted a six-year limit on service as a committee or subcommittee chair. (Senate Republicans also did so effective for the 105th Congress.) They gave full-committee chairs the power to appoint subcommittee chairs, to assign members to subcommittees, to hire staff for the majority party, and to control the committee's budget. Collectively, those changes basically repealed the so-called *Subcommittee Bill of Rights* installed by Democrats in the 1970s. Republicans also limited members to two full-committee or four subcommittee assignments, consistent with the 1993-1994 recommendation of the Joint Committee on the Organization of Congress. Furthermore, they restricted all members to one full-committee or subcommittee chairship. These changes represent the most comprehensive committee reform effort since the Legislative Reorganization Act of 1946.

TYPES OF COMMITTEES

Standing Committees

The *standing committees* are responsible for processing most of the legislation introduced each year. They are what Woodrow Wilson had in mind when he wrote about "committee government." Standing committees are created by public law or chamber rules; they are organized around broad public policy areas, such as agriculture, banking, or foreign relations. They have *legislative authority*, which gives them the right to receive and report bills in their jurisdiction.

Table 5.2 summarizes the current House and Senate standing committee systems. The table lists the nineteen committees of the House and the seventeen of the Senate in the 105th Congress. Relative parity in the total number of committees is a recent thing, reflecting the abolition of three House committees in the 104th Congress. Prior to that change, the House had quite a few more standing committees, typically with narrower jurisdictions.[44]

Some parallelism clearly exists between the House and Senate structures. Both chambers have committees with the same title and general responsibilities, such as Appropriations, Budget, Small Business, Judiciary, and Veterans' Affairs; in other cases, the titles differ but the responsibilities closely correspond, such as the House International Relations and Senate Foreign Relations Committees. One result of the committee reconfiguration in the House in the 104th Congress, however, was to make the structures appear less similar. Committees like Education and the Workforce or Transportation and Infrastructure seem to lack a corresponding committee in the Senate, even though Labor and Human Resources and Environment and Public Works are their actual counterparts. In a few cases, no parallel committee does exist (for example, Senate Indian Affairs), making it somewhat awkward to negotiate House–Senate differences on bills in those areas.

Table 5.2 also highlights the disparate size of committees. House committees ranged from 13 to 73 members in the 105th Congress, while Senate committees ranged from 12 to 28. Another way to look at size is to calculate the average number of committee seats. The House had a total of 789 seats on nineteen committees, for an average size of 42 members; the Senate had 312 seats on seventeen committees, for an average size of 18 members. House committees are therefore more than twice as large as their Senate counterparts, although they constitute a much smaller proportion of the chamber's total membership. About 10 percent of all members serve on a typical House committee, compared to about 18 percent in the Senate. The differential explains why representatives average fewer committee and subcommittee assignments than senators.

The difference in the number of assignments has significant consequences. The career of the average representative is likely to be defined by his or her committee assignments, with only limited opportunity to stray outside one or two policy areas. The lack of breadth means that representatives are less likely than senators to emerge as national figures or to seek the presidency. In the last four election cycles, only three representatives have sought the presidency, as compared

Table 5.2   Standing Committees of the 105th Congress (1997–1998)

HOUSE	Total Members	PARTY RATIO		Subcommittees
		Republicans	**Democrats**	
Agriculture	50	27	23	5
Appropriations	60	3	26	13
Banking and Financial Services	53	29	24	5
Budget	43	24	19	0
Commerce	51	28	23	5
Education and Workforce	45	25	20	5
Government Reform and Oversight	43	24	19	7
House Oversight	8	5	3	0
International Relations	47	26	21	5
Judiciary	35	20	15	5
National Security	55	30	25	5
Resources	50	27	23	5
Rules	13	9	4	2
Science	46	25	21	4
Small Business	35	19	16	4
Standards of Official Conduct	14	7	7	0
Transportation and Infrastructure	73	40	33	6
Veterans Affairs	29	16	13	3
Ways and Means	39	23	16	5

to nine senators. Representatives are viewed more as specialists while senators are seen more as generalists, partly because of the disparate pattern of committee assignments.

Table 5.2 also shows that the majority party exercises its prerogative to control all of the committees (except ethics). Theoretically, seats are apportioned according to party ratios in the chamber; Republicans occupied 52 percent of seats in the House for the 105th Congress, for instance, so by that standard they should have received 52 percent of the seats on all of the committees. Yet, the reality differs from the theory. The House follows an established tradition of the majority party giving itself lopsided margins in the major committees. The majority party does so on the grounds that it is principally responsible for enacting legislation, and so deserves slightly padded margins on certain committees. In the 105th Congress, Republicans gave themselves 57 percent of seats on Appropriations, 59 percent on Ways and Means, and a whopping 69 percent on the Rules Committee. The minority party complains bitterly about the practice, but without success because a straight party vote decides committee ratios. In the

Table 5.2   continued

SENATE	Total Members	PARTY RATIO Republicans	Democrats	Subcommittees
Agriculture, Nutrition and Forestry	18	10	8	4
Appropriations	28	15	13	13
Armed Services	18	10	8	6
Banking, Housing and Urban Affairs	18	10	8	5
Budget	22	12	10	0
Commerce, Science and Transportation	20	11	9	7
Energy and Natural Resources	20`	11	9	4
Environment and Public Works	18	10	8	4
Finance	20	11	9	5
Foreign Relations	18	10	8	7
Governmental Affairs	16	9	7	3
Indian Affairs	14	8	6	0
Judiciary	18	10	8	6
Labor and Human Resources	18	10	8	4
Rules and Administration	16	9	7	0
Small Business	18	10	8	0
Veterans' Affairs	12	7	5	0

1980s, Republicans tried unsuccessfully to rally public support for their crusade to end stacked committees. It is unlikely that Democrats will fare better if they try to do so in the 1990s. The issue is simply too convoluted for all but the most interested citizens.

Finally, Table 5.2 outlines the subcommittee structure of the House and Senate. It shows that an average committee has three to five subcommittees. Some committees have no subcommittee structure, such as the Budget Committee, whose one major task is to produce a comprehensive budget package each year. By contrast, the Appropriations Committees use thirteen subcommittees corresponding to the number of appropriations bills that Congress must pass each year to fund the federal government.

One thing Table 5.2 does not show is the relative sanctity of committee decisions. Richard Fenno did pioneering work in this area by analyzing the success of committees in getting the parent chamber to pass their bills.[45] He discovered widespread variation across committees, with Appropriations and Ways and Means having much better success than Education and Labor or Foreign Affairs.

He concluded that different types of committees exist in the House. *Corporate committees* enjoyed autonomy and success in passing their bills, but they were not very responsive to the membership; *permeable committees* were open and responsive, but they exerted less influence in the parent chamber and sometimes encountered difficulty passing their bills. In general, corporate committees were those atop the House hierarchy, such as Appropriations, Ways and Means, and Rules. Permeable committees were the less prestigious House and the Senate committees. Even the permeable committees prevailed most of the time on the floor, though—a testament to the sanctity of committee decisions.[46]

The institutionalization of "subcommittee government" in the 1970s challenged the sanctity of committee policy-making. Members responsible for reforming an unresponsive committee system wished to scrutinize committee bills and to add amendments on the floor. Soon, an identifiable pattern of floor decision making arose.[47] Recentralization of power in the "money committees" in the 1980s reestablished the autonomy of committees somewhat, but nothing approaching their pre-1970s levels.[48] In the 104th Congress, Republicans chipped away at committee autonomy by centralizing power in the speakership. Of course, a diminished ability of committees to prevail on the floor did not prevent committees from quashing legislation. That negative role alone makes them key actors in the legislative process right up to the present.

Select Committees

Select committees are created by a resolution to perform a specific task; thus, they supplement the standing committee structure. They are distinguishable in two ways. First, they lack legislative authority, so they are unable to receive and report bills in their jurisdiction. Instead, they customarily study a pressing issue and then make legislative recommendations to their chamber. Second, they are temporary, lasting as long as an investigation warrants up to a maximum of the two-year cycle of a given Congress. Select committees may take on the appearance of standing committees because they may be renewed over successive congresses, but they are not as important. Select committees are like understudies in theater—part of the act and ready to perform, but rarely commanding center stage.

Select committees serve both individual members and the institution.[49] They provide a platform for members to ingratiate themselves with particular constituencies or to pursue an issue of personal interest. For years, Charlie Rangel (D., N.Y.), who represents a district in Harlem, used his chairship of the House Select Committee on Narcotics Abuse and Control to promote an antidrug message. As recently as the 102nd Congress (1991–1992), the House and the Senate each had select committees on Aging; Indian Affairs; Children, Youth, and Families; Hunger; Narcotics Abuse and Control; and Intelligence. Most of those were abolished in subsequent congresses as cost-saving measures.

Select committees also serve the institution. For one thing, they provide flexibility to tackle issues that require attention but do not warrant a permanent committee. The Watergate scandal of the 1970s provides an example. Congress had to investigate allegations that President Nixon participated in a cover-up of criminal conduct, so the Senate created the Select Committee on Presidential

---

BOX 5.3   In with the Frosh, Out with the Select Committees

The House freshman class of the 103rd Congress (1993–1994), at 110 members, was the largest in the post–World War II period. Many of the freshmen pledged during the campaign season to bring greater fiscal discipline to the House and to reduce the cost of government. They soon delivered on that promise.

In the opening days of the new Congress, the freshmen spearheaded opposition to reauthorization of the Select Committee on Narcotics. The freshmen lobbied rank-and-file members of both parties; they recruited the standing committee chairs who stood to benefit if rival select committees were shut down. Their side argued that select committees duplicated tasks already performed by the standing committees, burdened taxpayers with unnecessary costs, and produced symbolism rather than substance because the select committees lacked legislative authority. A bill renewing the House Select Committee on Narcotics lost by a 180–237 vote.

Democratic leaders were dumbfounded. The reauthorization had been routinely approved for years. Speaker Tom Foley (D., Wash.) quickly pulled the reauthorization of the other select committees off the floor while he assessed the political situation. Republican Leader Robert Michel (Ill.) suggested a possible solution. He proposed a one-year rather than a two-year reauthorization for all four select committees: Narcotics; Hunger; Aging; and Children, Youth, and Families.[1] He figured a one-year reauthorization would fly with House Republicans, who would combine with members on the select committees and Democratic leaders to provide a majority.

Yet, rank-and-file members rebelled. The cost of maintaining the four select committees over the years totaled $44.7 million.[2] The freshmen and their allies wanted to defund select committees, and they demanded a separate reauthorization vote on each one. President Clinton helped their cause by announcing a 25 percent cut in White House staff and then challenging Congress to follow suit. Democratic leaders planning to put forward a resolution extending all four select committees for one more year delayed while they worked to build political support. They failed.

When Democratic leaders finally brought a bill to the floor to fund the standing committees, they had acquiesced to the rank and file. Their $52.3 million budget for the operations and staff of the standing committees incorporated only ninety days of funding for the four select committees. The bill terminated select committees that had existed in the House for over a decade. The resolution passed by a 224-196 margin.[3]

The abolition of select committees in the 103rd Congress set the stage for additional cuts in the Republican-controlled 104th Congress by focusing attention on institutional costs. During the fight over reauthorizing select committees, Jennifer Dunn (R., Wash.) proposed a 25 percent reduction in standing committee budgets. Republicans dismissed that idea once they became the majority party, but they did abolish three standing commitees.

---

1. Jeanne Ponessa, "Fate of Select Panels in Doubt After House Rejects One," *Congressional Quarterly Weekly Report,* January 30, 1993, 207.
2. Ibid.
3. "House Votes, 120," *Congressional Quarterly Weekly Report,* April 3, 1993, 868.

Campaign Activities (1973–1974), whose inquiry paved the way for impeachment proceedings. Once it finished its investigation, the select committee dissolved.

Second, select committees provide a solution to the problem of issues cutting across standing committee jurisdictions. The sale of arms to Iran and the diversion of profits to the Contras in the 1980s, known as the Iran–Contra affair, raised legal and foreign policy issues involving as many as ten separate standing committees. The creation of a select committee in each chamber, and their subsequent agreement to hold a joint inquiry, prevented a logistical and jurisdictional nightmare.[50] The use of select committees to head off jurisdictional disputes is rare, because hundreds of issues cut across standing committee lines. Congress cannot create select committees every time, and so uses them only when major issues are involved. It refers bills to multiple committees in most instances.

Third, select committees mollify organized interests. The American Association of Retired Persons (AARP), for instance, is a powerful senior citizen's lobby whose agenda ranges from Social Security benefits, to affordable health care, to insurance costs. The Senate Special Committee on Aging gives the AARP a legislative access point and symbolic reassurance; it gives senators a forum to ingratiate themselves with a powerful lobby. Those who serve on less prestigious committees are sometimes compensated by a plum select committee post.

A hybrid of the select committee system is the House and Senate Intelligence committees. Created in the 1970s to oversee the operations of the CIA, they are distinguished by legislative and budgetary authority, as well as a rotating membership.[51] The House even acknowledges the special status by conferring the odd title *Permanent* Select Committee on Intelligence. Its position is somewhere above select committees but below standing committees.

Joint Committees

Joint committees consist of equal numbers of senators and representatives, with the chairship rotated between them. Four such committees operated in the 105th Congress. The Joint Printing Committee monitored the *Congressional Record* and oversaw the work of the Government Printing Office. The Joint Library Committee oversaw the work of the Library of Congress. The Joint Economic Committee gathered data on the state of the economy and evaluated the president's annual economic message. The Joint Taxation Committee backstopped the revenue committee in each chamber. Joint committees typically have a mildly partisan flavor, with several more majority- than minority-party members on each one. Yet, their operations are mostly bipartisan.

Joint committees ostensibly facilitate coordination in the bicameral Congress. However, their potential "for enhancing the efficiency and effectiveness of the legislative process" is often illusory, because they meet infrequently and have only a limited legislative role.[52] They become important only when the two economic committees produce data that are a catalyst for legislation, such as the Joint Taxation Committee paving the way for tax reform in 1986 by publicizing inconsistencies in the tax code.[53] If select committees are like theater understudies, joint committees are like bit players on stage.

Conference Committees

The Constitution requires that bills be passed in identical versions by the House and Senate before they are forwarded to the president either for his signature or veto. Because the two chambers are so distinctive, they frequently change each other's bills, if not pass altogether different versions. *Conference committees* are temporary panels of representatives and senators, chosen by the Speaker of the House and the presiding officer of the Senate. They meet to reconcile differences in House and Senate bills. If conferees reach agreement, their handiwork is presented to their respective chambers for ratification and for transmission to the president. A conference committee dissolves once its work is completed.

At first glance, conference committees may seem mundane. Chamber leaders invariably select the chair and the ranking minority member of the committee with jurisdiction to lead their chamber's delegation (most of whom are from the standing committee). The conferees negotiate over language and dollar amounts, trying to uphold both their chamber's position and a partisan position. They end up agreeing to a compromise package, which is usually accepted by both chambers as the best deal that can be negotiated.

Upon closer scrutiny, however, the conference committee is a fascinating hybrid. The precise content of bills and the roster of conferees is never the same, giving each conference committee a unique flavor. Moreover, even though they are only temporary panels, conference committees are empowered to resolve major differences on important bills. Although conferees are supposed to negotiate within the parameters of the bills passed by their chambers, they are not required to do so. The results can be surprising. To cite an example, the fiscal year 1992 Interior Appropriations bill, funding the National Endowment for the Arts (NEA), prohibited the NEA from supporting any artistic projects that "promote, disseminate, or produce materials that depict or describe in a patently offensive way sexual or excretory activities or organs." Both the House and Senate included the same language in their differing versions of the appropriations bill; they inserted the language because of public outcry over NEA-sponsored projects of questionable taste. What happened to the language in the conference committee? House conferees ignored it because most of them disliked that specific provision. Senate conferees sacrificed it in exchange for lower grazing fees for cattle ranchers whose livestock roamed on public land.[54] Representative Bill Dannemeyer (R., Calif.), a harsh critic of the NEA during his time in office, labeled the agreement the "corn for porn" deal. An identical provision initially passed by both chambers ended up being dropped in conference. It confirmed President Reagan's quip that "if an orange and an apple went into conference consultations, it might come out a pear."[55]

The surprises sprung over the years have caused scholars and politicians alike to dub conference committees the "third house" of Congress.[56] Senator George Norris (R., Nebr.) summarized their importance decades ago: "The conference committee is many times, in very important matters of legislation, the most important branch of our legislature."[57] And Senator William Fulbright (D., Ark.) once sarcastically observed that conferees on an appropriations bill deserved commendation for "so forthrightly disregarding the wishes of the common lay members of the Senate and the House." Fulbright added that "to save the world and the people of this country, all that is needed is to reconvene, preferably in secret, only those incomparable sages, the conferees of the Appropriations Committee."[58]

Today the concerns expressed by Fulbright are less relevant. The practice of conferees deliberately thwarting the will of the full membership is the exception, not the rule, and the practice of secret negotiations is mostly gone. In 1975, each chamber adopted a measure requiring conferees to hold open meetings unless they voted publicly to close them; in 1977, the House followed up with a provision forcing conference committees to be open unless the full chamber voted to close them.[59] Now, virtually the only closed conference committees involve national security.[60]

Conference committees are discussed more completely in Chapter 8, which focuses on the legislative process and addresses bicameral issues, such as the ability of one chamber to dominate the other during negotiations. At this point, in keeping with the previous analogies, think of conference committees as the supporting players who appear on stage every so often to steal the show.

COMMITTEE ASSIGNMENTS

Members of Congress have a stake in securing desirable committee posts. They need slots that serve their constituencies and assist their prospects for reelection. They need satisfactory positions because they will invest time and effort in their committee work. They seek forums that allow them to focus on the issues they care about most. Members' committee assignments may define their congressional careers and determine their contribution to posterity.

The process of doling out committee assignments in each new Congress is greatly simplified by the practice of permitting returning members to reclaim their seniority on standing committees. Thus, a member serving on the Senate Agriculture Committee in the current Congress will be allowed to reclaim that same seat in the next. That practice benefits the institution by promoting continuity and marshaling expertise on committees. Yet, each new Congress raises assignment issues, as returning members strive to upgrade their position in the chamber and as new members manuever for desirable posts. The complex machination of fitting people and positions together has been labeled "the giant jigsaw puzzle."[61] The two chambers and two political parties assemble their committee rosters somewhat differently.

Assignment Process

House Democrats relied on their colleagues on the Ways and Means Committee to review and distribute committee assignments from 1911 to 1974. As part of the revolt against committee chairs, that authority was reassigned to a *Steering and Policy Committee* in 1975.[62] The move simultaneously slashed the power of the Ways and Means members and increased the Speaker's power because he chaired the Steering and Policy Committee. Reformers struck at a time when Ways and Means Chair Wilbur Mills (D., Ark.) was embroiled in ethics problems that diminished his ability to fend off an attack on his committee.

Since Democrats became the minority party in the House, they have used the simplified title *Steering Committee*. In the 105th Congress, the committee was headed by Minority Leader Richard Gephardt (Mo.) and Steny Hoyer (Md.); it had thirty-nine members in all. For assignment purposes, it divides standing committees into three types: exclusive, major, and nonmajor. Any member receiving an *exclusive* assignment (Appropriations, Ways and Means, and Rules) is not allowed a seat on any other significant committee. All Democrats without an exclusive assignment are usually given a *major* (for example, Agriculture, Commerce, International Relations) and a *nonmajor* post (for example, Small Business, Veterans' Affairs). The entire slate of assignments is transmitted to the Democratic Caucus for approval. The loss of majority-party status and the abolition of several standing committees has compressed the number of prized slots for Democrats in recent years, making the assignment process especially difficult.[63]

House Republicans determine their assignments in a similar way. They also use a *Steering Committee,* which is headed by the Speaker. (Before they became the majority party, Republicans used the descriptive but awkward title "Committee on Committees.") The Speaker controls one-fourth of all votes on the Steering Committee through appointments. In the 105th Congress, key members included Majority Leader Richard Armey (Tex.), Majority Whip Tom DeLay (Tex.), and several committee chairs; it had twenty-five members in all. It uses the classification scheme employed by Democrats, although in the past it has used the patriotic symbolism of "red, white, and blue" to refer to exclusive, major, and nonmajor committees. Members with an exclusive assignment are prohibited from serving on any other significant committee; the Speaker is allowed to pick the members of the Rules Committee. All remaining Republicans receive a major and nonmajor assignment. The entire slate is ratified by the Republican Conference.

In the 104th Congress, the power and prominence of the GOP freshman class was evident in the committee assignment process. One-third of all House Republicans were newly elected in 1994. They were strong supporters of Speaker Gingrich, and he rewarded them with excellent committee assignments.[64] Republican freshmen received many seats on committees with broad jurisdiction, such as 6 seats on Budget, 8 on Commerce, 15 on Government Reform and Oversight, and 13 on Resources. Freshmen also received 11 seats on the three exclusive committees—7 on Appropriations, 3 on Ways and Means, and 1 on Rules. Two freshmen even received subcommittee chairships. With fewer choice seats available, a more conventional pattern emerged in the 105th Congress.

The Democratic and Republican Steering Committees are fairly representative of their respective party caucuses. They mirror their parties' ideological composition and their regional party strength. Table 5.3 provides data on the two Steering Committees relative to their respective party caucuses for the first session of the 104th Congress.

The most striking feature of the data is the congruity of scores between members of the Steering Committee and their party caucus. Party unity scores reflect the percentage of recorded votes in which members voted in agreement with their party. In the 104th Congress, members of the Republican Steering Committee voted in agreement with their party 94 percent of the time, compared to 91 percent of the time for all Republicans; members of the Democratic Steering Committee voted in agreement with their party 82 percent of the time,

Table 5.3 Representativeness of the House Steering Committees in the 104th Congress (1995–1996)

	PARTY UNITY SCORES	
	Steering Committees	Party Caucus
Republicans	94%	91%
Democrats	82%	80%
	PRESIDENTIAL SUPPORT SCORES	
	Steering Committees	Party Caucus
Republicans	19%	22%
Democrats	73%	75%
	CONSERVATIVE COALITION SCORES	
	Steering Committees	Party Caucus
Republicans	94%	90%
Democrats	41%	57%SD/28%ND[a]

[a] SD = Southern Democrats; ND = Northern Democrats.

SOURCE: *Congressional Quarterly Almanac* 51 (Washington, D.C.: Congressional Quarterly, 1996), C15–C33.

compared to 80 percent of the time for all Democrats. Presidential support scores measure the percentage of recorded votes in which members voted in agreement with President Clinton's stated position. Once again, the figures are closely grouped, with Republican Steering Committee members supporting the president 19 percent of the time, compared to 22 percent for all Republicans, and Democratic Steering Committee members supporting the president 73 percent of the time, compared to 75 percent for all Democrats. Finally, conservative coalition scores gauge the percentage of recorded votes in which a majority of Republicans voted in accordance with a majority of southern Democrats. Republican Steering Committee members voted with the conservative coalition 94 percent of the time, compared to 90 percent for the Republican Caucus. Democratic Steering Committee members voted with the conservative coalition 41 percent of the time, a figure wedged in between the 28 percent and 57 percent totals for the northern Democrats and southern Democrats, respectively.

What does the close congruence of scores indicate? The House Republican and Democratic Steering Committees are very representative of their respective party caucuses in terms of ideology and partisanship. The Steering Committees are not a demographic microcosm of their party caucuses, but they represent a cross-section of members in key respects.

Once both parties complete their work, before or early into a new Congress, they forward their assignments to the full House, which ratifies them in a pro forma vote. Minority-party complaints about lopsided committee ratios are voted down, and the process ends for the duration of that Congress.

The Senate's committee assignment process is straightforward and flows from chamber rules. The Senate classifies committees as major or minor. Thirteen major committees exist, four of which are considered "elite" (Appropriations, Armed Services, Finance, and Foreign Relations). Senators may not serve on more than one elite committee or on more than two major committees, and no senator may receive a second major committee post until every senator has one. Known informally as the *Johnson Rule,* because it was inaugurated by Majority Leader Lyndon Johnson (D., Tex.) for Democrats in the 1950s, this practice is widely adhered to by both parties. Still further decentralization occurred in the 105th Congress because of limitations on the number of subcommittee chairships per member. This Republican provision dropped the proportion of subcommittees being chaired by the leader of a full committee from 40 percent to 19 percent in two years.[65] Now, even first-term senators in the majority party serve as subcommittee chairs.

The restrictions placed on committee service by Senate rules are mostly advisory, because they are routinely waived to accommodate specific senators. For instance, Senator Charles Grassley (R., Iowa) served on one elite committee, three major committees, and one joint committee, and headed one select committee in the 105th Congress; Senator John Warner (R., Va.) served on seven committees, chairing two of them; and Senator Robert Byrd (D., W. Va.) served on two elite committees. Technically, these assignments violated Senate rules, but the norm in the more informal and collegial Senate is to bend the rules to accommodate the individual member. For the same reason, the Senate often increases the number of seats on key committees. Barbara Sinclair explained the expansion of committee seats back in the 1960s as a way to accommodate an infusion of northern Democrats and, more recently, as a way to cope with the incentives for senators to be involved with a broader range of issues.[66]

A chamber rule more important than numerical restrictions is one prohibiting a senator from serving as chair of more than one major committee. This rule periodically puzzles senior members, whose seniority positions them to head two major committees in a new Congress. When facing that situation, senators usually weigh the prestige of the assignments, the potential benefits to constituents, and the potential for drastic policy change if the person next in seniority rises to the chairship.[67] The last dimension creates ideological cohesiveness among committee leaders, because they try to advance the careers of members with goals similar to their own.[68] The most celebrated case in recent years involved Senator Jesse Helms (R., N.C.), who was forced to pick between chairship of the Agriculture and the Foreign Relations Committees. In the 1980s, facing a difficult reelection fight, Helms picked the constituency-oriented Agriculture Committee, leaving Foreign Relations to Senator Richard Lugar (R., Ind.). When presented the same dilemma in 1995 after Republicans regained control of the Senate, Helms picked the more prestigious Foreign Relations Committee. Helms and Lugar held the first and second positions on both committees in the 105th Congress.

The committee assignment process followed by the two parties is very different in the Senate than in the House. Democrats use a *Steering and Coordination Committee*. In the 105th Congress, it was chaired by Senator John Kerry (D., Mass.) and consisted of twenty members, nearly half of all Senate Democrats. Republicans employ a *Committee on Committees,* which was chaired by Slade Gordon (R., Wash.); it had no other members. What explains these odd structures? They are essentially coordinating bodies, with decision-making authority residing in the Democratic Caucus and the Republican Conference. It is possible for the party caucuses to make committee assignments because of their small size (usually about 45–55 members). Once again, the relative informality and intimacy of the Senate vis-à-vis the House is apparent.

Attractiveness of Assignments

Not surprisingly, members typically want seats on powerful and prestigious committees. Representatives seek assignments on exclusive committees, and senators on elite committees. Members file an inordinately large number of requests for a small subset of committees.[69] They want to spend their time on major legislative committees and avoid the drudgery of minor committees.

The rush to gain slots on a restricted number of committees places the party "committee on committees" in a tough situation, because it is impossible to accommodate everyone. This dilemma is lessened by restrictive rules governing assignments, such as representatives having either an exclusive or one major and one minor assignment; it is also lessened by the steadily expanding number of seats on the committees in high demand. This practice of "seat inflation" has a rich history in Congress. The House membership grew by 48 percent from 1875 to 1921, for instance, while the number of committee slots grew by 82 percent.[70] The pressure to add seats in desirable committees has continued in modern times.[71] Ironically, expanding the number of seats actually diminishes the value of a seat on a prestigious committee.[72] What is the value of serving on the Senate Appropriations Committee when nearly one-third of all senators serve on it?

The combination of restrictive rules and larger committees has made it possible for chamber leaders and their "committees on committees" to accommodate many members. The assignment process follows a general pattern of "interest–advocacy–accommodation," in which members register committee preferences, receive support from supportive colleagues, and garner acceptable assignments. The result is that "most members for most of their careers are on the committees they want."[73] Not everyone can be satisfied, but members benefit from the flexible assignment processes they have devised.

Factors in Assignments

Members seeking assignments and those responsible for doling them out approach the matter differently. In his classic study of committees, Richard Fenno suggested that members seeking assignments are primarily motivated by one of three goals: (1) getting reelected, (2) gaining influence within the chamber, or (3) determining public policy.[74] Those focused on reelection will gravitate toward "clientele" committees, where they can pander to interested constituencies; those seeking chamber influence will opt for powerful "insider" committees like Appropriations or Rules; those pursuing policy goals will seek committees with public policy jurisdictions. Of course, the goals are not mutually exclusive. A seat on the Ways and Means Committee can ensure chamber influence and enhance prospects for reelection, because the position virtually guarantees a steady flow of campaign contributions.

In contrast to the members seeking assignments, those doling them out begin with the seniority principle, which allows returning members to reclaim their committee seats. Other assignments are meted out after several factors are weighed.

One factor is a member's ideology. In some cases, the focal point becomes ideological balance. Republicans strike a balance between their conservative and moderate factions, and Democrats between their moderate and liberal factions, by placing members of all ideological stripes on committees. In other cases, the focal point becomes a lack of balance. Remember the case of the House Judiciary Committee, which routinely buries legislation on social issues? It is usually stacked with conservatives by Republicans and with liberals by Democrats. The Rules Committee is another example of a committee intentionally skewed toward a particular viewpoint because it is a tool of the party leaders.

A second factor in committee assignments, one that coincides with individual member goals, is whether an assignment will boost prospects for reelection. Both parties want to maximize their number of seats, so they try to place members on electorally beneficial committees.

The case of Tom Allen (D., Maine) illustrates the point. He was a liberal Democrat who knocked off a conservative Republican incumbent in the 1st District in 1996. Democrats promptly placed him on the House National Security Committee, where he could lobby to bring defense contracts back to Bath Iron Works, a shipbuilding company that was his district's largest employer. Along the same lines, members from oil-producing states seek and receive seats on committees with energy jurisdiction, and members from western states get seats on committees with authority over public lands. In fact, some committee posts are informally reserved for states or districts, such as members from New York City holding seats on the Banking Committee so that they can look out for Wall Street.

This arrangment makes sense although it is not an absolute guarantee of influence or reelection.[75] It is also inimical to the public interest. When members serve on committees affecting their states or districts, they too often become advocates rather than evaluators of programs. Thus, members of the Agriculture Committee become apologists for price supports, and members of the Banking Committee become advocates for banks and financiers. The public interest suffers when that tendency is multiplied across policy domains.

A third factor in committee assignments is racial and gender balance. The limited number of minority and female members makes it impossible for committees to have representation according to proportions in the general population; in lieu of proportional representation, most committees have one or some minority and/or female members. An obvious example of race being weighed is the chairship of the Indian Affairs Committee by Senator Ben Nighthorse Campbell (R., Colo.), the only Native American in the Senate.

Following consideration first of seniority and then such factors as ideology, electoral benefit, and racial/gender balance, the "committees on committees" face a bewildering set of questions about individual members: Does a person's background suggest a particular assignment? Will a person do the work if he or she is selected for an important post? How intensely does a person feel about a particular post? Answers to these questions can be highly impressionistic, which is why chamber rules lock in place the major pieces of the jigsaw puzzle.[76]

What emerges from the complicated mix of factors is a slate of committee assignments that tends to place personal preference and political calculation ahead of institutional effectiveness. The focus is on meeting the personal and electoral needs of the individual member, not fulfilling the responsibilities of the institution to function efficiently and legislative effectively. We cannot readily criticize those priorities—meeting personal needs is humane, and satisfying electoral needs adheres to acknowledged democratic traditions. Yet, Congress's decision to place individual needs before institutional performance has a price.

Committees are the core of the legislative process. They are sometimes called the "little legislatures" because of their vital role in processing legislation.[77] Committees are also responsible for structuring congressional careers, particularly among representatives. In the 104th Congress, committees sometimes took a back seat to the leadership-driven Contract With America, but in the 105th Congress, their traditional place as the center of legislative initiative returned.[78] More than a full century after Woodrow Wilson's observations about the centrality of committees, they remain the heart of the legislative process.

NOTES

1. Woodrow Wilson, *Congressional Government* (Baltimore: Johns Hopkins University Press, 1981), 24.

2. Matthew C. Moen, *The Christian Right and Congress* (Tuscaloosa: University of Alabama Press, 1989), 95–96.

3. P. J. O'Rourke, *Parliament of Whores* (New York: Vintage Books, 1992).

4. Steven S. Smith and Christopher J. Deering, *Committees in Congress,* 2d ed. (Washington, D.C.: CQ Press, 1990), 25–26. Chapter 2 of this book contains an excellent discussion of the evolution of the committee system in Congress.

5. *Origins and Development of Congress* (Washington, D.C.: Congressional Quarterly, 1976), 174–175.

6. *How Congress Works,* 2d ed. (Washington, D.C.: Congressional Quarterly, 1991), 76. The information is partly compiled from George Goodwin, Jr., *The Little Legislatures* (Amherst: University of Massachusetts Press, 1970).

7. A recent examination of the importance of policy and committee jurisdictions, based on hearings from 1947 to 1993, may be found in Frank R. Baumgartner, Bryan D. Jones, and Michael C. Rosenstiehl, "Shepsle Meets Schatt-schneider: The Structural Dynamics of Committee Jurisdictions," paper presented at the Annual Meeting of the American Political Science Association, San Francisco, August 29 to September 1, 1996.

8. Smith and Deering, *Committees in Congress,* 27–32.

9. Calculated from data found in *The World Almanac* (New York: Newspaper Enterprise Association, 1986), 259; Roger H. Davidson and Walter J. Oleszek, *Congress and Its Members,* 3d ed. (Washington, D.C.: CQ Press, 1990), 26.

10. Joseph Cooper, *The Origin of Standing Committees and the Development of the Modern House* (Houston: Rice University Studies, 1970), 56.

11. Smith and Deering, *Committees in Congress,* 29–30.

12. Ronald M. Peters, Jr., *The American Speakership* (Baltimore: Johns Hopkins University Press, 1990), 58.

13. Wilson, *Congressional Government,* 58.

14. Ibid., 69, 146; Roger H. Davidson and Walter Oleszek, *Congress Against Itself* (Bloomington: Indiana University Press, 1977), 22.

15. Ibid., 24.

16. Ibid., 26.

17. *How Congress Works,* 77.

18. For a historical overview of the committee assignment process since the 1890s, see Jonathan N. Katz and Brian R. Sala, "Careerism, Committee Assignments, and the Electoral Connection," *American Political Science Review* (March 1996): 21–33.

19. Smith and Deering, *Committees in Congress,* 37–39.

20. See Roger H. Davidson, "The Legislative Reorganization Act of 1946," *Legislative Studies Quarterly* 15 (August 1990): 357–373.

21. For a recent study challenging the importance of written committee jurisdictions in the referral of legislation, see David C. King, "The Nature of Congressional Committee Jurisdictions," *American Political Science Review* (March 1994): 48–62.

22. *Guide to Congress,* 2d ed. (Washington, D.C.: Congressional Quarterly, 1976), 52–53.

23. Cited in Christopher J. Bailey, *The U.S. Congress* (New York: Basil Blackwell, 1989), 108.

24. Barbara Sinclair, *The Transformation of the U.S. Senate* (Baltimore: Johns Hopkins University Press, 1989), 31.

25. Arthur G. Stevens, Jr., Arthur H. Miller, and Thomas E. Mann, "Mobilization of Liberal Strength in the House, 1955–1970: The Democratic Study Group," *American Political Science Review* 68 (1974): 667–681.

26. *Guide to Congress,* 616.

27. Norman J. Ornstein, Thomas E. Mann, and Michael J. Malbin, *Vital Statistics on Congress 1997–1998* (Washington, D.C.: Congressional Quarterly, 1998), 126.

28. See Leroy L. Rieselbach, *Congressional Reform* (Washington, D.C.: CQ Press, 1986), 155–158; an excellent overview of the entire 1970 Reorganization Act may be found in Walter Kravitz, "The Legislative Reorganization Act of 1970," *Legislative Studies Quarterly* 15 (August 1990): 375–376.

29. Smith and Deering, *Committees in Congress,* 50–51.

30. Davidson and Oleszek, *Congress Against Itself,* 220–261.

31. The "Obey Commission" of 1976–1977 and the "Patterson Committee" of 1979–1980, named after the members who chaired them, focused on further refinements to the 1970s reforms.

32. Sinclair, *The Transformation of the U.S. Senate,* 34.

33. Cited in Goodwin, *The Little Legislatures,* 1970.

34. Roger H. Davidson, "Two Avenues of Change: House and Senate Committee Reorganization," in *Congress Reconsidered,* 2d ed., ed. Lawrence C. Dodd and Bruce I. Oppenheimer (Washington, D.C.: CQ Press, 1981), 127–128.

35. Rieselbach, *Congressional Reform,* 9–15.

36. Steven S. Smith, "The Senate in the Postreform Era," in *The Postreform Congress,* ed. Roger H. Davidson (New York: St. Martin's Press, 1992), 190–191.

37. See Norman J. Ornstein, "The House and the Senate in a New Congress," in *The New Congress,* ed. Thomas E. Mann and Norman J. Ornstein (Washington, D.C.: AEI, 1981), 378–380.

38. George H. Gallup, Jr., *The Gallup Poll: Public Opinion 1979* (Wilmington, Del.: Scholarly Resources, 1980), 186-187.

39. C. Lawrence Evans and Walter J. Oleszek, *Congress Under Fire* (Boston: Houghton Mifflin, 1997), 22.

40. C. Lawrence Evans and Walter J. Oleszek, "The Politics of Congressional Reform: The Joint Committee on the Organization of Congress," in *Remaking Congress,* ed. James A. Thurber and Roger H. Davidson (Washington, D.C.: Congressional Quarterly, 1995), 73–98.

41. Evans and Oleszek, *Congress Under Fire,* 60.

42. Ibid., 60–61.

43. "Foley on Congress and the Executive," *National Journal,* April 29, 1989, 1037.

44. For an informative recent study of the ongoing redefinition of committee jurisdictions, see Bryan D. Jones, Frank R. Baumgartner, and Jeffrey C. Talbert, "The Destruction of Issue Monopolies in Congress," *American Political Science Review* (September 1993): 657–671.

45. Richard F. Fenno, Jr, *Congressmen in Committees* (Boston: Little, Brown, 1973).

46. Ibid., 235. See also James W. Dyson and John W. Soule, "Congressional Committee Behavior on Roll Call Votes: The United States House of Representatives, 1955–1964," *Midwest Journal of Science* 14 (November 1970): 626–647.

47. Steven S. Smith, *Call to Order: Floor Politics in the House and Senate* (Washington, D.C.: Brookings Institution, 1989), 24–48.

48. Lawrence C. Dodd and Bruce I. Oppenheimer, "Consolidating Power in the House: The Rise of a New Oligarchy," in *Congress Reconsidered,* 4th ed., ed. Dodd and Oppenheimer (Washington, D.C.: Congressional Quarterly, 1989), 39–64. See also James A. Thurber, "If the Game Is Too Hard, Change the Rules: Congressional Budget Reform in the 1990s," in *Remaking Congress,* ed. James A. Thurber and Roger H. Davidson (Washington, D.C.: Congressional Quarterly, 1995), 131–144.

49. V. Stanley Vardys, "Select Committees of the House of Representatives," *Midwest Journal of Political Science* (August 1962): 251–252.

50. Bahman Baktiari and Matthew C. Moen, "American Foreign Policy and the Iran–Contra Hearings," *Comparative Strategy* 7 (1988): 428.

51. Frank J. Smist, Jr., *Congress Oversees the United States Intelligence Community 1947–1989* (Knoxville: University of Tennessee Press, 1990), 217.

52. Robert C. Wigton, "Joint Legislative Mechanisms: An Untapped Reform Potential?" *Polity* 24 (Winter 1991): 323.

53. Jeffrey H. Birnbaum and Alan S. Murray, *Showdown at Gucci Gulch* (New York: Vintage Books, 1987), 7. On the Joint Taxation Committee's historic role, see John F. Manley, "Congressional Staff and Public Policy-Making: The Joint Committee on Internal Revenue Taxation," *Journal of Politics* 30 (1968): 1046–1067.

54. Matthew C. Moen, "Congress and the National Endowment for The Arts: Institutional Patterns and Arts Funding, 1965–1994," *Social Science Journal* 34 (1997): 185–200.

55. Cited in Lawrence D. Longley and Walter J. Oleszek, *Bicameral Politics: Conference Committees in Congress* (New Haven, Conn.: Yale University Press, 1989), 1.

56. *Congressional Record,* March 8, 1955, 2553. This remark and those following on conference committees were part of a statement read into the record by Senator Everett Dirksen.

57. Ibid., 2557.

58. Ibid.

59. Rieselbach, *Congressional Reform,* 157.

60. House Republicans adopted a related "sunshine reform" in the 104th Congress that requires committee hearings to be open as a matter of right, rather than as part of a committee authorization.

61. Kenneth Shepsle, *The Giant Jigsaw Puzzle* (Chicago: University of Chicago Press, 1978).

62. For an overview, see Rieselbach, *Congressional Reform,* 93–94.

63. Matthew C. Moen, "The House Freshmen of the 104th Congress," paper presented at the Annual Meeting of the New England Political Science Association, Portland, Maine, May 5–6, 1995.

64. Ibid., 8–9.

65. Jackie Koszczuk, "A Full Circle," *Players, Politics, and Turf of the 105th Congress* (Washington D.C.: Congressional Quarterly), March 22, 1997, 10.

66. Barbara Sinclair, "The Distribution of Committee Positions in the United States Senate: Explaining Institutional Change," *American Journal of Political Science* 32 (1988): 276–300.

67. Melissa P. Collie and Brian E. Roberts, "Trading Places: Choice and Committee Chairs in the U.S. Senate, 1950-1986," *Journal of Politics* 54 (1992): 231–245.

68. Ibid., 242.

69. Charles S. Bullock III, "Committee Transfers in the United States House of Representatives," *Journal of Politics* 35 (1977): 85–120; "U.S. Senate Committee Assignments: Preferences, Motivations, and Success," *American Journal of Political Science* 29 (1985): 789–808. For excellent related work by Bullock, see "Freshmen Committee Assignments and Reelection in the U.S. House of Representatives," *American Political Science Review* 66 (September 1972): 996–1007; "The Motivations for U.S. Congressional Committee Preferences: Freshmen of the 92nd Congress," *Legislative Studies Quarterly* 1 (May 1976): 201–212. See also Gary W. Copeland, "Seniority and Committee Transfers: Career Planning in the Contemporary House of Representatives," *Journal of Politics* (May 1987): 553–564.

70. Charles Stewart III, "The Growth of the Committee System, From Randall to Gillett," in the *The Atomistic Congress,* ed. Allen D. Hertzke and Ronald M. Peters, Jr. (Armonk, N.Y.: Sharpe, 1992), 185.

71. Michael C. Munger, "Allocation of Desirable Committee Assignments: Extended Queues Versus Committee Expansion," *American Journal of Political Science* 32 (1988): 317–344; see also Tim Groseclose and Charles Stewart III, "The Value of Committee Seats in the House," paper presented at the Annual Meeting of the American Political Science Association, San Francisco, August 29 to September 1, 1996.

72. Munger, "Allocation of Desirable Committee Assignments: Extended Queues Versus Committee Expansion," 317.

73. Shepsle, *The Giant Jigsaw Puzzle,* 236. The same is true for state legislatures. See Ronald D. Hedlund and Keith E. Hamm, "Leader Accommodation to Members' Committee Requests," 27, paper presented at the Annual Meeting of the American Political Science Association, Chicago, September 1992.

74. Fenno, *Congressmen in Committees,* 1.

75. Linda L. Fowler, Scott R. Douglass, and Wesley D. Clark, Jr., "The Electoral Effects of House Committee Assignments," *Journal of Politics* 42 (1980): 307–319; Valerie Heitshusen, "Do Committee Members Get a Bigger Piece of the Pie?" paper presented at the Annual Meeting of the American Political Science Association, Chicago, September 1992.

76. On the overall representativeness of committees relative to the political parties and parent chamber, see Tim Groseclose, "Testing Committee Composition Hypotheses for the U.S. Congress," *Journal of Politics* 56 (May 1994): 440–458.

77. Goodwin, *The Little Legislatures.*

78. Koszczuk, "A Full Circle," 9–10; for an alternative view on the importance of committees in the 104th Congress, based on examination of reproductive policy-making, see Noelle H. Norton, "Continuity in Legislative Committees: Making Controversial Policy in the 104th Congress," paper presented at the Annual Meeting of the American Political Science Association, San Francisco, August 29 to September 1, 1996.

6

Leadership and Parties

I t is a wonder that anything gets accomplished in the U.S. Congress. In Chapter 4, we examined member characteristics and how individual members strive to accomplish personal goals. In Chapter 5, we considered the role that committees and subcommittees play in the legislative process and their traditionally independent policy-making within their jurisdiction. In fact, the forces that pull Congress apart are tremendous, so much so that two leading scholars of the body refer to it as "atomistic": "Congress is, in the final analysis, a group of individuals rather than a collective whole."[1]

In this chapter, we consider how this collection of individuals is brought together to accomplish the nation's business. They do, after all, work together well enough to pass hundreds of bills each session and to fulfill many other responsibilities. Much of that success can be attributed to leadership, both informal and formal, in the House and the Senate, as well as to the willingness of members to sacrifice some of their individuality so that the body can collectively govern the nation. We begin our exploration of leadership by looking at the formal positions of leadership in the House and Senate and examining what resources are available to them. Next, we discuss how leaders are selected and look at historical trends in leadership, especially in the House of Representatives. Finally, we consider why members of Congress provide leadership resources to a few in their midst and how it is reflected in partisanship within each body.

CONGRESSIONAL LEADERSHIP STRUCTURE

Leadership is essential for Congress to confront the nation's problems and to accomplish any collective goals. However, the two chambers stand in sharp contrast to each other in terms of the nature and powers of their leadership. The relatively large House requires more formal leadership and a capacity to control the flow of legislation if it is to function effectively—if not efficiently. The House also has a strong tradition of deference to seniority. In general, one becomes a House leader through extended service and gradual movement up the leadership ladder, although seniority is generally less important within the Republican party. The Senate, by contrast, can tolerate individuals who exercise more discretion and leadership with more limited formal powers. In fact, the Senate norm of "unlimited debate," which ensures the prerogatives of every member in the legislative process, is so established that leadership must control the flow of legislation through very inclusive bargaining and compromise.

The other important point is that leadership in these bodies comes in various forms. First, there is institutional leadership over both bodies as established in the Constitution. For example, the vice-president of the United States is the president of the Senate. Second, there is leadership that is elected by and responsible to the individual parties. Its task is to ensure that party interests are served in the legislative process. Third, there is the committee leadership that we saw as critically important in Chapter 5. Finally, there is informal leadership from individuals who are able to make things happen without the benefit of formal leadership positions under them. In this chapter, we focus on the first two types of leadership.

In terms of the formal leadership structure of the two chambers, size alone would lead one to expect different leadership structures in the House and Senate. A primary difference is that the House is structured so as to allow the Speaker of the House, in consultation with the majority and minority leaders, to manage the business of that chamber. The Senate has less structure and less control. Turn on C-SPAN during important proceedings in the House and you will see the Speaker actually presiding. Turn on C-SPAN 2 during an important debate in the Senate and you are likely to see a junior senator presiding. In this section, we will explore the differences in leadership between the two bodies.

Senate

The Senate's presiding officer (the president of the Senate) is the vice-president of the United States, but one can watch that body closely for a long time and never see the vice-president anywhere in the chamber. Theoretically, the vice-president is always welcome in the Senate, and periodically a newly elected vice-president will suggest that he will spend more time in the Senate than his predecessors. Al Gore, moving from senator to vice-president, initially thought that might be a good idea, but he was quickly discouraged by some senators who suggested that they really did not want him hanging around on a regular basis.

More importantly, it quickly became clear to the vice-president that the position lacked meaning.

The vice-president will be found in the chamber during important ceremonial events. For example, during the president's annual State of the Union address to a joint session of the Congress, you can see the vice-president and the Speaker of the House seated behind the president. The vice-president is on the rostrum not because he is the vice-president of the United States, but rather under his other hat, as president of the Senate. The vice-president might also be present when a vote important to the administration is coming up in the Senate and the outcome is expected to be close, because in the event of a tie, he is authorized to cast the deciding vote. Vice-President Gore, for example, cast the decisive vote on President Clinton's first budget plan, which ultimately became a cornerstone of his presidency's economic and budget policy.

The only other officer of the body is the *president pro tempore* of the Senate. According to the Constitution, this officer is responsible for presiding over the Senate in the absence of the vice-president. The president pro tempore is also third in line to succeed to the presidency, behind the vice-president and the Speaker of the House. A careful look, though, indicates that this position is also honorific. What is the evidence? First, there is no competition for the position. The most senior member of the majority party, by tradition, is elected to this position. Therefore, in the 105th Congress (1997–1998), it was held by nonagenarian Senator Strom Thurmond (R., S.C.), who was first elected to the Senate in 1954 on a write-in campaign. Second, you would rarely see Senator Thurmond standing at the podium. Instead, he normally allowed rotating junior members of his party to preside. Third, the holder of the gavel clearly has little in the way of significant discretion in the conduct of the Senate's business.

In sum, the two officers of the body are not the primary reservoirs of leadership in the Senate. Rather, the true leadership in the Senate is found within the party structures and within the committees. The most significant of these leaders are the majority leader and the minority leader. But before exploring these positions, it is worth reviewing the context in which they operate.

First, individual senators have great discretion and leeway to pursue their own agendas, and they only very reluctantly yield that power. The rules provide much protection for the rights of individual senators, and they guard those rights jealously. Besides the practice of unlimited debate, under normal rules, senators are free to offer amendments, even nongermane amendments, to force consideration of their proposals.

Second, the Senate is a body in which the majority party is not certain of being able to work its will. Debate remains unlimited (unless, as explained shortly, there is unanimous consent to structure and limit it), so everyone has the opportunity to participate in the deliberation process. Through a *filibuster,* an individual can bring the entire body to a temporary standstill (a filibuster occurs when one or more senators gain the floor and refuse to relinquish it). It can be ended by a cloture vote, but that requires the consent of 60 senators. The consequence of this is that it takes 60 votes, rather than 51, to effectively manage the Senate. Therefore, the leaders of the majority party may not be able to control the Senate even if they can win the votes of all senators from their party.

The majority and minority leaders are selected by their respective party caucuses to work on behalf of their party and facilitate the efforts of party members. However, the importance of these party leadership positions did not develop until the end of the nineteenth century. At that point, the two parties provided a significant basis for organizing the body, and each party found it beneficial to select one of its members to serve as the advocate for its party and the individuals within it.[2]

The majority and minority leaders serve a variety of roles, but in all cases both their resources and their functions are limited. Foremost, they are the center of communications regarding both policy and procedure for members of their party. They need to be able to advocate on behalf of party members and to ensure membership awareness of the status of issues important to both individual members and the party as a whole. Through negotiations, the majority and minority leaders try to develop some elements of predictability regarding floor activities. Because individual members can disrupt the Senate, the majority party will negotiate mutually satisfactory arrangements with the minority party regarding what items will be brought before the Senate and how debates will be handled. In fact, much Senate business is conducted under *unanimous consent agreements* reached in this way.

Unanimous consent agreements are similar to House rules in that they establish a calendar and limit debate and amendments.[3] But, unlike the House, where a rule is enacted by majority vote, unanimous consent agreements are just what their name implies—that is, a single member can block such an agreement. The task of the majority and minority leaders is to find an arrangement that accommodates the membership while allowing the policy process to move forward predictably.

These floor leaders are watchdogs over floor activity to ensure that the interests of their party and its membership are protected. The floor leaders or a substitute must be present and vigilant whenever the Senate is in session. As Figure 6.1 shows, the floor leaders are actually in the middle of a substantial leadership structure designed to facilitate the governance of the Senate. In the 105th Congress, on the Republican side of the aisle, Majority Leader Trent Lott (R., Miss.) was assisted by Assistant Majority Leader Don Nickles (R., Okla.). Nickles filled the role traditionally held by the party whip. The whip serves as the conduit through which information flows to and from the leadership. While the term *whip* may conjure up images of a leader forcing her or his party rank and file in line, the reality is that the whip explains the party position and tries to find ways to accommodate the membership to maintain as many votes as possible. To achieve that goal, Nickles is aided by a chief deputy whip and eleven deputy whips.

Further, the Republican Conference (or party caucus) has a chairman and a secretary. Under their auspices, there is also a campaign committee (National Republican Senatorial Committee), a Policy Committee, and a Committee on Committees. These various leadership opportunities provide a total of 56 slots for 55 Republican senators. While not everyone serves in one of these slots, the opportunities for formal leadership are broadly distributed.

On the Democratic side, Senator Tom Daschle (D., S. Dak.) served as the minority floor leader, with Wendell Ford (D., Ky.) serving as his top assistant in

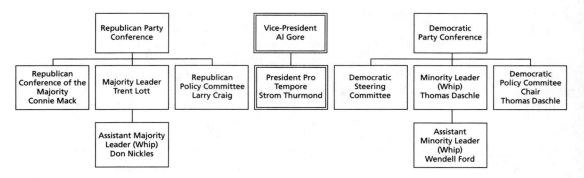

FIGURE 6.1 Senate Leadership, 105th Congress

the position of minority whip.[4] The Democrats also had an assistant floor leader, Byron Dorgan (D., N. Dak.), a chief deputy whip, and three deputy whips, along with an array of positions and committees within the Democratic Caucus.

Some conclusions about Senate leadership are fairly obvious at this point. First, power is widely spread in the Senate. Second, leadership is primarily a matter of negotiation, compromise, and accommodation. Leaders have few resources—either threats or inducements—to persuade a senator to behave in other than her or his own best interest. Even the committee assignment process provides little in the way of resources to the leadership. On the Republican side, committee appointments are initiated by a seven-person Committee on Committees that has none of the top party leadership on it, with the exception of the floor leader, who is an *ex officio* member. On the Democratic side, those decisions fall into the hands of a twenty-person Steering and Coordination Committee.

House

Leadership in the House is much more bureaucratized and routinized than in the Senate. Trying to manage a body of 435 individuals who are up for reelection every two years poses a much greater challenge. But there are also greater resources available to House leaders than Senate leaders. Simply managing the House organization is more complex because it is larger and more diffuse, but the Speaker—who is entrusted with that responsibility—has a substantial professional staff to help in that regard. Moving toward staff professionalism and accountability was one of the goals of the Republican party leadership when they gained control of the House at the outset of the 104th Congress (1995–1996). But the leadership issues that most concern us here relate to controlling the flow of legislation though the process and achieving party policy goals. We will begin, though, by considering the structure of the House leadership.

At the top of the House leadership is the *Speaker of the House.* The Speaker is different from any officer of the Senate in that he or she serves as both the leader of the body—in both formal and informal senses—and the leader of her or his party. In the formal sense, the Speaker manages the body by overseeing tasks such as payroll, maintenance, and supplies. He or she also schedules when the body will meet. In a less formal sense, the task of being advocate for both the House and the legislative branch falls onto the Speaker's shoulders. This responsibility becomes particularly important in the event of conflict with another branch of government. When there is interinstitutional conflict, there will always be many voices emanating from the Congress, but the Speaker's will rise above all others and carry extra weight. At the same time, the Speaker is often called on to play a partisan role as spokesperson for her or his party. Needless to say, the roles may come into conflict at times.

The Speaker is also the presiding officer of the body. Unlike in the Senate, there is no norm that everyone in the House will have her or his say; consequently, the power of recognition is critical and provides the Speaker with a way to control the flow of House business. Therefore, when the House is in session, the Speaker often occupies the chair. (We will see in Chapter 8 that the House normally considers legislation initially while sitting as the Committee of the Whole House, rather than as the House of Representatives. But the Speaker does not preside over the Committee of the Whole.)

Beyond the powers given to the Speaker by the rules, he or she accrues great power through control over various aspects of the party apparatus. We will look at many of these powers of the Speaker later in the chapter when we address the reformed House of the 104th Congress, but some general comments are appropriate at this point. Speaker Newt Gingrich has influence within the Republican party because he exercises various amounts of control over the committee appointment process, the selection of committee and subcommittee chairs, committee agendas, and the Rules Committee. When we review the history of House leadership, we will see that there has been a constant tension between the Speaker and his party members in these areas. If the Speaker attempts to exercise too much authority, he risks losing his position as members rebel against autocratic rule. If the Speaker exercises too little authority, he risks being labeled a failure and perhaps also being subject to replacement.

Before looking at that history, the rest of the House leadership merits attention. As Figure 6.2 shows, both parties have floor leaders with tasks similar to those in the Senate but operating under a different set of constraints. Their tasks are to oversee what happens on the floor, to protect the interests of their party, and to negotiate on behalf of party members for fair treatment in the legislative process. On the majority side, though, the floor leader is second in command in her or his party. The majority leader, then, is an aide to the Speaker (but not always the loyal lieutenant the Speaker might hope). The majority leader serves as the focal point for communication with the Speaker (and through the party's whip organization) and helps oversee the details of managing the flow of legislation.

But the majority leader is also constrained by the *Rules Committee*. It is very appropriate to consider the Rules Committee as part of the leadership structure because, on the one hand, it has so much influence over the flow of legislation and, on the other, it is clearly an arm of the Speaker and his control over the legislative process. You will learn more about the Rules Committee when we dis-

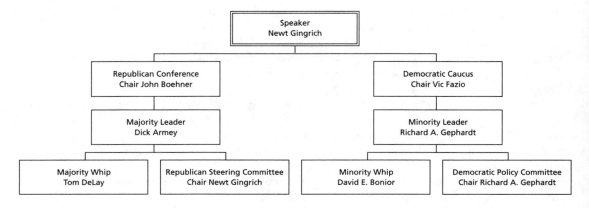

FIGURE 6.2   House Leadership, 105th Congress

cuss the legislative process in Chapter 8. For now, it is enough to know that few
bills are considered in the House that have not first gone before the Rules
Committee and received a recommendation from it for a rule. The *rule* governs
the length and terms of debate for the legislation, including who will manage the
debate and what amendments can be offered. So, even though the majority leader
may manage the floor, it is actually the Speaker who presides and the Rules
Committee that controls the flow of legislation.

The minority leader, unlike the majority leader, is the top official in her or
his party and therefore has responsibilities similar to a combination of those held
by the Speaker and majority leader. Of course, being in the minority party means
that he or she is not responsible for organizing and managing the House and that
any success in affecting the scheduling and flow of legislation will be through
bargaining and compromise. But the minority leader is responsible for ensuring
that her or his party is informed and that its individual and collective interests are
protected on the floor. The minority leader also tends to be the best spokesperson for the party within the House. How visible that person is outside of
Congress depends on the relative visibility of other party leadership. Richard
Gephardt (D., Mo.), the minority leader in 1998, had to contend for the spotlight
with Tom Daschle in the Senate and the Democrat-controlled White House. He
benefitted, though, from the general knowledge that he is a presidential candidate
for the year 2000.

The floor leaders of both parties are aided by a substantial whip system that
helps keep them in touch with 200 or so members of their party. The whip structures can be quite complicated, including individuals from regions, classes (for
example, freshmen in the 104th Congress), demographic groups, and just about
any other relevant bloc of members. There are approximately 100 individuals in
the Democratic whip structure. In the 105th Congress, Representative Tom
DeLay (R., Tex.) served as the majority whip, and Representative David Bonior
(D., Mich.) was the minority whip. Each party also formally organizes as a party

caucus composed of all members. The caucuses have chairs and a number of committees to help organize or advance the interests of the party.

SELECTION OF LEADERS

Part of the precarious nature of leadership in the Congress can be traced to the selection process. For the positions we have discussed, a critical point of decision making is the party caucus. The very people whom the leaders attempt to lead, whom they may try to persuade to walk the party line, and whom they might even consider coercing, are the same people who elected and will be called upon to reelect the leaders at the start of the next Congress.

In the Senate, the two formal leaders are the vice-president, who is selected elsewhere, and the president pro tempore, who is elected by the entire body. But we know that by tradition, the president pro tempore is the most senior member of the majority party and usually is elected by a voice vote.

In contrast, the selection of the floor leader can be very contentious. The majority and minority leader are elected by their respective party caucuses, and these elections often involve quite a bit of campaigning among contenders for the positions. The same can be said about the whip positions and even lower party offices. Although these may not seem to be positions of great power, they do provide a number of perks, allow senators to participate in key decision-making meetings, and may provide stepping-stones to higher office. Contests, then, may focus on personality or policy.

Those on the leadership ladder who want to advance either themselves or their policy preferences are constantly aware of the fact that they need the support of their caucus to do so. The nature of the selection process, then, reaffirms the notion that these leaders are negotiators and compromisers who must try to gain victory through accommodation of their colleagues.[5]

In the House, the Speaker is elected by the entire body. Each party conference first determines who will be its nominee; then the Speaker is elected on a straight party vote by the entire body. Once the party selects its nominee, the election is, of course, a foregone conclusion. The nominee of the majority party wins. At least, that is the way it normally goes.

At the advent of the 105th Congress, though, we saw a historical anomaly. Speaker Gingrich's position within his own party was seriously weakened for a variety of reasons, primarily concern over ethics violations and a perceived abuse of power. Added to that situation was the narrow majority the Republican party held in the House. Gingrich, then, needed nearly all Republican votes to gain reelection, but it was clear that a number of his Republican colleagues would not support him. In fact, a number of discontented Republicans did cast votes against Gingrich, but by a narrow margin, he maintained his position even though he did not win majority support.

The House majority and minority floor leaders are selected by their respective party caucuses, as in the Senate. For Democrats, in particular, the races for lower offices are quite important because they allow movement up the leadership ladder in predictable ways. While such progression is also important for Republicans, there are many instances of someone climbing onto the ladder at a higher rung, and even near the very top.[6]

The nature of leadership contests has changed in recent decades, in part because the nature of the jobs have changed. For a long time, the key to success in both bodies, but especially the House, was to be an effective "insider" and to campaign as one.[7] Success on the job required leaders to have good interpersonal skills and to interact effectively with members on a one-on-one basis. Selection contests reflected that same bias. In a well-known 1962 battle for majority leader, Carl Albert, the sitting party whip, was opposed by Richard Bolling, the "outsider." Albert resorted to the sort of personal campaigning among members that he had used as the party whip, while Bolling's campaign was much more public. But Bolling foresaw the outcome and withdrew before the caucus vote, leaving insider Albert unopposed.[8]

Since then, both the nature and expectations of the job and the style of campaigns for leadership positions have changed. To be effective, contemporary party leaders have to maintain a much higher public profile and utilize the mass media more effectively.[9] They also need to help candidates from their own party get elected to the Congress. They must be able to help recruit strong candidates, must be willing to travel around the country to appear on behalf of candidates, and must be able to raise money to help fund those campaigns.[10]

Success in gaining election to leadership positions can be traced, in part, to members' gratefulness for electoral support, especially at early and critical stages of their political careers.[11] Success is also found among those who can effectively use the media to reach fellow members and the general public and who are perceived by those members as able to successfully sell the party program to the public.[12] The visibility accorded to Speaker Thomas P. "Tip" O'Neill (1977–1987) as the top elected Democrat in the country was a major step toward a more public congressional leadership. It is likely that we have seen a full transition in the last few years. Bob Dole, who resigned as majority leader to seek the presidency in 1995, will probably be seen as the last congressional leader who was not particularly effective on television. At the same time, Speaker Gingrich is viewed as someone who made his reputation through the media. Rather than being known as a legislator (not having his name attached to any substantial legislation), he instead was valued by his colleagues as an aggressive and effective spokesperson for his party. How could the man credited with creating the Republican majority through long and tireless efforts to sell his program both to his party leaders and to the public not be put in charge of the House?

THE LEADERSHIP CONTEXT IN
HISTORICAL PERSPECTIVE

Having discussed congressional leaders, their resources, and their selection process, we return to the question of how Congress manages to achieve anything. The powers available to congressional leaders might seem so limited that one would doubt that anything could ever be accomplished. Yet, we know that the Congress does govern. While people disagree about whether Congress moves as effectively or as expeditiously as it should in addressing public issues, it has managed to draft and enact the set of public policies that have governed the nation for over 200 years.

Still, there is a constant tension in Congress between members and leaders. The viewpoint of the leadership is easy to understand. The leaders assume the greater obligations, workload, and perhaps electoral risk in order to have more power, more influence over public policy, and greater prestige and status. But why would members—also motivated by a desire for power, policy preferences, prestige, and electoral security—voluntarily sacrifice potential control to the leadership? The short answer is that leadership is essential if members are to accomplish their personal goals. We will address that question in more detail in a later section. But first, we will look at how members' willingness to invest power in leadership has ebbed and flowed over the course of congressional history.

The history of leadership in the House has been much more carefully examined than that of the Senate, so this discussion will focus on the House; however, some references will be made to the Senate.[13] It is worth remembering as we address the House that the Senate has always been a smaller and more collegial body, with rules that facilitate full participation and equality among its members. The leadership in the Senate is much more the result of personal skills and natural party cohesion than leadership resources.

ERAS OF THE SPEAKERSHIP

In the definitive work on the speakership in the House, Ron Peters argues that the speakership should be understood "within the context of its own history and that of the political system of which it is a part."[14] The speakership has been transformed over time, and these changes, according to Peters, reflect developments taking place within the broader political system and in society more generally. What follows is an overview of the periods identified by Peters.

Parliamentary Speakership

The first period, that of the parliamentary speakership, lasted until the Civil War. In parliamentary governments, the Speaker tends to be a nonpartisan presiding officer who is expected to be fair and not to engage in partisan leadership. During this period, the Speakers of the House had those characteristics. They tended to be weak, with their primary responsibility being to preside fairly over the body. Fairness was critical because parliamentary procedure was still being created due to the sparsity of precedents.

This was also an era of both a weak national government and weak political parties. The speakers seemed doomed to relative impassivity because there was no strong partisan faction and no strong sense of national mission for leadership to

BOX 6.1   Henry Clay: The Charismatic Compromiser

Henry Clay's political career is one of the most amazing in American history. His life spanned the years from the Revolution until nearly the Civil War and consequently reflects much of that era. Born in Virginia, he trained to be a lawyer and moved to Kentucky at the age of twenty. After having been elected to the Kentucky state legislature in his mid-twenties, he was appointed to the U.S. Senate and took office in 1810, even though he was younger than the constitutionally prescribed age. He ran for the U.S. House and was elected later that same year. Upon his arrival at the Capitol, he was elected Speaker of the House.

Clay's ambition, however, was not simply to be Speaker of the House. He had policy ambitions as well. Although a moderate in many senses, he was a firm believer in the "American system" and worked to promote America's greatness. He was a war hawk in the War of 1812, believing that America's destiny as a sovereign nation needed to be fulfilled. He promoted what he saw as the economic destiny of the nation through the imposition of tariffs, the establishment of a strong national bank, and improvements in the infrastructure. But as discussed in the text, the speakership was hardly a source of power to achieve those goals.

As Speaker, Clay was expected to preside in a fair and impartial manner, but his strong personality made him a forceful leader in the Congress. Over his long career, he is credited with many substantial policy successes. He was particularly talented at finding common ground and brokering compromises, he possessed renowned oratorical skills, and he had the ability to charm those with whom he crossed paths.

Still, the speakership was not sufficiently powerful to hold Clay. Barely two years after assuming the office, he resigned to help negotiate the end of the War of 1812. But after a one-year hiatus negotiating the Treaty of Ghent, he returned to the House and was once more elected Speaker. Still, contrary to his well-known comment that "I would rather be right than be president," Clay coveted that position and sought it five times. Meanwhile, he held the position of Speaker through 1820 and again in 1823. Over the next thirty years, he held a number of positions, including sitting in the Senate and serving as secretary of state.

His service as speaker during this period was unique because he was able to use the position to achieve significant policy goals. But his service did not remake the position or serve as a model for those who followed; rather, he stands as an exception. While most speakers simply presided over the body, Clay used it as a forum. When the House met as the Committee of the Whole House, he would often step down from the chair and hold his colleagues spellbound with his oratory. Beyond that, he was able to negotiate and compromise his way to significant legislative victories, including the Missouri Compromise and the chartering of the Second National Bank. But the powers of his office contributed little to his success.

Other speakers in this era had less success, and turnover in office was frequent—from 1800 to the Civil War, twenty different men held that position. Few great men seemed called to the position, and, if called, they seemed unlikely to consider it a final destination from which to carry out their ambitions. Politics were increasingly difficult in this period as leaders struggled simply to hold the nation together. Clay's great capacity both to persuade and to forge compromise shaped his reputation during this era. But it was not until later in the nineteenth century that the potential of the office was more fully developed so that others might take advantage of it.

rally around. But as serious regional divisiveness escalated into the secession movement, speakers were not able to manage conflict and focused simply on presiding over the body.

During the parliamentary period, many precedents were established including dictates that the speaker would not debate from the chair and would vote only in the case of ties. But the committee system also developed, allowing the speaker some basis to influence both the agenda and the behaviors of others.

Though speakers were relatively limited during this period because of weak parties and the lack of a substantial national agenda, one speaker stands out. In fact, many consider Henry Clay the greatest Speaker in American history. Peters attributes Clay's success to his strong personality and leadership skills and to the fact that he had a national agenda around which he rallied support.

At the end of this period, the Civil War split the nation and left scars on both its social and political character. Moreover, according to Peters, after the Civil War, a national agenda revolving around westward expansion and industrialization gave shape to political conflict that was somewhat enduring. The largely unified and philosophically cohesive Republican party, the majority party throughout this era, favored national expansion. The Democratic party was the party of state's rights and, increasingly, of minority rights as more immigrants arrived in this country. Uniting inhabitants of the post-Reconstruction South with immigrants and workers as a political force left the Democrats with some cohesiveness difficulties, but even then they were reasonably unified on many key philosophical issues.

Partisan Speakership

These forces led to what Peters labels the period of partisan speakership. The speakers not only presided over the House but clearly acted as leaders of their parties. This period featured true party government more than any other time in American history. Parties offered alternative programs, and the majority party was relatively effective in enacting its proposals. Speakers led strong party caucuses; they generally controlled the agenda; and they largely controlled the flow of legislation through recognition, control over the Rules Committee, and other parliamentary resources such as multiple referrals and the use of task forces.

Unlike the previous era, when speakers had to be concerned with establishing precedents and ruling in ways that would be considered fair, speakers now were much more comfortable using the rules to achieve their goals. Over time, power increasingly flowed into the hands of the Speaker (and, by implication, out of the hands of the average member). The effectiveness of the majority party in achieving its policy goals took its greatest toll on the minority. A series of speakers established their power of recognition without appeal, established the Rules Committee as a permanent committee and gained control over it, ended obstructionism by the minority, and (under Speaker Joseph Cannon) dominated appointments of committee members and their chairs.

Initially, the minority party feared a loss of influence. But as the Speaker gained more and more power, members of the majority party also began to fear the loss of their capacity to achieve their policy and personal goals. The membership of the House soon rebelled and reasserted the prerogatives of individual members. The revolt against Uncle Joe Cannon was one of the most dramatic actions in the annals of the Congress. However, in many ways, it can be seen as the natural result of the constant struggle to find a balance between the need for individual members to act freely and the need for them to collaborate to set policy.

BOX 6.2   The Revolt Against Uncle Joe Cannon

The speakership of Joseph Cannon in the early 1900s illustrates the potential of the office, but the revolt against him demonstrates what can happen to a speaker who tries to tap the office's full potential. The twenty years prior to the revolt against Uncle Joe, as he was known to friend and foe alike, saw the power of the House leadership go from one extreme to the other. This period illustrates the difficulty in finding a reasonable balance between the prerogatives of individual members and the power of capable leaders. While the ultimate showdown under Cannon was over the power of the speakership, the original struggle was between a minority seeking protection and a majority seeking empowerment.

Those representing the minority had gradually institutionalized a number of devices for protection from majority dominance. The tactics of the minority varied, but primary among them were the disappearing quorum[1] and the persistent use of floor motions designed solely to slow or obstruct business. These actions led many to conclude that the minority had achieved too much protection.

In response, slowly at first but then more substantially, the balance of rights shifted from the minority to the majority. Among the first steps was the assertion of the recognition power (determining who can speak from the floor) of the Speaker without appeal. Moreover, recognition preference was informally given to committee chairs. The Rules Committee was also made a permanent standing committee of the House and began to assume its gatekeeping role in 1880.

The tools for a more powerful speaker began to come into being, but the norms of the institution initially prevented any ambitious use of them. The first breakthrough came under Speaker Thomas Reed (R., Maine), who asserted that the majority must have the capacity to govern. First, he simply refused to allow dilatory motions, and then he eliminated the disappearing quorum. (Members found it difficult to claim that they were not there when the Speaker identified them as present in the chamber!) These new practices were enough to shift the balance greatly toward the majority. They also laid the groundwork for a very strong speakership.

When Joseph Cannon (R., Ill.) became speaker in 1903, the resources were available for him to become a domineering leader. Moreover, he was a believer in party government and had some strong policy preferences. He used his various powers—including those of recognition, control of the calendar, and dominance of the Rules Committee—to the point that members felt threatened. In reaction, some members of his own party joined forces with Democrats to undermine his authority. Barely surviving that effort, he sought retribution by stripping three fellow Republicans of their committee chairs.

Cannon clearly had gone too far. Because the Rules Committee was considered to be a major source of the Speaker's control, the House stripped the speakership of control of the committee's membership and chair. With his powers taken away, Cannon surrendered himself to his colleagues. While many would gladly have removed him from his position, the majority voted to let him complete his term as Speaker, and his constituents returned him to Washington for several more terms.

In a relatively short period, the House had moved from minority obstructionism, to majority governance, to what some saw as the tyranny of the speakership. Balance is, indeed, difficult to find. Members want to protect their rights, but they also want to be able to achieve their policy goals. The latter requires some capacity for majorities to be found and necessitates some leadership. But if that leadership is too strong, members again start to feel that they have lost their rights. Under Cannon, members felt the clamps tightening and so took away some of the tools of their dungeon master. A new and more equitable balance would have to be achieved.

---

1. The term *disappearing quorum* refers to a tactic that works only when the House is closely divided. Because a majority of the House must be present to conduct its business (a quorum), a minority could stop action if the minority plus the number of members not present constituted a majority (a quorum) of the body. They could do so by disappearing. In fact, it was easier than that: They did not even have to disappear; all they had to do was not answer a quorum call—even if physically present. Speaker Thomas Reed broke practice by calling out the names of those in the chamber and instructing the clerk to record them as present.

Neither all the vestiges of Cannonism nor the desire for effective governance died with the revolt against Cannon. Gradually, however, members undermined most of the significant powers of the speakership. They gained access to the floor for minor legislation. They liberated the Rules Committee from dominance by the Speaker. The seniority rule became nearly inviolable, providing protection for committee appointments and the designation of chairs. At the same time, the policy agenda evolved, changing the nature of political conflict and hampering the ability of the parties, especially the Democratic party, to sustain a high level of cohesion.

Feudal Speakership

The next period (1911–1961) is labeled the period of feudal speakership by Peters because powers largely devolved to little fiefdoms known as committees. The independence of committees was guaranteed in a variety of ways. First, of course, the seniority rule prevented not only the speaker but even the majority party from exercising any great influence over who would become the committee chair. It also prevented any recourse to the chair's actions. Under the seniority rule, the member with the longest service on the committee (in the majority party) was entitled to the chairship. Seniority was also a major force in the selection of subcommittee chairs and in the making of committee assignments. Even though the seniority rule was more of a norm that could have been violated at any time (as it ultimately was in the 1970s), it was such a strong norm that the cost of doing so was quite high.[15]

Another source of independence for committees was the independence of the Rules Committee itself. Although getting a rule from an independent Rules Committee could be as challenging as it was from one dominated by the Speaker, at least the committees felt they could attempt to pursue their own agenda.

Committees had firm control over their own agendas in a variety of other ways as well. They had complete authority to schedule legislative hearings and markups so they could control the movement of any legislation within their jurisdiction. Moreover, virtually nothing made it to the floor that had not gone through committee, so the power to block legislation was very strong. Jurisdiction was firmly established in the rules of the body, and multiple referral was not available throughout this period. Consequently, working around committees was very difficult.

There was still the question of getting legislation passed once it reached the floor. Some committees were very adept on the floor, but regardless of the committee, there remained the need to find a majority. Here, the membership valued the leadership by asking it to negotiate and bargain among these fiefdoms so that a majority could be achieved on the floor. Sam Rayburn (D., Tex.) defined the speakership during this period, serving from 1940 until his death in 1961 (with two one-term interludes when his party was in the minority). Routinely ranked as one of the top speakers of all time, Rayburn managed the House with much skill and little power. His interpersonal skills and his dedication to detail provided him with some resources, but much of his time was spent trying to work out deals among his feudal barons, that is, his committee chairs.

One of his last acts, though, was to lessen the independence of the Rules Committee. Newly elected President John F. Kennedy pushed Rayburn to break the conservative monopoly of power on the panel so that he might have a better chance to enact his programs. Rayburn acceded to the president's wishes. In an unpleasant battle with one of his most powerful chairs, Judge Howard Smith (D., Va.), Rayburn found a majority of votes to enlarge the committee and then appointed members loyal to him rather than Smith. More often, Rayburn's style and the style of the other speakers in the feudal period was to try to accommodate as many members as possible. Majorities were found a few votes at a time through quiet diplomacy.

During this same period, the Senate was seen as a "Gentleman's Club" where members' behavior was constrained by a strong set of norms designed to allow broad and fair participation within a civil environment. Leadership, as in the House, was a matter of finding points of agreement and building from them. Donald Matthews, a leading student of the Senate at the time, identified the Republican party leadership as formal, institutional, and decentralized, with power dispersed within a formal organization. On the Democratic side of the aisle, power was "highly personalized, informal, centralized in the hands of the floor leader."[16] Matthews' description of the circumstances facing party leaders speaks volumes about leadership in both parties:

> Senate party leaders generally conceive of their jobs not as creating an over-all party program . . . , but as achieving as much party unity as possible on discrete pieces of legislation. Under modern conditions, the more ambitious role is no doubt beyond their power. Even the limited goals they set for themselves are very difficult to achieve. They have no control over the raw material they are expected to unify; new party members appear on the Hill and old members are defeated quite independently of the leaders' actions or desires. They have no major sanctions to employ against party dissidents. . . . Often, the leader has little control over the content of the measures on which he seeks party agreement.[17]

As in the House, persuasion was the currency of Senate leadership during this time period. The majority leader had some control over when and if measures came to the floor, but discretion was limited by the reality of the Senate's rules. Anything, for example, could be offered as an amendment to other legislation. In the Senate, however, the seniority rule was less inviolable, in part because of confusion caused by the variety of committee appointments. Members might be deprived of a prized chairship, for example, by being given the chairship of a different committee or subcommittee.[18]

The strongest Senate leader during this period was Lyndon Johnson, whose leadership was primarily a reflection of the force of his personality. He was a master at all aspects of persuasion—both through inducements and through threats and coercion. Those who received it did not easily forget the "Johnson treatment." Consider this description of how Johnson achieved his ends:

> The psychological warfare he waged depended upon a communication system that bordered on the psychic. If Johnson was ever caught off guard, no one survived to tell about it. During critical periods, such as that of the civil

rights fight, he was all over the place, cornering colleagues and talking incessantly. One long arm draped over a fellow-senator's shoulder, his head alternately thrown back and then thrust up close to his victim's as he rammed home his points, he appeared to work a kind of hypnosis.[19]

But Johnson also played the rules to his advantage. When he became the floor leader, he established himself with junior members by instituting the "Johnson rule" requiring that each member receive a major committee assignment before senior members could receive a second one. Not only did this rule slightly disperse power in the Senate,[20] but it ingratiated Johnson with junior members.

In sum, leadership in the Congress during the early part of this century was generally a matter of bargaining and persuasion. Still, real differences existed between the two bodies and between the two parties. The House was more feudal, with leaders relying on committee chairs and ranking minority members, while in the Senate success and votes came one by one. Also, in both the House and the Senate, Republicans tended to be more formal and institutional in their approach to leadership, while Democrats tolerated diversity and utilized a more personal approach to leadership. On a formal basis, few resources existed to help any of the party leaders in their quest to become effective mangers of their bodies. Yet, leaders did not fail, and the institution continued to operate. But as the century wore on, even greater challenges confronted congressional leadership.

Democratic Speakership

The five Democrats who served as speakers between Sam Rayburn and Newt Gingrich oversaw a period of great transition in the House. During this period, the considerable power of committee chairs was broken, with power being further decentralized to subcommittees and to individual members themselves, even as the speakership gained some important powers. Speaker Carl Albert (D., Okla.), who served from 1971 to 1977, presided over the most substantial of these changes.

In brief, during this period, both members and subcommittees gained some rights and some protections from abusive chairs. The iron-clad seniority system was broken, raising the possibility that chairs could be replaced if they failed to meet the expectations (needs) of their colleagues. The Speaker also gained more influence over committee appointments and acquired some tools to help control the agenda and the flow of legislation to the floor. Power was removed from the hands of a small number of committee chairs and spread far more broadly among the membership. At the same time, however, it was recognized that power would have to be simultaneously centralized to facilitate the passage of legislation.

Even with their new power, House leaders no longer could hope to succeed by dealing with a small number of feudal lords (committee chairs). Instead, they were forced to work with more members and subcommittees and with an increasing number of organized informal groups. Peters labels this as the period of democratic speakership, with power spread among relatively equal members.

Under these conditions, then, a House of Representatives emerged in which the floor became much more the focus of activity. The drama might unfold behind the scenes, but the finale usually played out on the floor, with majorities

constructed anew on each vote. Although members certainly were policy oriented, reelection usually was the primary concern. It became the job of the leadership, then, to find a majority by meeting policy preferences and/or electoral
needs. For "Tip" O'Neill the position was even more demanding because for all
but the first two years of his ten-year term as Speaker, he served under a
Republican president, Ronald Reagan. To accomplish anything, he not only had
to accommodate his party in the House but also to survive a Republican Senate
and president. In many ways, his success as Speaker can be traced to his roots as
an old-style pol who was sensitive to the needs of his party members. He was
willing to help them achieve their individual goals even as he moved toward
achieving party goals.

It was also under O'Neill that the speakership was established as a television
presence.[21] During much of his time in office, O'Neill was the top elected
Democrat in the country and, therefore, looked to as party spokesperson on a
regular basis. His large physical stature, white hair, and craggy features also made
him a popular target for cartoonists.

Television provides many resources to speakers in their battle to lead, but they
are intangible resources. Television appearances allow speakers to communicate
with their members indirectly. It also provides a major tool for controlling and
advancing the agenda by affecting what both members and the public think.
Because television provides access to the constituents of all members, it is a
potential source of influence on members and their reelection bids. Finally, to the
extent that the party leadership has control over press coverage, such as through
staged events, leaders may be able to provide benefits to party members by gaining television appearances for them.

O'Neill's successor, Representative Jim Wright (D., Tex.), was much more
aggressive in promoting his agenda and less sympathetic to the needs of members. He pushed the limits of the powers of the office and used whatever tactics
were necessary to win. Regardless of the value of his accomplishments, he alienated most Republicans and lost footing among many Democrats. Further, his successes came at an increasingly high price. House members began to see too much
influence flowing to the Speaker and became distressed about what it would
mean to them. As a result, Republicans had a strong incentive to undermine him
in any way they could. And when Republicans raised questions regarding the
legality and ethics of a book deal, few Democrats felt any urgency to come to
Wright's defense. Wright, a gifted orator, was successful on television and in many
other ways, but his colleagues considered him insensitive to their needs, leaving
him vulnerable to challenge. Recognizing his lack of support, Wright resigned
from his position after less than two-and-a-half years in office.

Further damaging Wright's capacity to survive was the knowledge that his
successor would be Tom Foley (D., Wash.). Foley seemed to possess the complete
package of traits sought by his colleagues. Unfortunately, the level of partisan rancor continued to rise as years of divided-party government seemed to take its toll.
Republicans remained irritated over the treatment they received under Wright,
and Democrats blamed the Republicans for bringing down their speaker. Policy
differences were substantial, and compromise and bargaining were constrained by
the huge budget deficit.

Added to that mix was the continued rise of Newt Gingrich (R., Ga.) within Republican party ranks. Unlike many who preceded him, Gingrich's goal clearly was to return the Republican party to majority status. Accommodation and compromise was not the route to majority status, so Gingrich worked to further heighten partisanship in the House. In the end, of course, he succeeded. And Tom Foley's reign ended in a way that no speaker's had since the Civil War—he was defeated at the polls by his own constituents.

Gingrich Speakership

Upon achieving the speakership, Gingrich sought to remake it and much of the House. The reforms enacted at the start of the 104th Congress were substantial, and he promised more as he continued in office. Through both strong leadership and rules reforms, Gingrich put himself more fully in charge of the House than any Speaker in memory.[22] First, he attacked the committee system, which had been a constant source of difficulty for Democratic speakers. He eliminated three committees, clearly demonstrated that loyalty would be as strong a criterion for committee chair appointment as was seniority, established a limit of three terms as chair, eliminated proxy voting in committees, and dramatically cut committee staff. Next, he relied heavily on task forces to develop legislation, particularly for that related to the Contract With America. Removing control of major legislation from the hands of the committees was a frontal assault on their prerogatives, and one that Gingrich suggested might be greatly expanded in the future.[23]

He also reestablished the Speaker's Advisory Group to unite the party leadership and provide it with greater control over the agenda, committees, and most other aspects of House life. He gained firm control of the Rules Committee, as well as effective command of the committee entrusted with making committee appointments. Further, he sought help in managing the business of the House by, among other things, creating an Office of Chief Administrator answerable directly to the Speaker.

How this Gingrich-led Republican revolution will be perceived in the long run remains to be seen. But some observations are appropriate. First, Gingrich was phenomenally successful in pushing the priorities specified in the Contract With America through the House and in holding his party together on other critical votes. Yet, his ability to remake America was severely limited by his failure to consider the fact that the House does not operate in a vacuum, independent of the less impassioned Senate, to say nothing of the president. Because Gingrich's legislation did not undergo the normal processes of negotiating, bargaining, and compromising, it was much more difficult to find common ground with the Senate and the White House.

Second, the House does operate in a manner quite different than it did under its Democratic predecessors. How these changes evolve will determine their lasting effects, but for now it is clear that the power and independence of committees have been undermined. However, with the advent of the 105th Congress, it was also clear that committees had staved off some of the threat from the task force concept and had regained some control over their own agendas. The next critical juncture will come as chairs begin to be term-limited out of their

---

BOX 6.3   Speaker Newt Gingrich: The Trials and Tribulations of a Revolutionary

---

His beginnings hardly suggested that he would reshape American politics. But Newt Gingrich (R., Ga.) found a way to build a Republican majority in the Congress. As part of his desire to lead a revolution in American politics, he enhanced the powers of the leadership in the House of Representatives.

Gingrich grew up in a military family, attended Emory University in Georgia, and received a Ph.D. in history at Tulane. He then got a job teaching history at West Georgia College. But politics had been in his blood since childhood, and within four years he was running for Congress. He was not successful in his challenge to a long-time Democratic incumbent in 1974, a good year for Democrats. Undeterred, he tried again in 1976, only to confront a ticket headed by a Georgia Democrat running for president. Still determined, he ran again in 1978, finally winning the Sixth District of Georgia.

From the beginning, Gingrich had a number of distinctive traits. He was routinely described by supporters as a big-picture person, intelligent, and with grand ideas—and as a gadfly by detractors. He also seemed particularly attuned to strategy, and that is where he attracted serious attention. Unlike many in his party, he had little interest in being an effective member of the minority party—he wanted to be in the majority party.

From the beginning, his prime goal was gaining control of the House for the Republicans. He was, for example, appointed to the House Administration Committee because the leadership knew he would protect the party's interests during campaign finance reform debates.[1] More notably, his style was one of drawing distinctions between the parties rather than cooperating. He, and others who agreed with him, turned to using the House's Special Order provisions and one-minute speeches to gain access to the floor and to the growing C-SPAN audience. With little in the way of legislative goals, he could focus on embarrassing the Democratic party and drawing distinctions

between the parties favorable to the Republicans.[2] Not surprisingly, partisanship began to rise during this period.

Gingrich also learned the lesson of communicating directly with the public. Democratic speakers were slowly learning the lessons of governance during a media age, but Gingrich learned them more quickly. He found that being critical of established policies and patterns of governance struck a chord with voters as well. What changed the course of history, though, was his ability to sell a vision for the future to his party and to the American public.

Gingrich's opportunity came when the country elected a Democratic president, Bill Clinton. As a skilled strategist, Gingrich knew that the congressional party of the president is vulnerable during the midterm election. He pulled out all stops. He gathered money from contributors who might normally support Republicans but who were reluctant to invest in the minority. He recruited good candidates around the country. He even scripted the language candidates should use to denigrate Democrats and advance the Republican cause. But most importantly, he spearheaded the Contract With America, a list of issues that polls showed the public widely supported.[3]

A number of things made the Contract distinctive. First, it was presented to the public as a binding written commitment with no fine print.[4] The language was strong and left the voters feeling empowered. Second, Gingrich succeeded in getting widespread Republican commitment to the Contract. In 1994, Republicans spoke with one voice. Third, he fed on voter cynicism and anger in a variety of ways. The outcome, of course, is well known—Republicans gained a majority in the House for the first time since the 1952 election.

For Gingrich, majority status was not his end goal, but rather the means to reshape politics and policy in America. Upon achieving majority status, he sought to reshape the House. He wanted to rid it of the entrenched characteris-

BOX 6.3 continued

tics of Democratic party dominance and replace it with his own model of governance. In a variety of ways, he increased the power of the speakership. Due to his mastery of informal powers, he was virtually beyond reproach early in the 104th Congress. He set the agenda, established priorities, determined the details of legislation, and delivered the requisite votes.

For a brief time, Gingrich was as powerful as a Speaker of the House is likely ever to be. Eventually, however, too many people felt run over; intraparty tensions began to exert cross-pressures on him; and he made mistakes, including being considered culpable for the government shutdown. Charges of campaign and ethics violations provided an opportunity for opponents to begin the process of undermining his power. At the start of the 104th Congress, many considered him the most powerful man in America; at the start of the 105th Congress, he barely was reelected speaker after a number of Republicans abandoned him. As part of the deal over his ethics charge, he apologized to the House and agreed to pay a substantial fine. Through all of this, his public approval ratings plunged.[5]

Gingrich's stature declined so severely during the 105th Congress that his party, including some top party officials, plotted to remove him from office. Fueled by discontent on the part of junior, ideologically driven conservatives within their own party, these dissidents decided it was time for a change.[6] After some quiet agitation, the rebels met with much of the top party leadership—excluding, of course, Gingrich. During a series of meetings, Majority Leader Dick Armey, Majority Whip Tom DeLay, and Representative Bill Paxon (who chaired Republican leadership meetings) all flirted with supporting the overthrow movement and allowed their names to be discussed as composing a new leadership team.[7] DeLay suggested that a successful palace revolt would have to unfold quickly and should take the form of a motion to vacate the chair. Not overly concerned about the transition itself,

the rebels evidently assumed that they would join a united group of Democrats to remove Gingrich. Whether the Democrats would have helped the Republicans out of their own mess is uncertain. When the coup attempt was uncovered, Gingrich and his supporters managed to defeat the effort. But it became clear that the Gingrich revolution had suffered another setback.

Gingrich's legacy may endure well beyond his term. He threatened the basis of the committee system in the House and much of what gives members their independence. Committees stemmed that tide and, in some significant ways, managed to reverse it. The long-term consequences of Gingrich's efforts to remake the House will be determined by whether power stays concentrated in the leadership or whether it devolves back to the committees. Regardless, Gingrich's accomplishments, both before he became Speaker and afterwards, are a testament to what leadership can do in the House— whether that leadership is informal or is based on the advantages of formal office.

1. Gary W. Copeland, "The House Says 'No' to Public Financing of Congressional Campaigns," *Legislative Studies Quarterly* 9 (August 1984): 487–504.

2. Stephen Frantzich and John Sullivan, *The C-SPAN Revolution* (Norman: University of Oklahoma Press, 1996), esp. 255–293.

3. Ronald M. Peters, Jr., *The American Speakership: The Office in Historical Perspective*, 2d ed. (Baltimore: Johns Hopkins University Press), 287–322.

4. Ed Gillespie and Bob Schellhas, eds. *Contract With America: The Bold Plan by Rep. Newt Gingrich, Rep. Dick Armey and the House Republicans to Change the Nation* (New York: Times Books, 1994), 7.

5. Peters, *The American Speakership*, 311–316.

6. Jackie Koszczuk, "Party Stalwarts Will Determine Gingrich's Long-Term Survival," *Congressional Quarterly Weekly Report*, July 26, 1997, 1751–1755.

7. Jackie Koszczuk, "The Gingrich Coup, Hour by Hour," *Congressional Quarterly Weekly Report*, July 19, 1997, 1673. The details in this paragraph of the events surrounding the coup attempt are drawn from that account.

positions. Will the rule be modified, perhaps establishing loopholes? Will some chairs simply slide over to become chairs of other committees?

Third, as an office, the speakership clearly is more powerful. The modernizing of the management of the House helps provide control to the speaker. The Speaker's Advisory Group serves as a great resource for the Speaker to manage the agenda of the House, the flow of legislation, and the distribution of rewards and sanctions. But the concentration of powers and resources in the hands of Gingrich also put in his lap a higher level of responsibility. Coupled with his high profile in this media age, the Speaker is destined to be carefully scrutinized.

As a result, Gingrich's speakership became vulnerable. His attention to the needs of individual members was never high, and as he focused his eyes on other prizes, it slipped even more. When Republicans were blamed for failures in governance, especially those resulting in government shutdowns, Gingrich was singled out. Perhaps his greatest sin, however, was that he became an electoral liability to many in his party. Ethics charges became one basis for attacking the Speaker and nearly led to his defeat for reelection to that position at the start of the 105th Congress. Months later, he barely survived an overthrow attempt by some fellow Republicans, including some of his top lieutenants.

Many lessons can be drawn from Gingrich's speakership. One of the most important is that it is difficult to lead an institution like the Congress. Members are present on the authority of their constituents and are ultimately responsible for their behavior to them—not to the leadership. The powers that the leadership has are granted to it by its members and are revokable by them. This reality provides a constant source of tension that we will discuss shortly.

LEADERSHIP IN THE CONTEMPORARY SENATE

One can no longer think of the Senate as a Gentlemen's Club.[24] Not only does its membership include a number of women, but the norms that governed that club have evolved, the way it conducts its business has changed.[25] The norm of specialization has been changed through a wider distribution of prize committee assignments, and large staffs allow members to wander into areas beyond their specialization. Widespread access to the media also provides individual senators with the capacity both to help shape the agenda and to frame the debate. Greater use of the filibuster and even the threat of its use provide great power to a minority. It is said that to win in the Senate, one must be able to find a sixty-vote majority (to support a cloture vote ending debate).[26] At the same time, the norm that every senator should have her or his say and have an opportunity to affect the course of a piece of legislation remains very firmly ingrained.

Leadership in the Senate, then, faces challenges that in many ways are greater than those in the House.[27] One advantage that Senate leaders have, though, is that they need to deal with only 100 individuals rather than 435. Whatever inducements they might have to offer go further because they do not need to be spread as broadly. The desire to make things happen in a reasonable manner has led to increased use of unanimous consent agreements that determine the rules of debate on any particular piece of legislation. Because this is the Senate, however, any single senator can undermine such an agreement.

Leadership remains extremely difficult in a body whose members jealously guard their personal prerogatives to influence public policy and whose members have the resources and capacity to delve into nearly any issue, force debate, and shape the discussion of it. The leadership challenge is exacerbated by the fact that members are accountable only to constituents and only every six years. Thus, the question becomes not why the leadership is weak, but why there is any leadership at all. It is that question to which we now turn.

THE NEED FOR LEADERSHIP
VERSUS INDEPENDENT MEMBERS

In both chambers, we see a constant tension between, on the one hand, the need for leadership privy to resources and, on the other, the desire of members for independence and personal discretion.[28] Both representatives and senators in the contemporary Congress have strong policy orientations. They want to be able to shape policy; but they also want to meet the needs of their constituents and to be able to win reelection.

To succeed in these goals, legislation must be passed and laws must be made. To do so, priorities must be set, procedures followed, and majorities found or created. The tasks of leadership are to lead members through a series of policy debates and to facilitate the passage of laws in the desired form.[29] Leadership needs some control over the agenda and over the rules of debate to enable laws to be passed and members to achieve their goals.

In considering leadership in the contemporary Congress, keep in mind that it exists to allow members to achieve their goals. Few in Congress are there to serve the president or to be a party loyalist. The specific goals of members vary widely, but they do have personal goals. As Glenn Parker points out, the members sacrifice some discretion in these matters because they need help achieving goals.[30] Without leadership, they are unlikely to achieve any goals, they may lose reelection, and they will rarely affect public policy.

Members, then, face a dilemma. They need to give up enough power to their leadership so that it can be effective enough to allow the members to achieve their goals. At the same time, the leadership cannot be so powerful that it begins to infringe on the ability of members to pursue individual goals. In the late nineteenth century, Speaker Reed argued that the majority must be able to govern, but in doing so he took away some of the obstructionist prerogatives of the minority. In the early twentieth century, when Speaker Cannon moved to accrue even more power to the speakership, he severely infringed on the power of the membership of the House at large. House members accepted much of what Reed did because it allowed them to achieve policy goals and promote reelection. But they revolted against Cannon because they felt that they had lost too much capacity to affect policy and risked losing the ability to control their own reelection fate.

In the House, is it a coincidence that the two recent speakers who have had their leadership positions seriously challenged were the two who tried to most firmly use and expand the powers of the office? Wright's support had been weakened by his aggressive pursuit of policy goals, and he had created an angry minority party by his tactics. Many members had reason to go after Wright, and few felt much need to fight for him. In the end, the ethics charges undermined his speakership, but the lack of support from those who voted for him as Speaker left him unable to survive the charges. The attacks on Gingrich can also be interpreted as a method to prevent Gingrich from going further and even served to reverse the trend toward greater accrual of power in the speakership.

In the Senate, we have seen a series of leaders who have not tried to stretch their leadership beyond what their colleagues preferred. If anything, recent Senate leaders have been criticized for not being aggressive enough in the use of power. Senators who feel frustrated in their attempts to legislate because of the lack of collective action often criticize the leadership. But Senate leaders are constrained not only by the individualistic nature of their body but also by the fact that a working majority in the Senate is sixty votes, and neither party has achieved that number for quite some time. Legislative success in the Senate, then, requires not only accommodating one's own party but also reaching across the aisle to find votes on a regular basis.

Still, if House leaders periodically err on the side of too aggressively pursuing leadership, Senate leaders surely take a cautious approach. But the dynamics that set the contours within which leaders must operate are extraordinarily fluid. The majority/minority status of one's party makes a big difference. An effective balance for a minority leader may be dramatically out of alignment for a majority leader. The status of one's party in the other body and the party in control of the White House also affect the demands on and expectations of a leader. Even more intangible variables can make a difference. If a Congress runs the risk of being labeled "do-nothing" or obstructionist, the importance of passing legislation increases. The flurry of legislation passed in the waning months of the 104th Congress may have spared many Republicans defeat at the polls. Recognizing that threat, many members at that point were willing to grant more authority to their leadership. Members' expectations of their leaders might even change from month to month.

Members will generally look first at reelection needs and then at policy goals. Their view is that the leadership should facilitate success in both areas. To the extent it does, they are willing to sacrifice some personal discretion. To the extent that leadership does not facilitate the pursuit of personal goals, authority is only reluctantly given to leadership. To the extent that the leadership stands in the way of goals achievement, leaders themselves become vulnerable. The tension is inherent in the process, and the relationship between leaders and followers is fluid. Regardless of the personal skills of leaders, however, they are unlikely to be much more successful than their followers allow them to be.

PARTY UNITY

As we have seen, the leadership has limited capacity to control the outcome of public policy deliberations. That is, it has only modest influence over the content of legislation and only partial ability to set the agenda. Members of the Congress like it this way because they want discretion in both areas. These constraints on the leadership's ability are, then, normally acceptable to party membership. But what members want is for their leaders to deliver votes on legislation they, the members, have drafted and are promoting. Leadership is expected to deliver votes.

Like all other aspects of leadership, however, the expectation for delivering votes is constrained by members' willingness to accept it. When a vote confronts them, members immediately assess the electoral consequences. If following the party line might hamper their chances of reelection, they are likely to abandon their party. Moreover, they expect to do so with impunity. The belief is that the leadership should understand their electoral needs and work to accommodate them. Ideally, members will not be put into a position where they face cross-pressure, but if they are, they expect to be able to cast a vote for their constituents and not suffer for it within the party. There should be no sanctions or repercussions for such a vote.

Still, the leadership is expected to identify party issues and positions that will aid members in obtaining reelection. Leadership should pick and promote policies that separate and enhance the two parties.[31] That is, they should find issues that are important to voters and that will help party incumbents with their constituencies. So, if leadership is succeeding in both parties, we should see a large number of issues come before the Congress that differentiate the two parties. Moreover, when that happens, the leadership should be able to deliver large numbers of votes for the party's issue.

Even the expectation that leaders actively seek to differentiate the parties is relatively new. In fact, during the era when a conservative coalition between southern Democrats and Republicans was a major force in the Congress, leadership often sought to avoid such divisive issues. Figure 6.3 shows how frequently party votes have occurred in the Congress in recent decades. Those figures are based on *Congressional Quarterly's* tabulation of the percentage of time the majority of Democrats in the body stood in opposition to the majority of Republicans.

From the late 1960s to the early 1980s, those party votes occurred infrequently. From 1966 through 1982, the percentage was never more than 50 percent in the House, and it did not go over 50 percent from 1967 through 1985 in the Senate. Since the mid-1980s, however, the frequency of party votes has increased rather consistently. Throughout the 1990s, about two-thirds of the votes in each house have been party votes—generally a little higher in the House than the Senate. The higher frequency of partisan voting has also been reflected in greater partisanship in a variety of other ways, including deadlock on some critical legislative matters and more acrimonious rhetoric.

It would not be appropriate to attribute the increase in partisanship simply to the actions of the leadership. The changing partisan alignment in the South, Republican party electoral strategy, and presidents who have served as partisan

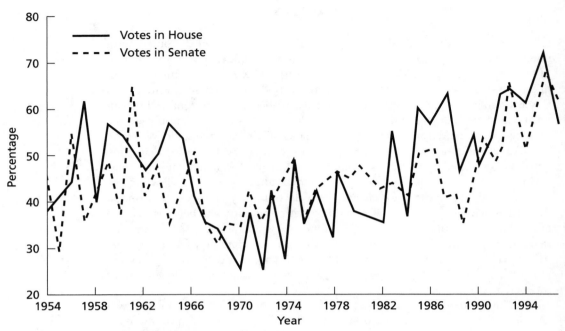

FIGURE 6.3   **Percentage of Partisan Votes, 1954–1996**

SOURCE: *CQ Weekly Report.* December 21, 1997, 3462.

lightening rods deserve much of the credit. But leadership was needed to structure this conflict. It is probably not a coincidence that the 64 percent of party votes in 1987, Jim Wright's first year as speaker, was notably higher than the numbers for the years preceding it. In fact, for all the years we have party voting data, it was at its peak (up to that point) in both chambers. Further, it seems that the leadership of at least the Republican party has used this strategy with reasonable effectiveness. The Republican success in wresting majority status from the Democrats can be attributed in part to this approach.

Partisan voting, then, is the result of structuring conflict between the two parties within Congress. If done well, partisan voting may provide electoral benefits. The other part of the process is enacting policy preferences. Once party votes are shaped, the question becomes whether the leadership can hold the party together enough to win. Legislating by unanimity within the majority party is rare. Success comes, then, from getting a large portion of fellow partisans and the requisite number of converts from the opposition party on one's side. Critical to this process is keeping a large portion of one's party together.

Congressional Quarterly tracks data that help us judge how well the party leadership keeps its troops in line. Taking only party votes into consideration, *CQ* calculates the percentage of the time all members of the party vote with their party. Thus, a party unity average score of 90 would mean that 90 percent of the time, members of that party voted with their party majority; only 10 percent of the

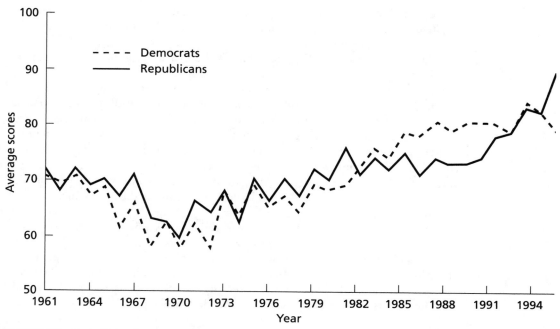

FIGURE 6.4   Party Unity Scores, 1961–1994

SOURCE: *1995 CQ Almanac* (Washington D.C.: Congressional Quarterly, 1995), C21.

time did members either vote against their party majority or not vote at all. Figure 6.4 shows trends in party unity scores in recent decades for Republicans and for Democrats from both chambers combined.

The average unity score has consistently increased since the early 1960s and at times has been extraordinarily high. During their first year in the 104th Congress, Republicans achieved an amazing unity score of 91 percent. Further, of the remaining 9 percent, 2 percent reflect absences, so only 7 percent of the time did a Republican vote against the party majority on these party votes. The overall increase in these scores reflects the changing characteristics of our party system, including overall increases in partisanship and in the effectiveness of party leaders.

With the task of constructing a majority falling to the party's leadership, the ability to keep votes within the party is important. It is less important, of course, when the majority is large. In fact, the leadership has the luxury of letting members stray for electoral advantages when the majority is large. Allowing members to do that may provide an electoral cushion for members should the leadership need them on a subsequent vote. Therefore, while it would be misleading to interpret these numbers as a direct indication of leadership effectiveness, the data in the two figures do suggest that party leadership in both bodies and in both parties oversees a partisan membership who can reliably be expected to line up on opposite sides of issues.

Leadership is a complicated matter in any body, but in Congress it is especially difficult. Members agree on the need for leadership and are willing to grant leaders certain powers to facilitate the effective conduct of business. But if leadership begins to look as if it might hinder the reelection efforts of members or stand in the way of policy enactment, members may withdraw support for or strip powers from speakers. Further, the formal powers given to leaders at the top of the hierarchy are quite modest. Leadership has little control over the calendar, over the content of legislation, over rewards or punishments for members, or over members' electoral futures. At the same time, circumstances are quite different for leaders in the House and Senate. In the Senate, each member is afforded tremendous leeway and individual influence. By contrast, in the House, leaders have more formal powers, particularly through their control over the Rules Committee, but even in the House leaders are constrained by the expectation of interest accommodation.

A prime lesson of this chapter is that leadership is a persistent challenge in a collective body like the Congress. When members are formally equal and accountable primarily to their own constituents, leadership will result primarily from perceived common needs. As those needs change, leadership and expectations for it also evolve. The tension is constant because the stakes are high both for the careers of members and for our nation's public policies.

NOTES

1. Allen D. Hertzke and Ronald M. Peters, Jr., *The Atomistic Congress: An Interpretation of Congressional Change* (Armonk, N.Y.: Sharpe, 1992), 3.

2. Randall B. Ripley, *Power in the Senate* (New York: St. Martin's Press, 1969), 21–52.

3. See Walter J. Oleszek, *Congressional Procedures and the Policy Process,* 4th ed. (Washington, D.C.: CQ Press, 1996), 235–238.

4. Senator Ford did not seek reelection in 1998.

5. Tip O'Neill, "Rules for Speakers," in *The Speaker: Leadership in the U.S. House of Representatives,* ed. Ronald M. Peters (Washington, D.C.: Congressional Quarterly, 1994), 202–221. See also Barbara Sinclair, "Congressional Leadership: A Review Essay and A Research Agenda," in *Leading Congress: New Styles, New Strategies,* ed. John J. Kornacki, Jr. (Washington, D.C.: Congressional Quarterly, 1990), 97–162.

6. While a bit dated, a good overview is Robert L. Peabody, *Leadership in Congress: Stability, Succession, and Change* (Boston: Little, Brown, 1976). More recently, see Lynne P. Brown and Robert L. Peabody, "Choosing the Speaker," in *The Speaker,* ed. Peters, 18–39.

7. Nelson W. Polsby, "Two Strategies of Influence: Choosing a Majority Leader, 1962," in *New Perspectives on the House of Representatives,* 2d ed., ed. Robert L. Peabody and Nelson W. Polsby (Chicago: Rand McNally, 1969), 325–358.

8. Ibid. See also Albert's own account in Carl Albert with Danney Goble, *Little Giant: The Life and Times of Carl Albert* (Norman: University of Oklahoma Press, 1990), esp. 243–257.

9. Cokie Roberts, "Leadership and the Media in the 101st Congress," in *Leading Congress,* ed. Kornacki, 85–96; and Joe S. Foote, "The Speaker and the Media," in *The Speaker,* ed. Peters, 135–156.

10. Ronald M. Peters, Jr., *The American Speakership: The Office in Historical Perspective,* 2d ed. (Baltimore: Johns Hopkins University Press, 1997), 291–293.

11. Although it would be very difficult to demonstrate that members support individuals for party leadership positions because of contributions given by their leadership PAC, most observers see that pattern. It was also a substantial part of the Gingrich strategy. Moreover, it is clear that leadership PACs contribute their money in a strategic way. See Clyde Wilcox and Marc Genest, "Member PACs as Strategic Actors," *Polity* 23 (Spring 1991): 461–470.

12. Karen M. Kedrowski, *Media Entrepreneurs and the Media Enterprise in the U.S. Congress* (Cresskill, N.J.: Hampton Press), 166–169.

13. Recall, also, that floor leadership positions did not evolve as important offices until the end of the nineteenth century. Prior to that time, most of the Senate leadership was informal or found in the leadership structure of its committees. Ripley, in *Power in the Senate,* refers to these as individualistic and decentralized leadership patterns.

14. Peters, *The American Speakership,* 16.

15. See also H. Douglas Price, "The Congressional Career: Then and Now," in *Congressional Behavior,* ed. Nelson W. Polsby (New York: Random House, 1971), 14–27.

16. Donald R. Matthews, *U.S. Senators and Their World* (New York: Vintage Books, 1960), 123.

17. Ibid., 126.

18. It is not always clear when senators choose to move and when they are forced to do so. Senator Jesse Helms (R., N.C.) moved from being the chair of Foreign Relations to Agriculture and back to Foreign Relations, all voluntarily. See also the concept of compensated violations discussed in Nelson W. Polsby, Miriam Gallaher, and Barry Spencer Rundquist, "The Growth of the Seniority System in the U.S. House of Representatives," *American Political Science Review* 63 (September 1969): 787–807.

19. Douglass Cater, *Power in Washington* (New York: Random House), 164. See also the discussion of Johnson's various "treatments" in Ralph K. Huitt, "Democratic Party Leadership in the Senate," *American Political Science Review* (June 1961): 333–344.

20. See Leroy N. Rieselbach, *Congressional Reform: The Changing Modern Congress* (Washington, D.C.: Congressional Quarterly, 1994), 26.

21. Joe S. Foote, "The 'Outside' Role: A Leadership Challenge," *Extensions* (Norman, Okla.: The Carl Albert Congressional Research and Studies Center, Fall 1996), 4–6.

22. John E. Owens, "The Return of Party Government in the U.S. House of Representatives: Central Leadership—Committee Relations in the 104th Congress," *British Journal of Political Science* 27 (April 1997): 247–272.

23. For an overview, see C. Lawrence Evans and Walter J. Oleszek, *Congress Under Fire: Reform Politics and the Republican Majority* (Boston: Houghton Mifflin, 1997).

24. Nelson W. Polsby, "Goodbye to the Senate's Inner Club," in *Congress in Change: Evolution and Reform,* ed. Norman J. Ornstein (New York: Praeger), 208–215.

25. A good, concise overview of the changes in the Senate can be found in Norman J. Ornstein, Robert L. Peabody, and David W. Rohde, "The U.S. Senate: Toward the Twenty-First Century," in *Congress Reconsidered,* 6th ed., ed. Lawrence C. Dodd and Bruce I. Oppenheimer (Washington, D.C.: CQ Press, 1997), 1–28. See also Barbara Sinclair, *The Transformation of the U.S. Senate* (Baltimore: Johns Hopkins University Press, 1989).

26. An excellent treatment of this and related points is Barbara Sinclair, *Unorthodox Lawmaking* (Washington, D.C.: Congressional Quarterly, 1997).

27. Samuel C. Patterson, "Party Leadership in the U.S. Senate," in *The Changing World of the U.S. Senate,* ed. John R. Hibbing (Berkeley, Calif.: IGS Press), 87–108.

28. Glenn R. Parker, *Institutional Change, Discretion, and the Making of Modern Congress* (Ann Arbor: University of Michigan Press, 1992), esp. 49–66.

29. David W. Rohde, *Parties and Leaders in the Postreform House* (Chicago: University of Chicago Press, 1991). See also Barbara

Sinclair, *Legislators, Leaders, and Lawmaking* (Baltimore: Johns Hopkins University Press, 1995).

30. Parker, *Institutional Change,* 95–108.

31. Rohde, *Parties and Leaders,* 105–119.

7

Staff:
The Unelected Legislators

Forty years of Democratic rule in the House ended on January 4, 1995, when a Republican majority took control. Forty years of hiring practices and staffing patterns abruptly changed.

For Donnald K. Anderson, Clerk of the House, the day brought an end to a career that began as a Capitol Hill page in 1960 and culminated in the position of chief administrative officer of the House. The clerk is elected by the majority party; Anderson's last official act before he stepped down was swearing in members of the 104th Congress (1995–1996). Another 600 legislative aides working for House committees also lost their jobs when members voted to reorganize the committee structure and to reduce support staffs by one-third.[1] The Office of the Doorkeeper was abolished and its custodial responsibilities transferred to other offices. The House historian and his staff were fired.[2] Committee chairs were given authority to conduct all staff hiring, with that right simultaneously revoked from the subcommittee chairs and ranking minority member. Recall from Box 4.1 that the Legislative Service Organizations were defunded, causing a loss of ninety-six staff positions.[3]

Republican control changed the lives of hundreds of legislative aides in the House. The careers of many long-term Democratic appointees ended, while opportunities for Republican appointees opened up. The rules package instituting the changes on the opening day of the 104th Congress passed overwhelmingly. Democrats voted for the package because staff cuts would undermine the support system of the new Republican majority. Why not cut positions that were going to be filled by the other party if they were left intact? Republicans backed structural reorganization to justify release of hundreds of aides hired by Democrats and to deliver on their promise to shrink the size of government.

Senate Republicans took control of their institution on the same day. They, too, bounced some of the Democratic administrative appointees, such as the Senate parliamentarian. Over the course of the 104th Congress they cut 226 committee staff slots; in contrast to the House, though, the cuts were temporary. Senators restored more than 200 committee positions in the 105th Congress (1997–1998). They also increased the number of personal aides. In fact, senators added more than 250 new positions in the 105th Congress, topping a record for the number of personal aides in the Senate.[4]

The new Republican majority in the House and Senate clearly perceived staffing issues differently. Representatives believed their chamber was overstaffed, particularly with committee aides; senators believed their chamber was understaffed, especially with personal aides. Members responded to their own chamber's needs. In this chapter, we trace the historical growth of the legislative branch, outline the various staff positions and functions, and discuss the legislative branch appropriation.

GROWTH OF THE LEGISLATIVE BRANCH

The U.S. Congress is the most heavily staffed legislature in the world.[5] The Canadian Parliament, by contrast, employs 10 percent as many people.[6] Of course, any comparisons between congressional and parliamentary staffing levels are imprecise; the executive and legislative branches are separated by a written Constitution in our system, while they are unified in a parliamentary system. Congress needs more assistance because it is more autonomous by design.

Figure 7.1 provides perspective on staff size and growth by showing annual legislative branch appropriations since World War II. The graph starts from the time of passage of the Legislative Reorganization Act of 1946 because that represents the beginning of the modern era in congressional staffing.

The most striking feature of Figure 7.1 is the steady growth in legislative branch appropriations over time. In 1946, the appropriation was $54 million; by 1995, the figure was more than $2 billion. Adjusting for inflation, the appropriations for the legislative branch still grew by more than 700 percent!

A second feature is the steep rise following the Legislative Reorganization Act of 1970, which further increased staffing to help Congress compete with the executive branch in policy-making. Congress increased its budget by $400 million every five years.

What explains the skyrocketing number of legislative aides? First, Congress became a more attractive career. Members' salary, benefits, and power increased as the government grew in size and scope, and career-oriented members increased their staffs as part of an effort to win reelection.[7] Second, members pursued greater autonomy from the executive branch in the wake of the Vietnam War and the Watergate scandal. They constructed support agencies, such as the

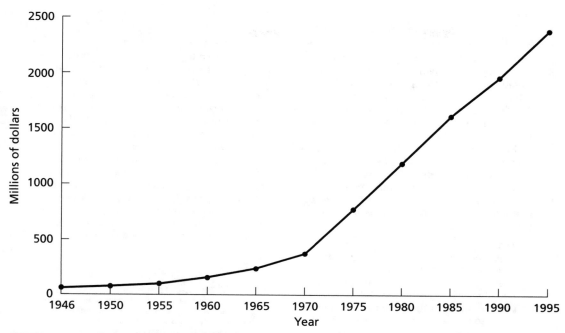

FIGURE 7.1   Legislative Branch Appropriation, 1946–1995

SOURCE: Norman J. Ornstein, Thomas E. Mann, and Michael J. Malbin, *Vital Statistics on Congress 1997–1998* (Washington, D.C.: Congressional Quarterly, 1998), 145–146.

Congressional Budget Office, to provide Congress with independent, reliable information. Third, members became overwhelmed with work. Congress appropriated more money, reported out more bills, cast more votes, and spent more days in session following each Legislative Reorganization Act. Congress added staff to cope with its workload.

In the immediate aftermath of the Legislative Reorganization Act of 1970, however, observers started questioning the unbridled growth. Political scientist David Price noted that entrepreneurial staff often pursued their own political agendas.[8] Senator Ernest "Fritz" Hollings (D., S.C.) expressed concern that staffers undermined the working relationship among senators:

> Everybody is working for the staff, staff, staff; staff driving you nutty in fact. It has gotten to the point where the senators never actually sit down and exchange ideas and learn from the experience of others and listen. Now it is how many nutty whiz kids you get on the staff, to get you [publicity in] magazine articles and get you headlines and get all these other [kind of] things done.[9]

At the end of the 1970s, political scientist Michael Malbin took the idea further, criticizing the "unelected representatives" of Capitol Hill for drafting and negotiating deals without adequate supervision from members. He also blamed staff

---

BOX 7.1   Staff in the Information Age

Congress may have to increase staffing levels in the future to cope with the additional workload created by the electronics revolution. The institution is more accessible than ever before. People are able to send e-mail messages to congressional offices and visit member Web sites from all around the world.[1]

Reliable data on the volume of citizen e-mail contact with members is not available, but anecdotal evidence provides reason to think that members are being inundated with messages. Here is the verbatim electronic reply of one senator to an e-mail message from a constituent:

> Thank you for your recent e-mail message. I appreciate hearing from you and have noted your comments. As you can imagine, my office receives hundreds of e-mail messages each week. It is a great way for my constituents to convey their views to me easily and quickly. While I am unable to provide a specific reply to your message at this time, state residents who have included a postal address will receive a reply via U.S. Mail as soon as possible. . . . Again, thank you for contacting me. I hope you will continue to provide me with your comments on issues of importance to you.

The reply makes it clear that the senator's office will not be providing an e-mail reply, nor will it be responding to nonresidents. Yet, the senator's office still has to sort through incoming messages and reply through regular mail to those who provide an address in the state. Those labor-intensive tasks suggest the need for more personal aides in congressional offices.

Congress will also have to hire techicians familiar with Web servers, Web pages, and electronic bulletin boards. It will need updated security systems to thwart computer hackers, and it will need experts knowledgeable about computer viruses. Simply put, a new breed of congressional staffer is appearing on the Hill.[2] Whether the new breed supplants or supplements existing staff remains to be seen.

---

1. Scholarship is just beginning to appear on electronic forms of communication with Congress. For instance, see John P. Messmer, "Early Politics on the World-Wide-Web," paper delivered at the Annual Meeting of the American Political Science Association, Washington, D.C., August 1997; E. Scott Adler, Chariti E. Gent, and Cary B. Overmeyer, "The Home Style Homepage: Legislator Use of the World Wide Web for Constituency Contact," paper delivered at the Annual Meeting of the American Political Science Association, Washington, D.C., August 1997; Matthew C. Moen, "World-Wide-Web Usage Among the New England Congressional Delegation," paper delivered at the Annual Meeting of the New England Political Science Association, Worcester, Mass., May 1998.
2. Chris Casey, *The Hill on the Net: Congress Enters the Information Age* (Boston: Academic Press, 1996).

---

for creating work to justify their existence.[10] In the early 1980s, two scholars described the modern congressional office as an "enterprise" needing constant supervision.[11] Their timing was exquisite—the Senate was involved in construction of an expensive new office building at the time.[12]

In the late 1980s and early 1990s, staffing levels became a partisan issue. Conservative Republicans argued that Democrats had increased staff to ensure the continuation of their majority in both chambers. Senator Hank Brown (R., Colo.), for instance, complained that staff levels outstripped legitimate institutional needs.[13] Kenneth Adelman pointed out that staff size had increased at six times the rate of the population since 1970, giving Democratic congresses a larger staff than General George Washington's army at Valley Forge![14] A conservative newspaper attacked the legislative branch appropriation one year with this sarcastic headline: "House Eliminates Four Positions, Will Get by With 31,751."[15] Republicans followed their attacks with a promise to voters in the 1992 elections to reduce the legislative bureaucracy if they gained majority-party control. Although that strategy did not bring about the desired result, it did encourage newly elected President Bill Clinton to call for a 25 percent reduction in legislative staffs on the Hill.[16] His message was carried forward by Senator David Boren (D., Okla.), one of the co-chairs of the Joint Committee on the Organization of Congress during the 103rd Congress (1993–1994).[17] Boren gained support from Republicans but convinced few of his Democratic colleagues.[18] Recall from Chapter 5 that the Joint Committee's recommendations, embodied in The Legislative Reorganization Act of 1994, died in both chambers.

During the 1994 campaign season, Republicans again pledged to cut the total number of congressional aides, making it part of their Contract With America. Once they gained a majority, House Republicans instituted their long-promised cuts. Their reductions approximated the 25 percent cut suggested by President Clinton, but the cuts were selective. Committees and support agencies lost people disproportionately compared to personal staffs.

PERSONAL STAFF

Numbers and Types of Positions

Most legislative aides work directly for members of Congress. In 1997, 7,282 people worked in the House and 4,410 in the Senate, for a total of 11,692.[19] The higher total for the House is a function of its size. When an average staff size is calculated, representatives have only 17 aides, while senators have 44. The differential reflects the fact that senators represent more constituents than House members. The extreme example is California, where a senator has about fifty times as many constituents as a representative.

The difference in staff size also reflects the reality that senators carry a heavier workload. They serve on more committees and subcommittees, and they spend more hours and days in session.[20] The Senate has only 100 members to carry the same workload as the 435-member House, which means that senators rely more heavily on staff.[21]

Chamber rules reflect and even institutionalize differences in bicameral staffing patterns. The House passed *Resolution 359* in 1979, for instance, capping the total number of personal aides at eighteen full-time and four part-time employees.[22] Most representatives hire the full complement of staff, but some positions are always vacant, keeping the average staff size at seventeen. In the 105th Congress, each House member received a "member's representational allowance" (MRA) averaging $901,771, from which they paid staff and office expenses.[23] Members are free to hire the maximum number of people allowed or to hire fewer and pay them better. Unspent allocations are returned to the U.S. Treasury.

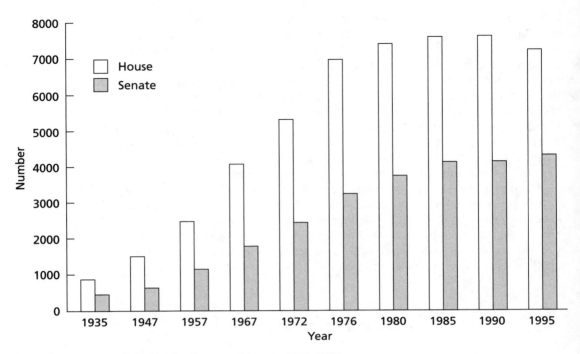

FIGURE 7.2   Personal Staff in the House and Senate, 1935–1995

SOURCE: Norman J. Ornstein, Thomas E. Mann, and Michael J. Malbin, *Vital Statistics on Congress 1997–1998* (Washington, D.C.: Congressional Quarterly, 1998), 135.

Senators face no technical limits on the number of personal aides, but they are constrained by an established allotment. In the 105th Congress, the allotment ranged from $1.1 to $1.9 million. The allotment is determined by the number of constituents a senator represents, so a senator from New York obviously receives more money than a senator from North Dakota.

Figure 7.2 summarizes trends in personal staff from 1935 to 1995, by plotting the total number of House and Senate aides. The most striking feature is a steady increase in staff from the 1930s through the late 1970s, when the numbers begin to level off for the reasons mentioned previously. The greater reliance on staff among senators is also evident, with the smaller Senate having proportionately more staff.

As Figure 7.3 shows, personal aides are divided between a member's home state or district and the Capitol. Senators usually deploy about one-third of their staff in their home state, while representatives typically deploy 40–48 percent in the district.[24] The likely explanation is that senators' six-year terms and heavier legislative responsibilities provide more reason to keep people on the Hill.

Considerable variation exists across states and districts, usually due to geographic considerations.[25] A representative from New York City may have one dis-

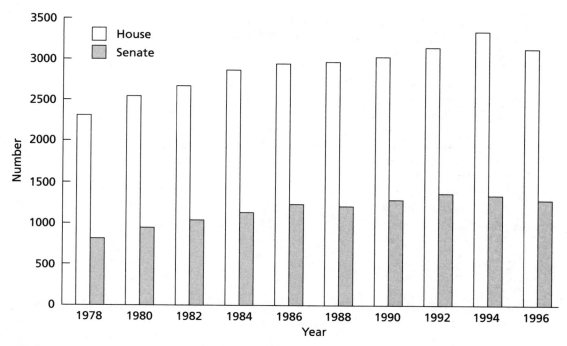

FIGURE 7.3   Staff Based in District and State Offices, 1978–1996

SOURCE: Norman J. Ornstein, Thomas E. Mann, and Michael J. Malbin, *Vital Statistics on Congress 1997–1998* (Washington, D.C.: Congressional Quarterly, 1998), 137–138.

trict office because his or her constituents are densely packed into a few square miles, while a representative from Montana will need numerous offices to cover the state's 147,000 square miles. Proximity to the Hill also influences deployment. Members representing states close to the capital find it easier to keep staff in Washington, D.C.

Allocation patterns obscure some differences between staff in the district and those on the Hill. A typical district staffer is a middle-aged woman who is connected to the local community and who spends most of her time resolving constituent problems.[26] Her work highlights member accessibility and translates into votes at election time.[27]

The situation on the Hill is much different, with a broader range of positions.[28] Although the structure varies, most offices have an administrative assistant (or "AA" in the lingo of Capitol Hill). The AA supervises operations and is responsible for personnel matters. A personal secretary schedules the member's time, while a press secretary handles media inquiries. A legislative director (or "LD") is responsible for legislative issues, monitoring the flow of legislation, researching bills scheduled for a vote, and updating an "issues notebook" with talking points on key issues. Several legislative assistants (or "LAs") report to the

**Table 7.1   Personal Staff Salaries for a Sample
Senator and Representative, 105th Congress**

Title	Senate Salary	House Salary
Member of Congress	$133,600	$133,600
Administrative assistant (AA)	99,500	105,000
Legislative director (LD)	72,000	45,000
Legislative assistant (LA)	45,750	33,400
Press secretary	54,000	30,500
Personal secretary	37,000	35,000
District director	51,000	33,800
District caseworker	33,500	23,300
Receptionist	21,500	23,000
Intern (6 months)	3,600	2,150

legislative director; LAs cover specific policy areas or committees. A computer operator and legislative correspondents ("LCs") spend the entire day answering constituent mail. Their work is unending, given that 35 million letters arrive at the Senate each year and another 185 million at the House.[29] Clerical staff and interns answer telephones and file papers.

The salary of these workers varies greatly according to the professionalism of the post. Table 7.1 lists staff salaries for one senator and one representative from the same state in the 105th Congress. These figures are merely illustrative, although they point to the general tendency of senators to pay aides more than do representatives. The salaries are far above average compared to most Americans, but so is the cost of living in the nation's capital. Those at the top of the pay scale fare well, but those in the middle and lower salary ranges tradition-ally seek positions in the private sector, where pay is commensurate with the cost of living. Capitol Hill is more of a training ground than a permanent place of employment, and salaries are one key reason.

Tenure and Turnover

In fact, job security for legislative aides generally is limited. Not only may they be fired for poor performance, but they automatically lose their job if their member dies, retires, or loses reelection. Over 50 percent of the House has turned over in the 1990s, causing hundreds of personal aides to lose their positions.

Until recent years, congressional staffers even lacked the legal protections given to most American workers. Congress often exempted itself from legislation regulating employment practices, such as the Civil Rights Act of 1964 and the Occupational Safety and Health Act of 1970, out of concern that executive branch officials might interfere with the legislative branch in the process of enforcing employment laws. Who wanted a Republican administration monitoring the employment patterns of a Democratic congress, or vice versa? Critics claimed that Congress exempted itself from employment practices simply to avoid the problems it created for others. Although this argument was weak intellectually, it was powerful politically. Congress came under fire, and so it began incorporating itself into national employment standards.

In 1988, the House adopted the *Fair Employment Practices Resolution,* which forbids members from discriminating against job applicants on the basis of race, color, sex, religion, national origin, age, or handicap. (The Senate left its informal rules in place). In 1989, Congress applied the Fair Labor Standards Act of 1938 to itself when it passed the *Minimum Wage Act,* requiring the federal minimum wage to be paid to legislative branch employees. It also mandated "equal pay for equal work" in an effort to raise the salaries of historically underpaid female employees. The *Americans with Disabilities Act* (1990), which prohibited discrimination against people with disabilities, applied to Congress as well as the nation. And the *Civil Rights Act of 1991* codified the Senate's existing rules against employment discrimination.[30] The result of these initiatives was greater security for workers, although the unsystematic character of the provisions across both chambers was confusing.

In 1993, Representative Christopher Shays (R., Conn.) and Representative Dick Swett (D., N.H.) introduced a bill requiring that workplace laws be applied to Congress. An independent office on Capitol Hill was supposed to oversee compliance (in order to circumvent the constitutional concerns of executive branch enforcement). The bill easily passed the House on a 427–4 vote, but the Senate never acted on it. The House responded by applying ten existing laws to its employees, without regard to the Senate.[31] This caused still more inconsistency in employment practices on the Hill.

Republicans pledged in the Contract With America to solve the issue by applying all relevant laws to Congress in a uniform manner. They moved swiftly to honor their pledge once they gained majorities in the 104th Congress. On the opening day—January 4, 1995—the House passed the *Congressional Accountability Act,* the same bill sponsored by Shays and Swett two years earlier. The Senate passed its own version about two weeks later, which the House approved and President Clinton then signed into law. Less than a month into the 104th Congress, workplace laws were finally applied in uniform fashion to Congress.

Despite increased protections for workers, a personal staff position on the Hill is a short-term career. One study by a nonpartisan foundation at the end of the 1980s showed that the average staff tenure was only 2.9 years, with almost one-half of House aides serving less than a year.[32] That rate of turnover forces the institution to constantly train people, which suggests that inexperience reigns in lower echelons. Serving as a personal staffer is the beginning rather than the culmination of a career.[33] Employees tire of the long hours, the tedium of answering endless constituent mail, and the lack of identity separate from the member. Aides usually recover from their initial bout with "Potomac fever."

COMMITTEE STAFF

Numbers and Types of Positions

Fewer people work for standing committees than for individual members. In the 105th Congress, the House had 1,250 committee aides and the Senate had 1,002, for a total of 2,252.[34] The difference reflects the higher number of standing committees in the House. Yet, the numerical advantage of the House is offset by the Senate's proportional advantage. The Senate makes up only 19 percent of the membership of Congress, but it has 45 percent of the committee staff positions. This maldistribution helps the Senate compete with the more specialized House in policy-making.

Figure 7.4 documents committee staffing trends in the 1990s. At the beginning of the decade, the House had approximately twice as many committee aides as the Senate. Following the dramatic reductions in the House during the 104th Congress, the chambers moved toward greater parity.

In general, the employment situation is better for committee than personal staff. Salaries are usually higher, and job security and working conditions are better. Recall from Chapter 5 that massive committee reorganization rarely occurs; absent shifts in partisan control, the standing committee system offers staffers a more secure employment situation. Their security is also greater because members who head committees/subcommittees usually occupy safe seats. They hire aides with similar political opinions and keep them on in subsequent congresses.[35]

The most precarious time for committee aides on Capitol Hill is when a new chair or a new political party takes control. The House Merchant Marine and Fisheries Committee illustrates the vulnerability of staff in those instances. For many years, the Merchant Marine and Fisheries Committee, headed by Walter Jones (D., N.C.), was a stable part of the standing committee structure. When Jones passed away, Gerry Studds (D., Mass.) became chair of the committee, and he released a dozen committee aides at the outset of the 103rd Congress.[36] A much more liberal member, from a different region of the country than Walter Jones, Studds wanted his own people in place. But when Republicans won control in the 104th Congress, they abolished Merchant Marine and Fisheries, transferring its jurisdiction into a subcommittee of the Resources Committee. People hired by Studds lost their jobs—part of the promised 25 percent staff reduction. Although it seems harsh to fire committee staff when political circumstances change, the majority party must be certain that it has loyal people. An inverse relationship exists between job security and professionalism, such that top-level aides are often victims of political purges while clerical workers may keep their jobs.

Standing committees usually have that dichotomy of clerical and professional aides. Clerical people handle mail and organize publication of committee documents, such as hearings on bills.[37] Professional aides are usually attorneys with expertise in the policy area of the committee. They perform two related functions. First, they do legislative work: conduct research on issues within the committee's jurisdiction, propose ideas for bills, and draft amendments to legislation. Their responsibilities are enormous when Congress is in session. Imagine the job

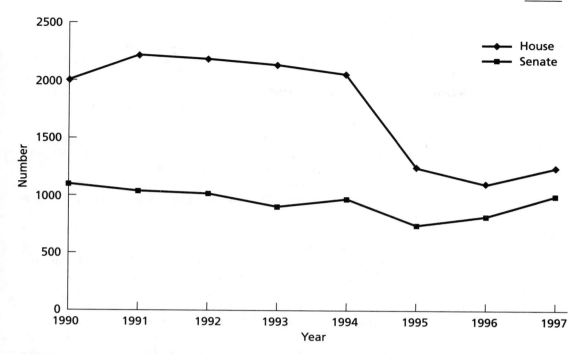

FIGURE 7.4   Committee Staff in the House and Senate, 1990–1997

SOURCE: Norman J. Ornstein, Thomas E. Mann, and Michael J. Malbin, *Vital Statistics on Congress 1997–1998* (Washington, D.C.: Congressional Quarterly, 1998), 139.

of the Senate Budget Committee, which analyzes hundreds of budget proposals. It's no wonder that Budget Committee aides once took advantage of a recess to craft proposals to balance the budget, such as forcing woodchucks to chuck more wood. Inserting that joke in a budget document, without telling the chair, drew hearty laughter from senators serving on the Budget Committee.[38]

Second, committee aides engage in oversight of the executive branch. They explore executive branch expenditures to ensure that money is being spent as Congress specified. They write letters to executive branch officials clarifying the intent of Congress when it passed a bill. They research the effectiveness of programs in their committee's jurisdiction. Although oversight typically is less exciting than legislating, it is a major component of committee staffers' responsibilities.

The work of committee aides technically is separated from that of personal aides, but in reality the distinction is blurred. The Legislative Reorganization Act of 1946 provided funds to hire experts for committees at record salaries, with the understanding that they would be nonpartisan.[39] Yet, the current practice of separate majority- and minority-party staffs eradicates the distinction between nonpartisan committee staffers and partisan personal aides. Members actually rely on both types of staff to promote their agenda and relay their accomplishments to constituents. Committee and personal aides remain in close contact.

Staff Allocations

The hundreds of people who work as committee aides are not evenly distributed across the standing committees. Powerful and prestigious committees understandably have the most staff. The House Appropriations Committee, for example, with jurisdiction over government spending, has 165 aides; the Veterans' Affairs Committee has 27 aides. Generally speaking, "elite" committees in the Senate and "exclusive" committees in the House average 30–50 more aides than minor committees. Table 7.2 breaks down standing committee staff for the 104th Congress.

Bicameralism also accounts for variation in committee staff deployment between chambers. The Senate Judiciary Committee, for instance, had 40 percent more staff (142 versus 85 people) than the House Judiciary Committee in the 105th Congress. It requires more staff in general because it is responsible for confirming judges and executive branch officials.

The House and Senate also differ in the way they allocate aides between full committees and subcommittees. The difference is not proportional—45 percent of House and 38 percent of Senate committee aides in the 1980s worked for the subcommittees.[40] Instead, the difference is distributional. Senate subcommittee staffers serve disproportionately on a few committees (such as Judiciary), while House subcommittee aides are distributed more evenly across the standing committees. The House reforms of the 1970s enshrined subcommittees and empowered subcommittee chairs to hire staff.[41] The reforms resulted in a 650 percent increase in the number of subcommittee aides during the 1970s, who were distributed across standing committees for egalitarian reasons.[42] Although House Republicans revoked the ability of subcommittee chairs to hire staff, they have yet to redesign subcommittee staffing patterns.

The principal factor in the maldistribution of committee and subcommittee aides, of course, is pure partisanship. The majority party hires a disproportionate share of committee staffers on the grounds that it is principally responsible for producing quality legislation. Once again, the Senate and House diverge on majority- and minority-party staff distribution. The Senate customarily allocates staff positions according to the ratio of majority- and minority-party seats in the chamber.[43] The situation in the House is more complex. The Legislative Reorganization Act of 1970 granted the minority party a one-third share of committee staff, but it gave the majority party the right to hire and fire those people. That situation proved unworkable. Democratic committee chairs did not like the one-third guarantee given to the minority party, while Republicans did not appreciate the lack of autonomy in personnel decisions. The following year, the Democrats granted autonomy in return for Republican concessions on the one-third guarantee. In recent years, the minority party typically has received between one-fifth and one-third of committee staff positions, depending on the partisanship of a given committee.[44] House Republicans have erred on the side of giving minority-party Democrats their fair share, partly because of the different situation faced by the parties when the GOP seized power in 1994. For Republicans, majority-party status meant a wholesale expansion of committee staff positions; for Democrats, minority-party status meant that many people were fired. Republicans erred on the side of generosity to mitigate the situation.

Table 7.2   Average Staff Sizes of Standing Committees, 104th Congress

	House	Senate
Exclusive/Elite Committees	110	61
Major Committees	94	79
Nonmajor/Minor Committees	82	35

SOURCE: Based on Norman J. Ornstein, Thomas E. Mann, and Michael J. Malbin, *Vital Statistics on Congress 1995–1996* (Washington, D.C.: Congressional Quarterly, 1996), 131–134.

The maldistribution of staff—across standing committees, chambers, and partisan lines—helps explain behavior on Capitol Hill. It explains why junior members focus on reelection, and why they are attracted to ancilliary operations like the Legislative Service Organizations (LSOs).[45] Compared to their senior colleagues, they lack access to legislative resources. It helps explain why minority-party members are strident partisans, especially in the House. They cannot compete with a staff-laden majority party in writing bills, so they opt for setting out alternatives. Conversely, staffing patterns help explain why senior members are sometimes vulnerable to the charge of forgetting "the folks back home." Once they ascend to a chairship, they are positioned to influence national policy. Members may become more attentive to their policy-making role than to their constituents. In those instances, committee aides inadvertently put themselves out of a job.

SUPPORT AGENCY STAFF

Three separate agencies backstop Congress. Each agency has a distinctive mission.

Congressional Research Service

Thomas Jefferson began the Library of Congress by donating his own books in 1800. During the War of 1812, the British burned the Capitol, along with most of the books that Jefferson donated. He restocked the Library by selling it 6,487 books at a cut rate. From that unlikely origin, the Library of Congress has developed an unsurpassed collection resting on 550 miles of bookshelves.[46]

A division of the Library of Congress called the *Legislative Reference Service* (LRS), created in 1914, was charged with providing reference and bibliographic services for members. The LRS employed librarians to "gather, classify, and make available, in translations, indexes, digests, compilations, and bulletins, and otherwise, data for or bearing upon legislation."[47]

BOX 7.2   THOMAS

On January 5, 1995—the day after he became Speaker of the House—Newt Gingrich (R., Ga.) held a press conference in the Library of Congress. He unveiled "The House Open Multimedia Access System" (THOMAS), which honors Thomas Jefferson, founder of the Library of Congress.

THOMAS is the principal Web site of Congress.[1] It contains information on the status of bills, the standing committees, the support agencies, and the legislative process. THOMAS also offers searchable electronic indexes, by bill number or keyword, making it easy for outsiders to stay updated on legislation in Congress. The one drawback of THOMAS is that its information is relatively recent. Searchable indexes go back only a few congresses.

The volume of contact THOMAS has received is astounding, as measured by Web site "hits." In its first full year of operation (1995), THOMAS sent 14 million files to Internet users totaling 136 billion bytes of information; in its second year, THOMAS sent 24 million files totaling 227 billion bytes; in its third year, THOMAS transmitted 102 million files totaling 337 billion bytes.[2] The numbers will only increase as the Web site becomes more user-friendly and as more people get on-line. Congress may need more staff to cope with the sharp rise in electronic inquiries.

---

1. Visit THOMAS at: http://thomas.loc.gov.
2. Usage statistics are published on the THOMAS Web page.

The Legislative Reorganization Act of 1946 altered the LRS, more than doubling its budget and redirecting the agency to work for congressional committees.[48] The policy specialist soon replaced the reference librarian. The Legislative Reorganization Act of 1970 made further changes, replacing the LRS with the *Congressional Research Service* (CRS) and again expanding its budget and its statutory obligation to the committees. In the 1970s and 1980s, requests from committees for research rose 460 percent.[49] Those demands caused the CRS to grow from about 300 employees in 1970 to more than 800 in the 1980s. Its staff now numbers about 750.

Most CRS employees are policy specialists who research and analyze information. They produce strictly nonpartisan reports, almost to the point of frustration. The CRS will analyze the sale of handguns, for instance, and explain the pros and cons of restricting sales, but it will not say whether that is a good idea. Such objectivity fulfills the CRS's mission and probably serves Congress well over the long term, but it sometimes frustrates members looking for short-term answers.

The CRS also serves members' personal offices as time allows. The CRS compiles and continually updates information on a range of public policy issues. Its information packets, or "info paks" as they are known, discuss the background and merits of an issue, along with any bills that have been introduced on it. Personal aides rely on these materials. Because legislative assistants are often new to their jobs, they need CRS publications to learn about their assigned policy areas; legislative correspondents regularly send info paks to constituents requesting information on some issue. Related to information services, CRS experts hold public policy briefings for personal aides at the start of congressional sessions. Their work for the committees thereby spins off to help personal aides.

The CRS handles several hundred thousand inquiries annually.[50] Most involve a quick response, such as sending an info pak or double-checking a quotation for a member's speech. Other requests involve months of meticulous research. The CRS employs prominent scholars in all fields to conduct its research, giving it an intellectual talent bank rivaling many universities.

General Accounting Office

The General Accounting Office (GAO) was created by the *Budget and Accounting Act of 1921* to oversee executive branch expenditures. It is directed "to investigate, at the seat of government or elsewhere, all matters relating to the receipt, disbursement, and application of government funds." Most of its early work consisted of recording expenses and conducting routine audits. In 1950, Congress shifted the responsibility of recording transactions to the executive agencies, under the supervision of an Office of Management and Budget. The shift caused a two-thirds cut in GAO personnel, from about 15,000 to 5,000.[51] The GAO's mission was also revamped at that time: It was asked to evaluate programs and to investigate waste or mismanagement. The GAO thus traded in "bean counting" for detective work.

The GAO is often called the "watchdog" of Congress because it keeps an eye out for malfeasance. Its investigators might be considered the "pit bulls" of legislative support staff because of their tenacity. They are trained in fields such as accounting and law enforcement, and their investigations are thorough. GAO personnel frequently are asked to testify in front of committees, giving them additional incentive to perform. GAO investigators ferret out information that allows Congress to take corrective action, even internally. A GAO investigation of the House bank in the early 1990s, for instance, helped set procedural reforms into place.

A majority of the approximately 3,500 GAO employees work in the Capitol, with the rest in regional offices. By law, they have access to the records of federal agencies, and they may undertake any investigation they believe is warranted. The common practice is to respond to requests from congressional committees. In addition to their investigative role, GAO personnel may write legal opinions on government policies or settle private claims lodged against the government.

The GAO balances its subordinate position as a support agency of Congress with its obligation to provide reliable and nonpartisan information. It is empowered to investigate any entity handling federal funds, including Congress. The GAO's obligation to find out the truth sometimes clashes with the desire of members to avoid negative publicity, as in the House bank scandal. In such cases, or when the GAO uncovers mismanagement in a favorite congressional program, it must weigh its obligation against sensible silence.

Congressional Budget Office

The Congressional Budget Office (CBO) was created under the *Budget Impoundment and Control Act of 1974*. Its staff works closely with the House and Senate Budget Committees, which were created by the same 1974 act to help

BOX 7.3   A Watchdog With Only One Master?

The General Accounting Office (GAO) is empowered to conduct nonpartisan investigations—a simple idea but a complex task. What happens when one party controls Congress while the other controls the executive branch? Is every GAO investigation a nonpartisan inquiry? What if the majority party in Congress tries to use the GAO to score political points against a president?

Republicans complained bitterly during the Bush presidency that Democrats used the GAO like an attack dog rather than a watchdog.[1] They conjured up a vision of a GAO prowling around the Bush administration, trying to dig up dirt to satisfy its Democratic masters.

Republicans laid out several pieces of evidence to support their claim. First, they noted that the GAO provided "detailees" to the committees—people specifically assigned to work for the chairperson. Republicans argued that this practice effectively turned nonpartisan GAO personnel into Democratic stooges, which was all the more outrageous because of the skewed distribution of staff favoring the majority party. Second, they noted that 810 of 990 (82 percent) GAO investigations conducted during President Bush's first year in office (1989) were ordered by Democrats. Third, they cited specific investigations, such as the ones into the use of military aircraft for personal trips by Bush administration officials and into the maldistribution of U.S. aid in Panama following a Bush-ordered invasion. Each investigation gave Republicans bad press.

Republicans seemed to prove partisanship by the GAO, but not conclusively. While the GAO provided committees with detailees, for instance, that practice was consistent with the GAO's obligation to help committees uncover wasteful spending. The fact that Democrats instigated most GAO investigations simply reflected their responsibilities as the majority party. Nosing around was part of their oversight obligation.

The GAO was stuck. It had to be responsive to Democrats, who controlled the committees and who determined the GAO's budget and activities. But it also had to be deferential to Republicans, who could be the majority party sometime in the future and who had every right to expect nonpartisan inquiries.

Republican displeasure with the GAO crested in the waning months of the Bush presidency. Republicans on the Senate Appropriations Committee demanded that $2 million be inserted into the fiscal year 1993 legislative branch appropriation to fund an independent audit of the GAO. The Republicans wanted to investigate the investigators. They also demanded that all detailees be paid from committee funds, thereby crimping the budgets of the House Democratic committee chairs who so often used them.

Although Democratic senators agreed to those demands, their House colleagues balked. These divergent views stymied passage of the legislative branch appropriation. Republicans kept pressing for concessions and threatening to hamstring the Senate; House Democrats especially kept resisting, and they outnumbered Republicans in the chamber.

Legislators eventually struck a classic compromise. The Republicans dropped their demands in return for a $7.5 million cut in the GAO's budget. The Republicans claimed that they had placed the congressional watchdog on a tight leash; the Democrats claimed that they had "tossed a bone" to the other side because the cut was 1.7 percent of the GAO's total budget.

Both sides started rethinking the role of the GAO after the 1992 and 1994 elections, which shifted majority-party control of the White House and Congress. Republican masters were now free to prowl a Democratic administration with the congressional watchdog.

---

1. This account draws on Beth Donovan, "The Diminutive Downsizing: Hill Funds Cut 1.25 Percent," *Congressional Quarterly Weekly Report,* September 26, 1992, 2915; and Beth Donovan, "Legislative Funding Total Is Less Than Last Year's," *Congressional Quarterly Weekly Report,* October 10, 1992, 3129.

Congress formulate an annual budget. The CBO's mission is broad. It analyzes data on the state of the economy, monitors congressional spending over policy areas, examines the budgetary implications of legislation, and forecasts trends in the economy, such as unemployment and productivity.[52]

Congress created the CBO to provide itself with an independent source of budgetary information. Prior to the CBO, Congress relied heavily on its executive branch counterpart, the Office of Management and Budget (OMB). Amidst political tussles with Republican President Richard Nixon, congressional Democrats saw the need to create an agency that could judge the validity of executive branch figures. Otherwise, Congress was relegated to tinkering with the budget submitted by the president.

The CBO began in 1974 with about 200 staffers, a number that has remained relatively constant over the years. Most CBO employees are economists, mathematicians, statisticians, and/or accountants. They run equations estimating the growth of federal spending and the size of the budget deficit based on particular economic assumptions, such as low unemployment. House and Senate leaders appoint the CBO director, with input from the two Budget Committee chairs.

The CBO has similarities to other support agencies. Its primary responsibility is to the committees, with the Budget Committee in each chamber receiving first priority, followed by Appropriations and Ways and Means (or Senate Finance). All other committees are second-tier priorities. The CBO will generate analyses for individual members, but only as time and resources allow. Like other support agencies, the CBO is nonpartisan, although as a practical matter, the CBO probably treats the majority party better because its members will formulate the agency budget in the following year. Finally, the CBO regularly compiles data without making specific policy recommendations. For example, it will forecast the amount of revenue lost by cutting the capital gains tax without taking a position on the cut.

The similarities the CBO shares with other support agencies also open it up to similar problems. Because its principal constituency is the Budget Committees, the CBO is easily caught in partisan budget fights. Members selectively cite its studies to justify political positions. Committees and individual members may also pressure the CBO to interpret data in partisan terms, as happened with a study of wealth going to upper-income earners during the Reagan/Bush presidencies.[53] The intrigue is particularly intense when the executive and legislative branches are controlled by different parties. The CBO and OMB then become pawns in a complicated public relations game.

APPROPRIATIONS AND ADJUSTMENTS

How is the $2 billion legislative branch appropriation spent each year? Figure 7.5 provides a breakdown of staff expenditures by category for 1997. It shows that 31 percent of the legislative branch appropriation paid the salaries of House employees. Congressional support agencies received another 24 percent, while the

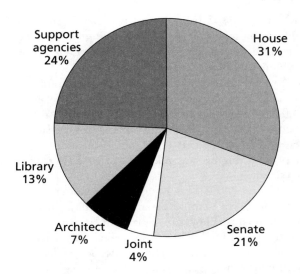

FIGURE 7.5   Congressional Staff Expenditures, 1997

SOURCE: Based on Norman J. Ornstein, Thomas E. Mann, and Michael J. Malbin, *Vital Statistics on Congress 1997–1998* (Washington, D.C.: Congressional Quarterly, 1998), 148.

Senate consumed 21 percent. Another 20 percent supported the Library of Congress and the Architect of the Capitol, which is an office responsible for a range of administrative functions. Joint expenditures by the House and Senate constituted 4 percent of the appropriation.

Although this finding cannot be discerned from Figure 7.5, the categorical expenditures of the Republican-controlled 105th Congress differed from those of preceding Democrat-controlled congresses. This is especially evident with support agencies. A new Office of Compliance exists to oversee administration of employment laws passed in the 104th Congress. (The Office of Compliance received its first appropriation in 1997; it does not appear in Figure 7.5 because it received less than .001 percent of the legislative branch appropriation.) The Office of Technology Assessment no longer exists. The General Accounting Office is operating with its lowest budget in years, reflecting Republican plans to have standing committees conduct comprehensive oversight.

Members have also made staffing changes within their respective chambers. Decrying legislative bureaucracy, representatives slashed committee staffs. They cut the number of personal aides, redeploying more of them to home districts. By contrast, senators quietly increased the number of personal and committee aides, as part of an effort to compete with the House in policy-making. The recent staffing changes demonstrate the continued applicability of a bicameral framework.

The recent changes also accentuate the uneasy place of staff on the Hill. Staff members are neither elected nor wholly secure in their positions, because they

---

BOX 7.4 Abolishing OTA

The Office of Technology Assessment (OTA) was created in 1972 to advise Congress of the "beneficial and adverse impacts of the applications of technology." The OTA engaged in long-term studies of the feasibility of new technologies, such as strategic defense missile systems. It also studied eradication of the rain forest, ozone depletion, and other global trends. The OTA was small compared to other support agencies of Congress, with only 150 employees and a $20 million annual budget. But the Republican-controlled Congress shut the OTA down in September 1995.

Why was the OTA abolished? As the smallest congressional support agency, it was vulnerable when Republicans started making good on their promise to institute staff reductions. Yet, the OTA's size was only part of the reason. Its vague mission compared unfavorably with other support agencies, which were more focused. During its last year, for instance, the OTA produced reports on nuclear fusion, resistant bacteria, electronic surveillance, and earthquakes. Its vague mission also prevented the OTA from being linked to a specific subset of congressional committees, so it had few defenders when it came under attack. Then, too, when they took control, House Republicans created a Science Committee that could commission necessary long-range studies.

True to its technological mission, the OTA placed its reports on the World Wide Web (http://www.access.gpo.gov/ota/index.html) before closing its doors.

---

may be sacrificed as pawns in a political game. Yet, their roles are so varied and indispensable to the institution that staff remain an integral part of Capitol Hill.

NOTES

1. Elizabeth A. Palmer, "Minute-by-Minute Through the GOP's Momentous Day," *Congressional Quarterly Weekly Report,* January 7, 1995, 10–11.

2. Janet Hook, "A New House Historian With a New Twist," *Congressional Quarterly Weekly Report,* January 7, 1995, 21.

3. James G. Gimpel, *Legislating the Revolution* (Boston: Allyn & Bacon, 1996), 39.

4. Norman J. Ornstein, Thomas E. Mann, and Michael J. Malbin, *Vital Statistics on Congress 1997–1998* (Washington, D.C.: Congressional Quarterly, 1998), 135.

5. An excellent comparative discussion is Gerhard Loewenberg and Samuel C. Patterson, *Comparing Legislatures* (Boston: Little, Brown, 1979); an excellent comparative review essay is Susan Webb Hammond, "Legislative Staffs," *Legislative Studies Quarterly* 2 (May 1984): 271–317; two dated but very informative overviews of congressional staffing are Kenneth Kofmehl, *Professional Staffs of Congress* (Lafayette, Ind.: Purdue University Studies, 1962), and Harrison W. Fox, Jr., and Susan Webb Hammond, *Congressional Staffs: The Invisible Force in American Lawmaking* (New York: Free Press, 1977).

6. Michael J. Malbin, "Delegation, Deliberation, and the New Role of Congressional Staff," in *The New Congress,* ed. Thomas E. Mann and Norman J. Ornstein (Washington, D.C.: American Enterprise Institute, 1981), 135.

7. David Mayhew, *Congress: The Electoral Connection* (New Haven, Conn.: Yale University Press, 1974), 84–85.

8. David E. Price, "Professionals and Entrepreneurs: Staff Orientations and Policy Making on Three Senate Committees," *Journal of Politics* 2 (May 1971): 316–336; David E. Price, *Who Makes the Laws?* (Cambridge, Mass.: Schenckman, 1972).

9. U.S. Senate, Committee on Appropriations, 94th Congress, First Session (1975), on H.R. 1221. Cited in Fox and Hammond, *Congressional Staffs*, 4–5.

10. Michael J. Malbin, *Unelected Representatives* (New York: Basic Books, 1979). For a description of life on the Hill as a legislative aide, see John L. Jackley, *Hill Rat* (Washington, D.C.: Regnery Gateway, 1992); Todd Richissin, "Congress' Big Turnover Has 'Hill Rats' Prowling for Jobs," Scripps-Howard News Service, November 20, 1992; Richard E. Cohen, "The Hill People," *National Journal,* May 16, 1987, 1171.

11. Robert H. Salisbury and Kenneth A. Shepsle, "U.S. Congressmen as Enterprise," *Legislative Studies Quarterly* (1981): 559–576; see also Robert H. Salisbury and Kenneth A. Shepsle, "Congressional Staff Turnover and the Ties-That-Bind," *American Political Science Review* (June 1991): 381–396.

12. *Congress A to Z,* Vol. 1 (Washington, D.C.: Congressional Quarterly, 1993), 165.

13. Hank Brown, "Staff Explosion on the Hill," *Washington Times,* April 11, 1991, G4.

14. Ken Adelman, "Gridlock on the Make-Work Hill," *Washington Times,* October 2, 1989, F1.

15. J. Jennings Moss, "House Eliminates Four Positions, Will Get by With 31,751," *Washington Times,* August 2, 1989, B5.

16. Pamela Fessler, "Clinton Cultivates Hill Soil for Early Start on Agenda," *Congressional Quarterly Weekly Report,* November 21, 1992, 3665.

17. Hearing before the Joint Committee on the Organization of Congress, S. 103-10, 103rd Congress, First Session, January 26, 1993.

18. C. Lawrence Evans and Walter J. Oleszek, *Congress Under Fire* (Boston: Houghton Mifflin, 1997), 67.

19. Ornstein, Mann, and Malbin, *Vital Statistics on Congress 1997–1998,* 135.

20. Ibid., 160–163.

21. Ross K. Baker, *House and Senate,* 2d ed. (New York: Norton, 1995), 95–100.

22. *How Congress Works,* 2d ed. (Washington, D.C.: Congressional Quarterly, 1991), 109.

23. Ornstein, Mann, and Malbin, *Vital Statistics on Congress 1997–1998,* 151.

24. Ibid., 137–138.

25. Steven H. Schiff and Steven S. Smith, "Generational Change and the Allocation of Staff in the U.S. Congress," *Legislative Studies Quarterly* (1983): 457–467; Glenn R. Parker, *Homeward Bound: Explaining Changes in Congressional Behavior* (Pittsburgh: University of Pittsburgh Press, 1986).

26. John R. Johannes, "Women as Congressional Staffers," *Women and Politics* 4 (Summer 1984): 69–81; for a comprehensive discussion of casework, see John R. Johannes, *To Serve the People* (Lincoln: University of Nebraska Press, 1984).

27. Morris P. Fiorina, *Congress: Keystone of the Washington Establishment,* 2d ed. (New Haven, Conn.: Yale University Press, 1989).

28. For a brief "insider's account" of personal staffs in each chamber, see John H. Oberg, "Senators' Staffs: A Reflective View," and Lee Godown, "Staff in the House: The View From the Hill," in *Congress and Public Policy,* 2d ed., ed. David C. Kozak and John D. Macartney (Prospect Heights, Ill.: Waveland Press, 1990), 121–127.

29. John S. Day, "Handling the Mail for the Hill," *Bangor Daily News,* July 15, 1992, 14. The author obtained the figures directly from the House and Senate post office directors.

30. "1991 Civil Rights Law Provisions," *Congressional Quarterly Almanac 1991* (Washington, D.C.: Congressional Quarterly, 1992), 258–260; *How Congress Works,* 122–124. For a discussion of discrimination issues, based on the underrepresentation of women in professional staff positions, see Sally Friedman and Robert K. Nakamura, "The Representation of Women on U.S. Senate Committee Staffs," *Legislative Studies Quarterly* 3 (August 1991): 407–427.

31. Evans and Oleszek, *Congress Under Fire,* 74.

32. Carleton R. Bryant, "Turnover High Among House Staffers, Report Says," *Washington Times,* October 23, 1990, A10. The organization was the Congressional Management Foundation.

33. Salisbury and Shepsle, "Congressional Staff Turnover and the Ties-That-Bind," 393.

34. Ornstein, Mann, and Malbin, *Vital Statistics on Congress 1997–1998,* 139.

35. Christine DeGregorio, "Professionals in the U.S. Congress: An Analysis of Working Styles," *Legislative Studies Quarterly* 13 (November 1988): 459–476; James D. Cochrane, "Partisan Aspects of Congressional Committee Staffing," *Western Political Quarterly* (June 1964): 338–348.

36. John McCaslin, "Lean and Mean," *Washington Times,* December 17, 1992, A6.

37. The *Washington Post* did an expose in the mid-1970s on the use of committee aides to perform personal tasks. See Stephen Isaacs, "Senators Using Committee Personnel for Own Work," *Washington Post,* February 16, 1975, 1.

38. Associated Press wire story, "Bogus Proposals Put Chuckle in Budget," March 15, 1986. On the Budget Committee and its chair at the time of the prank, Senator Pete Domenici (R., N. Mex.), see Richard F. Fenno, Jr., *The Emergence of a Senate Leader: Pete Domenici and the Reagan Budget* (Washington, D.C.: CQ Press, 1991).

39. Roger H. Davison, "The Legislative Reorganization Act of 1946," *Legislative Studies Quarterly* 15 (August 1990): 357–373; for a lengthy exegesis of the 1946 act, see Kofmehl, *Professional Staffs of Congress.*

40. Steven S. Smith and Christopher Deering, *Committees in Congress,* 2d ed. (Washington, D.C.: Congressional Quarterly, 1990), 152.

41. Ibid.

42. Leroy Rieselbach, *Congressional Reform* (Washington, D.C.: CQ Press, 1986), 155–156.

43. Smith and Deering, *Committees in Congress,* 152.

44. Walter Kravitz, "The Legislative Reorganization Act of 1970," *Legislative Studies Quarterly* 15 (August 1990): 379.

45. Arthur G. Stevens, Jr., Daniel P. Mulhollan, and Paul S. Rundquist, "U.S. Congressional Structure and Representation: The Role of Informal Groups," *Legislative Studies Quarterly* 6 (August 1981): 427.

46. Fred L. Worth, *Strange and Fascinating Facts About Washington D.C.* (New York: Bell, 1988), 161.

47. *Congressional Quarterly's Guide to Congress,* 3d ed. (Washington, D.C.: Congressional Quarterly, 1982), 550.

48. Davidson, "The Legislative Reorganization Act of 1946," 368.

49. Kravitz, "The Legislative Reorganization Act of 1970," 395.

50. *Congressional Quarterly's Guide to Congress,* 548.

51. Fredrich C. Mosher, *The GAO: The Quest for Accountability in American Government* (Boulder, Colo.: Westview Press, 1979), 124.

52. For a sophisticated discussion of the CBO's internal operations, see Stephen M. Miller, "Forecasting Federal Budget Deficits: How Reliable Are U.S. Congressional Budget Office Projections?" *Applied Economics,* December 1991, 1789.

53. For accusations of partisanship by a conservative economist, see Paul Craig Roberts, "The Congressional Budget Office's Skewed Numbers," *Business Week,* March 23, 1992, 20.

8

The Legislative Process

Scholars have penned many interesting tales of bills passed into law, but they always stress that most bills do not make it.[1] For a bill to become law, it must survive a complicated and often harrowing process, described colorfully by the dean of the House, John Dingell (D., Mich.): "It is a seemingly endless series of moves, until somebody prevails through exhaustion, or brilliance, or because of overwhelming public sentiment for their side."[2]

Bicameralism complicates the legislative process and often extends its duration as well. Bills must pass through two distinctive chambers, whose time tables and rules often differ. The much larger House needs rules and procedures that facilitate decisive action by the majority; by contrast, the smaller Senate uses rules and procedures that stress the rights of individual members. In other words, the House places a premium on procedure while the Senate protects personal prerogative.

The first budget fight of the Clinton presidency shows the chamber differences. In 1993, Clinton proposed a major deficit reduction bill that contained tax increases. It was opposed by some Democrats and virtually all minority-party Republicans in both chambers. House Democratic leaders aggressively lobbied the rank and file to support the new president, threatening to strip committee and subcommittee chairs of their positions in order to build political support; only 15 percent of House Democrats voted against the bill.

Senate Democratic leaders could not easily cajole individual senators. In fact, certain senators cut their own deals as part of their price for supporting the bill.

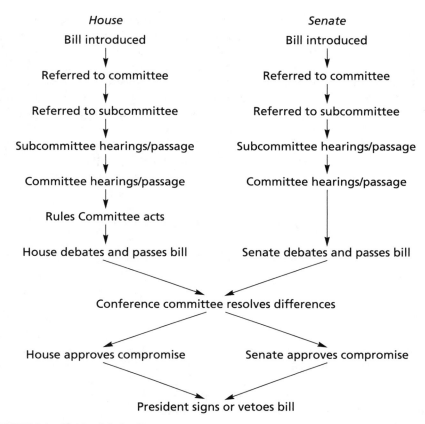

House

Bill introduced

Referred to committee

Referred to subcommittee

Subcommittee hearings/passage

Committee hearings/passage

Rules Committee acts

House debates and passes bill

Senate

Bill introduced

Referred to committee

Referred to subcommittee

Subcommittee hearings/passage

Committee hearings/passage

Senate debates and passes bill

Conference committee resolves differences

House approves compromise

Senate approves compromise

President signs or vetoes bill

FIGURE 8.1 The Legislative Process

David Boren (D., Okla.) demanded that a BTU energy tax be omitted; Dennis DeConcini (D., Ariz.) demanded that President Clinton sign an executive order creating a "deficit trust fund"; Bob Kerrey (D., Neb.) demanded that Clinton promise publicly to send a package of spending cuts to the Hill later in the year. Clinton's concessions to individual demands facilitated a 51–50 victory (with Vice-President Gore casting the tie-breaking vote).[3]

The different path that President Clinton's bill traveled in the House and Senate illustrates the complexity of bicameralism. In this case, a bill pushed through the majoritarian House was stalled, then altered, and almost derailed in the individualistic Senate. Endless variations exist when it comes to passing bills through two dissimilar chambers. A foreign observer once noted that bicameralism actually bends "the rules of logic . . . [forcibly reconciling] two theoretically irreconcilable systems."[4]

Figure 8.1 provides an overview of the legislative process, showing the long and difficult path a bill must travel in the House and Senate to become law. A small proportion of bills actually make it. In the 104th Congress (1995–1996), for instance, the House passed 611 of 4,542 (13 percent) bills introduced in it, while the Senate passed 518 of 2,266 (23 percent) bills; only 333 of those 6,808 (4.9 percent) total bills ultimately became law.[5] Recall from Chapter 5 that committees winnow out most of the bills introduced, removing from consideration bills that are poorly drafted, badly timed, or repetitious. Of course, even bills emerging from committees or a particular chamber face an uncertain future.

This chapter traces the rites of passage for a bill in the bicameral legislature, from introduction through a presidential signature. Figure 8.1 shows the parallel processes followed by the House and Senate, but it masks the differences between the two chambers as they handle legislation. This chapter will note those differences, as well as discuss legislative strategy, in the process of explaining how a bill becomes law.

INTRODUCING LEGISLATION

Bill introductions occur only when Congress is in session. The process is simple. Representatives place their bills in the *hopper*, a box at the front of the chamber; senators introduce bills from the floor or hand them to clerks. Only members can introduce bills.

The member introducing a bill is its *sponsor*. That person usually guides the bill throughout its legislative journey. *Co-sponsors* are members who add their names to a bill, rather than sponsor their own version. The practice of co-sponsorship lets individual members be associated with popular legislation; it serves the institution by decreasing repetitive printing costs. The rules change permitting co-sponsorship took effect in the 95th Congress (1977–1978), contributing to a 35 percent drop in bill introductions in the 96th Congress.[6]

Table 8.1 provides data on the volume of legislation that Congress has processed, by decade, over the last half-century. A total of 82,724 bills were introduced in the 1950s, for an average of 16,548 per Congress. Bill introductions rose sharply during the 1960s, accompanying the Great Society initiatives of President Lyndon Johnson. A total of 112,621 bills were introduced, for an average of 22,524 per Congress—a 36 percent increase over the 1950s. Bill introductions fell to 99,431 in the 1970s, and to 51,874 in the 1980s (with the sharp decline reflecting co-sponsorship). The figures for the 1990s parallel those of the 1980s.

Despite the drop in bill introductions, the sheer volume of legislative business has probably risen. Recall from Chapter 2 that a typical bill today is more complicated; the average bill was 3.3 pages in the 1960s, 6.5 pages in the 1970s, 8.7 pages in the 1980s, and 15.5 pages in the 1990s.[7] Multiplying bills introduced by average length in each decade casts a different light on the workload issue. Congress now handles fewer, but much more complex bills.

TYPES OF LEGISLATION

A *bill* is the most common form for legislation. Bills are identified by chamber and order of introduction, so the first bill introduced in the House in a new

Table 8.1   Bills and Joint Resolutions Introduced, 1951–1990

Decade	Total Bills Introduced	Average per Congress
1951–1960	82,742	16,545
1961–1970	112,621	22,524
1971–1980	99,431	19,886
1981–1990	<u>51,874</u>	<u>10,375</u>
Total	346,668	69,330

SOURCE: Based on Rozanne M. Berry, "Bills Introduced and Laws Enacted: Selected Legislative Statistics, 1947–1992," *Congressional Research Service Report*, January 15, 1993, 2.

Congress will be H.R. 1 while the fifth bill in the Senate will be S. 5. Low bill numbers are coveted for their symbolic value, with leaders often reserving those numbers for the significant initiatives of a session. Bills deal with public or private matters. They become law when passed by both chambers and approved by the president.

Joint resolutions may be used interchangeably with bills or for constitutional amendments. They are also identified by chamber and order of introduction, such as House Joint Resolution 4 (H. J. Res. 4). Constitutional amendments must receive a two-thirds vote in both chambers as a precursor to ratification by three-fourths of the states.

Concurrent resolutions are identified by chamber and sequence (for example, H. Con. Res. 6). They must pass both chambers in similar form, but they proceed no further because they lack the force of law. Concurrent resolutions are used in two different situations. First, they express the "sense of Congress" on issues for which the law is not applicable, such as condemning human rights violations in North Korea. Second, they facilitate institutional business, such as setting an adjournment date.

Simple resolutions are distinguished once again by chamber and sequence (for example, H. Res. 5). Simple resolutions establish or amend a chamber's rules, and apply only to the chamber passing them. The most frequent use involves the House Rules Committee, which employs simple resolutions to structure debate over bills it sends to the floor. Television coverage of proceedings went into effect when the House and Senate passed simple resolutions letting C-SPAN inside the chamber in 1978 and 1986, respectively.[8]

The *Legislative Counsel*'s office usually drafts legislation introduced by members. Created in 1919, the office consists of attorneys who are responsible for writing bills, resolutions, and amendments for the committees; the Legislative Reorganization Act of 1970 expanded their role to include support for members. Their technical work is done on a nonpartisan, confidential basis. It is commonplace for attorneys in the office to draft competing amendments for the same bill.

Drafted legislation faces an uncertain future. A sponsor may not actively promote a bill because she or he introduced it solely for credit-claiming purposes.

By contrast, a sponsor committed to passing a bill will take several steps to improve the odds. One tactic is to tailor a bill to appease the relevant committee chair, because he or she will control the legislation in the early stages. Another tactic is to introduce a bill early in a session, so it has adequate time to wind its way through the process. A third tactic is to build a bipartisan coalition. Members often circulate "dear colleague" letters that explain a bill and urge others to become co-sponsors. Before he became House majority leader, Dick Armey (R., Tex.) once circulated 126 "dear colleague" letters in a single year![9]

A sponsor's early efforts can be critical. Simple inertia or opposition can kill a bill, while assembling a winning coalition is necessary to pass one. Former House Speaker Sam Rayburn (D., Tex.) explained the principle colorfully: "A jackass can kick a barn down, but it takes a carpenter to build one."[10]

REFERRING LEGISLATION

The referral process offers an opportunity to shape a bill's fate. Clever sponsors insert language that helps determine which standing committee will receive a bill. Parliamentarians conduct the actual referral on the basis of a bill's language and written committee jurisdictions.

Some bills are referred to more than one committee. Consider a bill taxing goods purchased over the Internet. Should it go to the Commerce Committee, or the Ways and Means Committee, with its jurisdiction over taxation? Congress may use *multiple referral* in such instances. Two variations exist. In *split referral,* two or more committees receive appropriate parts of the bill at the same time; in *sequential referral,* the bill is sent first to one committee and then to another, usually within a specified time table. A third variation, called *joint referral,* involves a bill sent to two or more committees at the same time. House Republicans abolished it when they became a majority in the 104th Congress, arguing it was too inefficient. Typical of the complexity of rules in the House, though, they retained the right to send a bill to a second committee by calling the act an *additional initial referral.*

In 1975, the Speaker's referral powers were enhanced, making multiple referral more common.[11] (The Senate informally practices multiple referral, and its flexible rules reduce the significance of any particular referral). By the early 1990s, 18 percent of House bills were referred to multiple committees, compared to 6–10 percent a decade earlier.[12] These bills are often the most important of a session. The multiple referral process benefits the members of standing committees with broad jurisdiction, who receive many opportunities to scrutinize legislation.

Once a bill is referred, the relevant committee chair has principal say over its disposition. A chair's opposition can be fatal, because it occurs at a point in the legislative process at which the institution requires some winnowing and members expect it to occur. Then, too, the prerogatives of the chair have increased under the Republican majority, even as a term limit of six years was imposed. For instance, committee chairs are allowed to name subcommittee chairs, hire

---

BOX 8.1   A Wily Veteran Wins His Last Fight

"Uncle Carl" Perkins (D., Ky.) was the architect of many education programs during his sixteen-year tenure as chair of the House Education and Labor Committee. His final legislative achievement was aided by clever use of the referral process.

At issue was the right of voluntary student religious groups to use educational facilities on the same basis as other student groups. In *Widmar* v. *Vincent* (1981), the Supreme Court ruled that the University of Missouri had to offer student religious groups "equal access" to its facilities. Members of the 98th Congress (1983–1984), including Uncle Carl, wanted to extend the Supreme Court's decision into secondary schools.

Opponents argued that equal access violated the principle of church/state separation. They called it "son of school prayer." They were optimistic because any equal-access bill would probably be referred to the House Judiciary Committee, where it was likely to encounter strong opposition from civil libertarians.[1]

Yet, Perkins figured out a way to circumvent the Judiciary Committee. He helped write a bill that offered an administrative rather than a judicial remedy in any school district where equal access was denied. The penalty was a total cutoff of federal aid to the school district. By inserting a monetary penalty, rather than giving students the right to sue a noncompliant district, Perkins ensured that the bill would be referred to his Education and Labor Committee, rather than to the Judiciary Committee. Perkins was not going to follow through on the remedy he devised—he was too sympathetic to education to cut federal aid to schools. He simply wanted custody of the bill.

Perkins shepherded the bill through the Education and Labor Committee. During the hearings phase, the committee heard testimony from those serving on the Judiciary Committee, who griped about being circumvented. Uncle Carl smiled knowingly but kept pushing the bill along. It was reported out on a 30–3 vote.

Given the lopsided margin, Perkins asked Speaker Tip O'Neill for permission to bring the Equal Access bill to the floor under "suspension of the rules." This provision expedites consideration of a bill, but it also requires a two-thirds margin of victory. The Speaker agreed. During floor debate on May 15, 1984, Perkins acknowledged that a monetary penalty eventually had to be dropped in favor of a judicial remedy, but he argued that this could be done in House and Senate conference negotiations. The Equal Access bill received a majority, but it fell several votes shy of a two-thirds margin. It lost partly because a junior Republican named Newt Gingrich spent time earlier in that day questioning the patriotism of ten Democratic colleagues. Democrats were furious. Many decided to vote against equal access because so many Republicans backed it, despite Perkins' plea to keep the two issues separate.

Perkins knew that equal access had to be considered again, absent the two-thirds requirement and the partisan warfare. The opportunity arose when the Senate passed an equal-access bill that restricted equal access to noncurriculum hours and included a judicial remedy. Perkins went back to Speaker O'Neill, asking for another vote. The Equal Access Act passed by a 227–77 margin, and President Reagan signed it into law.

Through clever structuring of the referral process, Perkins built unstoppable momentum for equal access. He died a short time later, ending a remarkable thirty-two-year career in the House of Representatives.

---

1. This account draws from Matthew C. Moen, *The Christian Right and Congress* (Tuscaloosa: University of Alabama Press, 1989), 112–120, and Nadine Cohodas, "Two House Veterans Scrap on Issue of Equal Access," *Congressional Quarterly Weekly Report,* May 12, 1984, 1104.

---

subcommittee staff, and control the committee's budget. Those powers combine with the prestige of the position to place chairs in an enviable position. Sponsors solicit a chair's views on a bill for exactly that reason. There is no point in submitting a bill to raise income taxes, for instance, when Ways and Means Chair Bill Archer (R., Tex.) is on a campaign to abolish the Internal Revenue Service.

BOX 8.2   It Was Rocking, but It Got Rolled on the Hill

The early 1980s were boom times for the recording industry. Pop superstars such as Madonna, Prince, and Sheena Easton were wildly popular, perhaps in part because they dared to push the boundaries of good taste. They released songs like "Sugar Walls" and "Darling Nikki" that contained sexually explicit lyrics. Their work topped the "filthy fifteen"—a list of the fifteen most offensive songs according to critics.

The critics were mostly a group of influential women in the nation's capital. Dubbed the "Washington wives," they included Susan Baker (wife of White House official and future Secretary of State James Baker) and Tipper Gore (wife of Tennessee Senator and future Vice-President Al Gore). The two women founded the Parents Music Resource Center (PMRC), which supported voluntary restrictions on the recording industry. They wanted record producers to cover provocative album jackets, to print objectionable lyrics so that parents knew the words in songs, and to institute a ratings system for explicit music, like the system for motion pictures. The Washington wives staged a massive public relations campaign in 1985, winning accolades from members of Congress.

Performance artists were horrified. They attacked the PMRC for stifling artistic creativity and promoting censorship. They openly challenged recording industry executives to stand up to the pressure generated by the Washington wives.

Record companies were in a bind. On one side were outspoken and influential women with a popular cause; on the other side were artists whose work generated large profits. Industry executives tried to steer a middle course. Stanley Gorikov, president of the Recording Industry Association of America, wrote a letter to the PMRC proposing a sticker on albums with obscene lyrics but refusing to accept a voluntary rating system.[1]

The PMRC rejected the idea as completely inadequate, and its allies on Capitol Hill scheduled public hearings. The decision to proceed with hearings carried the implicit threat of restrictive legislation, which alarmed the recording industry. The Senate Committee on Commerce, Science, and Transportation addressed the issue in September 1985.

The hearings provided lively political theatre. Musicians and artists testifying before the panel dispensed with customary decorum. Artist Frank Zappa stated:

> The PMRC proposal (to institute a ratings system) is an ill-conceived piece of nonsense, which fails to deliver any real benefits to children, infringes the civil liberties of people who are not children, and promises to keep the courts tied up for years . . . the PMRC demands are the equivalent of treating dandruff by decapitation.[2]

He added a personal attack on Tipper Gore, whose husband Al Gore served on the commit-

---

Subcommittee Referral

A bicameral difference emerges once a bill has been referred to committee. In the House, bills are usually referred down to a subcommittee, if only to languish. Recall from Chapter 5 that the "Subcommittee Bill of Rights" provided for referral to well-established subcommittees. In its aftermath, during the years of Democratic control, about 80 percent of all legislation was referred and reported out of subcommittees.[13] Exceptions to the rule exist, of course, but most bills traditionally have passed through a House subcommittee at some point.

The Senate proceeds very differently, due mainly to its much smaller membership. Full committees study most proposals. Whereas a typical House subcommittee consists of 13–19 members, in the Senate it is more on the order of 7–9 members. Given senators' numerous committee/subcommittee assignments,

---

BOX 8.2   continued

tee. Senator Gore's colleagues were furious. Slade Gordon (R., Wash.) rebuked Zappa: "I can only say that I found your statement to be boorish, incredibly and insensitively insulting . . . you could manage to give the First Amendment to the Constitution of the United States a bad name, if I felt you had the slightest understanding of it, which I do not."[3]

The rhetorical pyrotechnics continued with other witnesses. Dee Snider, of the heavy-metal band Twisted Sister, whose song "We're Not Gonna Take It" was dubbed one of the "filthy fifteen," also insulted Tipper Gore. He said the "only sadomasochism, bondage, and rape" in his music was "in the mind of Ms. Gore." His comment sparked this exchange with Jay Rockefeller (D., W. Va.):

> *Senator Rockefeller:* Why did you feel it necessary to attribute some of the qualities to her as you did? Was that important to your testimony?
>
> *Dee Snider:* First of all, I was not attacking Senator Gore's wife. I was attacking a member of the PMRC.
>
> *Senator Rockefeller:* You were attacking Senator Gore's wife by name.
>
> *Dee Snider:* Her name is Tipper Gore, is it not? I did not say the senator's wife. I said Tipper Gore.[4]

The public hearings were a disaster for the recording industry. A group of articulate and well-mannered senators stacked up very favorably in the public eye against disrespectful rock musicians, whose attacks on Tipper Gore seemed mean-spirited. Shortly after the hearings, the recording industry gave ground. Record companies voluntarily attached a "parental advisory" sticker on albums with explicit lyrics. Although less than a complete victory for the PMRC, given the nature of its demands, the parental advisory sticker came about simply because of committee hearings. Congress never even passed a bill—the mere threat of regulation proved sufficient.

Technological advances soon took care of other concerns of the PMRC, such as provocative album jackets. Release of compact discs killed record albums and miniaturized pictures. Two months after Al Gore became vice-president, Tipper Gore resigned from the PMRC. The issue of sexually explicit lyrics faded from the public agenda.

---

1. Anne Gowen, "Tipper Gore Quits PMRC," *Rolling Stone,* April 1993, 20.
2. Committee on Commerce, Science, and Transportation, United States Senate, hearings on *The Contents of Music and the Lyrics of Records* (99th Congress, first session, September 19, 1985).
3. Ibid.
4. Ibid.

---

simply scheduling a session is often problematic. Only 30–40 percent of legislation is sent down to subcommittees.[14] The membership is too small to subdivide tasks as often as the House.

Once a subcommittee receives a bill, it may squelch it. The subcommittee chair exerts principal control on that point. Alternatively, subcommittees may serve as springboards for legislation, beginning with the hearings process.

Congressional hearings serve many purposes. They provide a forum to assess the merits of legislation, to fine-tune specific provisions, and to build momentum for passage. They offer members the opportunity to assess the acumen of executive officials. And they provide an important symbolic ritual in a democratic society. Many hearings will occur simultaneously on Capitol Hill when Congress is in session. For example, over a three-day period in 1991, a total of 143 hearings were held in the House and Senate![15]

Congressional hearings are tightly organized, and even partially orchestrated. The subcommittee chair opens up the hearings by reading a prepared statement outlining the issues at hand and signaling his or her thoughts about the bill being considered. The ranking minority member follows suit, with the other subcommittee members proceeding in order of seniority. Witnesses testify about the bill's merit, typically reading an opening statement into the record and then answering questions from members. Verbal exchanges between members and witnesses tend to be perfunctory, with some notable exceptions. The majority party may convene hearings in order to grill witnesses, such as tobacco company executives or television producers, who are called to testify on legislation designed to curb the delivery of their products to children. One of the powers of the majority party is its ability to schedule hearings to its political advantage.

Subcommittees typically hold two days of public hearings. Members subsequently meet to *mark up* a bill, which means making word-by-word revisions to improve it. Markup sessions attract lobbyists, who seize the opportunity to insert provisions into bills when few members are involved. It is easier to defend an embedded provision than to insert one later in the legislative process. The so-called Christmas tree bill (whereby every member receives a present for her or his district) often originates in a subcommittee markup session.

During markup, proponents will offer "friendly amendments" aimed at strengthening a bill's prospects. Opponents may offer a *killer amendment*—a single provision so objectionable that it stops the entire bill. In 1998, for instance, some Republicans tried to derail U.S. contributions to the United Nations by linking abortion restrictions to international family planning. They hoped to sink foreign aide by entangling it in the abortion issue. The resulting bill so infuriated Democrats and confused abortion factions within the GOP that Speaker Gingrich was forced to pull it from the floor until he could sort out the mess.[16]

Full-Committee Consideration

The full committee repeats the work of the subcommittee. It conducts another day or two of hearings, so those not serving on the subcommittee can shape the bill, and then it holds a markup session. Because additional members become involved with a bill at the full-committee stage, with a different chair presiding, the bill may undergo substantial revision. The Senate Labor and Human Resources Committee illustrates the potential for divergent outcomes. At the subcommittee level, in the 105th Congress, conservative Republicans such as Dan Coats (Ind.) and Judd Gregg (N.H.) presided. In the full committee, moderate Republican chair Jim Jeffords (Vt.) often worked closely with ranking Democrat Edward Kennedy (Mass.) on health and education issues.

If a bill is substantially altered from its original form, its sponsor may reintroduce a *clean bill,* which incorporates all of the changes made during subcommittee and committee markup. It then receives expedited treatment. Why introduce a clean bill? One reason is to present a polished product to members, instead of offering a draft loaded down with amendments. Another reason is to circumvent a House rule permitting only *germane* (related) amendments to a bill. A clean bill kills a parliamentary "point of order" against nongermane amendments by incorporating them into the substance of the bill. The Senate lacks a germaneness requirement, so clean bills are not an issue in that body.

Following consideration of a bill, committee members vote to report it out of committee. Usually, the bill is approved because a majority of members considered it worth their time to tackle. In some instances, committees may forward items they do not endorse, simply to give the full chamber the opportunity to vote on them. The Senate Judiciary Committee, for example, may forward a nomination for a judgeship even though it opposes confirmation.

A report accompanies every bill passing through a committee. It contains a legislative history, the exact wording of the bill, the major arguments for and against the bill, and a statement of its impact on existing law. Committee reports are identified by chamber and sequence, so the sixth report in the Senate in the 105th Congress will be designated S. Rept. 105-6. The committee report is an important historical document that judges and executive officials use to ascertain congressional intent as they hand down rulings or promulgate regulations.

THE CALENDAR SYSTEM

Bills reported out of committee are entered chronologically on a legislative calendar. Placement on a calendar is a routine parliamentary exercise, based on written committee jurisdictions and a bill's content.

Technically, the bill is now ready for floor consideration. Yet, too many bills are reported out of committees for all of them to be considered on the floor. The system of legislative calendars provides a mechanism to further winnow out bills.

The calendar system in each chamber is instructive because it dramatizes the House's greater reliance on formal rules and procedures. The House uses four different calendars. The *Union Calendar* receives major public bills that propose to spend or raise money. The *House Calendar* receives major public bills that focus on administrative or procedural matters. The *Private Calendar* is used for individual claims against the U.S. government, such as reimbursement for property damage, as well as for private immigration cases in which deportation might cause hardship. The *Corrections Calendar*, which was the brainchild of Speaker Newt Gingrich, is used for noncontroversial matters.[17] The Speaker wanted an easy way to abolish senseless federal regulations as part of his crusade to downsize government. The Corrections Calendar, which is used two days a month, allows a supermajority (three-fifths) to pass items, thereby short-circuiting the normal legislative process followed by other bills. The Speaker is given the power to determine which items are placed on the Corrections Calendar.

Another legislative shortcut in the House is *suspension of the rules,* which is also used in noncontroversial cases. During each Monday and Tuesday, a member may request "suspension of the rules" to pass a minor bill, such as naming a federal post office after a distinguished public official. Under guidelines adopted in the 105th Congress, only bills spending less than $100 million may be considered under the suspension procedure. Debate is limited to forty minutes, amendments are not allowed, and a two-thirds vote is required to pass legislation.

BOX 8.3   Extracting a Bill from Committee

The House has a complicated procedure for extracting a bill from a standing committee and bringing it to the floor. Any representative may file a *discharge petition* whenever a standing committee has not acted on a bill referred to it thirty days prior. The representative must collect the signatures of 218 members, a majority of the House. The logistics of simply gathering those signatures are daunting. Members usually circulate letters asking other members to sign their discharge petitions, or they have staffers call around to do the same. Since 1993, the names of members who sign discharge petitions are public information.[1] That provision was aimed at improving the slim odds for discharge petitions by applying public pressure to members not signing.

If the requisite number of signatures is gathered, the bill is placed on the *Discharge Calendar,* where it must sit for seven days. On the second and fourth Mondays of each month, bills may be taken off the Discharge Calendar and considered on the floor. If the motion to discharge a bill passes—and it probably will at that point because a majority of the House has already signed it—the bill is immediately taken up on the floor.

As a practical matter, this obtuse procedure rarely works. Committee chairs will ordinarily report out popular legislation, if only to avoid the humiliation of a bill being extracted from their committee. Those filing discharge petitions have trouble gathering enough signatures because majority-party members will not challenge their own committee chairs. When the provision to publicize names on a discharge petition was introduced, none of the four active petitions in the House had even 100 signatures.[2]

The typical pattern is that a member of the minority party files a discharge petition to extract a bill stalled in committee by the majority. The member labors to gather enough signatures but falls short by anywhere from one to many dozen members.

Discharge petitions can spur committees to act by showing the popularity of legislation, but usually they represent idle threats lodged by the minority party.

---

1. "Discharge Petitions Get GOP Attention," *Congressional Quarterly Weekly Report,* October 2, 1993, 2618.
2. Ibid.

The Senate calendar system is simple. The *Executive Calendar* receives treaties and nominations consistent with the Senate's "advise and consent" function. The *Calendar of General Orders* receives all other legislation, regardless of subject or significance. Bills are brought to the floor in two ways. First, a senator may motion to consider a bill. That right is guaranteed in the individualistic Senate, but it is rarely exercised. Prior approval from party leaders is usually obtained because they are free to table bills brought up without their consent. Under the rules, party leaders receive recognition before other senators.

Second, bills may come to the floor via *unanimous consent.* Senators simply agree on which bills to consider and how long to debate them, in an informal process negotiated by party leaders. According to Democrat Robert Byrd (W. Va.)—once majority leader of the Senate—about 98 percent of Senate business is handled that way.[18]

Unanimous consent operates at two different levels. *Simple unanimous consent* involves members' perfunctory requests during the legislative day, like placing material into the *Congressional Record.* Dozens of these minor requests are lodged daily when the Senate is in session, and they are unfailingly honored. *Complex unanimous consent* involves verbal or written agreement about the terms of debate on a bill. An agreement is typically crafted by the majority and minority leaders, and is then ratified by the full chamber. As the term implies, unanimous consent means that every senator concurs with the proposed course of action. A long-standing tradition of cooperation encourages (but does not require) individual senators to accept agreements they do not necessarily like. Consent agreements are binding once they are accepted.

Unanimous consent provides senators with a more flexible, relaxed, free-wheeling atmosphere than is found in the House. A senator who seeks two elite committee assignments in technical violation of Senate rules, for example, can easily obtain them by requesting and receiving unanimous consent. However, the senator who is willing to incur the wrath of his or her colleagues can derail unanimous consent agreements, frustrating the wishes of other senators. Venerable Senate traditions of minority rights and individual conscience counterbalance sanctions against obstructionism. Deadlock ensues when agreements are not reached.

The problem of procedural impasse has worsened over time. Senators cope with increasing demands by asking their leaders to schedule legislation at personally convenient times. Senator Byrd was well known for his gallant efforts to protect other senators' interests during his tenure as majority leader, but he confessed near the end that leadership had degenerated into balancing the whims of ninety-nine other senators.[19] The informal practice of *holds* compounds this problem by allowing individual senators the right to anonymously delay consideration of particular bills. (A hold is basically a threat to filibuster if a bill goes forward.) An attempt by Senator Ron Wyden (D., Oreg.) to make public the name of a senator placing a hold on legislation is instructive. Wyden's provision—attached to a spending bill in September—was conspicuously absent when the bill was brought to the floor by the Republican leadership in November 1997.[20] No explanation was given. The name of any senator placing a hold remains a secret.

The procedural gridlock in the Senate has caused unanimous consent agreements to become more elaborate over time, with the goal of expediting legislation.[21] This increased codification of Senate procedures is a point of convergence with the House.[22] Yet, the larger story is that the Senate is often unable to act, forcing its leadership to resort to unorthodox procedures to pass bills. According to political scientist Barbara Sinclair, "The Senate, in contrast [to the House has], failed to develop ways of coping effectively with the problems created by internal reforms and the political environment . . . legislating remains problematical in the Senate."[23] We will revisit that theme and the Senate shortly.

THE ROLE OF THE HOUSE RULES COMMITTEE

Once a bill is placed on one of the House calendars, it is ready for consideration. Sometimes, the bill will proceed swiftly to a vote, through some special route such as suspension of the rules. Typically, though, major bills will pass through the House *Rules Committee*. There is no comparable committee in the Senate.

The Rules Committee's initial task is to prioritize legislation. Presumably, bills are considered on the floor in the chronological order in which they were placed on the House calendars. Yet, such orderliness rarely happens. The Speaker may want particular bills considered before others, or some powerful committee chair may propose that his or her handiwork be placed ahead of a bill reported out of another standing committee. In those cases, leaders will ask the Rules Committee to send bills to the floor out of the order in which they were entered onto the calendars. Whenever the Rules Committee does so—and it does so all the time—it effectively prioritizes legislation.

The Rules Committee is especially responsive to the Speaker. Recall from Chapter 5 that when House Democrats decentralized political power to sub-committees in the 1970s, they concurrently strengthened the speakership. One way they bolstered the speakership was to grant it the power to nominate the majority-party members of the Rules Committee.[24] Democratic Speakers in the postreform era—Tip O'Neill, Jim Wright, and Tom Foley—used that power to exercise control over the flow of business. Republican Speaker Newt Gingrich followed suit. In the 104th Congress, he named Gerald Solomon (R., N.Y.) chair of the Rules Committee. The choice surprised some people, because Solomon had tangled with Gingrich in the past as part of intramural Republican party politics. Yet, Solomon proved a loyal and able subordinate, laboring to get the legislative components of the Contract With America sent forward to the floor quickly.[25] Solomon continued serving as chair in the 105th Congress before voluntarily retiring from Congress in 1998.

The Rules Committee is one of the most partisan committees in the entire House. It has thirteen members, with Republicans outnumbering Democrats by a margin of nine to four as of 1998. The lopsided ratio signals the Rules Committee's significance to the majority party. The committee has the power to halt the progress of some bills and to expedite others. In this sense, it is sometimes compared to a traffic cop.

Customarily, the Speaker or a chair of a standing committee asks the Rules Committee to craft a rule that will send a bill to the floor. The Rules Committee may hold hearings on that request, calling on members of the appropriate committee to testify about the need to send the bill forward. The hearings are similar to those in other committees. Opening statements by Rules Committee members are followed by question-and-answer sessions with witnesses.

The Rules Committee's power becomes evident once it has sifted through the many bills sitting on the House calendars and decided to proceed with one. The committee has many options. It can send a bill to the floor under an *open rule,* which means that germane amendments may be offered, or under a *closed rule,* which means that no amendments can be offered. Between those two extremes, a *modified open* or a *modified closed rule* (depending on its restrictiveness) allows amendments on some parts of a bill, but not on others. Finally, *waiving points of order* allows regular House procedures to be temporarily suspended. In addition to establishing the amending process for bills, the Rules Committee also sets time limits on debate. Thus, the committee quite literally decides the terms under which bills are debated on the House floor. Because legislative battles can

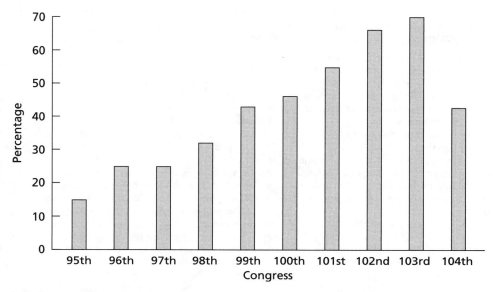

FIGURE 8.2   Bills with Restrictive Rules in the House, 1977–1996

SOURCE: U.S. Congress, *Congressional Record,* October 7, 1994, H11278; Roger H. Davidson and Walter J. Oleszek, *Congress and Its Members,* 6th ed. (Washington, D.C.: CQ Press, 1998), 232.

be decided by these early tactical manuevers, the Rules Committee is a potent force in the House.[26]

Once a rule is crafted (in the form of a simple resolution), it is sent to the floor for debate and a vote. It must receive a majority to take effect. The rule usually passes because majority-party members typically support it.

Ideally, the Rules Committee sends bills to the floor under open rules that give members the opportunity to participate fully in debate and in the amendment process. In reality, the committee often limits member participation, due in part to partisanship. The minority party, frustrated in the majoritarian House, often overloads bills sent forward under open rules with germane amendments. Exasperated majority-party members respond by sending fewer bills to the floor under open rules. This pattern emerged when Republicans were in the minority and Democrats in the majority, but it has continued since they switched positions. Further, the proportion of bills with restrictive rules has risen steadily over time. Figure 8.2 shows that the percentage of restrictive rules on major legislation has soared in the postreform era, from about 15 percent to 70 percent by the 103rd Congress. (The percentage dropped in the 104th Congress, but the figures are disputed by the Democrats, who claim that Republicans count unfairly.)

The Rules Committee is notoriously innovative in structuring floor debate. The *king-of-the-hill rule,* for example, specifies that the *last* amendment to a bill that receives a majority wins. The Rules Committee is so powerful because it decides the order of the amendments. It can place a preferred amendment first or

BOX 8.4   King-of-the-Hill Rescues the Arts

Congress created the National Endowment for the Arts (NEA) in 1965 to broaden appreciation of the arts in public life. The NEA was authorized to provide funds for local theater companies, symphonies, and museums, as well as for avant-garde performance artists.

The Reagan administration sought to change years of steady funding when it proposed a 50 percent cut in the NEA's budget in 1981, as part of its massive program of budget cuts. Congressional allies helped the NEA escape that draconian cut, but the stage was set for a decade of wrangling.

Matters crested in 1989 when the NEA was being reauthorized by Congress. Two highly questionable projects were linked to NEA sponsorship that year: a work by Andres Serrano that featured a crucifix submerged in the artist's urine, called "Piss Christ," and a photographic exhibit by Robert Mapplethorpe that included themes such as sadomasochism. Total NEA funding for the two projects was $45,000.

When the projects were publicized, a firestorm erupted. Conservatives attacked the principle of taxpayer dollars subsidizing questionable art; they wanted a vote to slash the NEA's budget. Liberals defended the principle of artistic expression and argued that the vast majority of funds were well spent.

Both sides headed for a showdown on the House floor. Luckily for the NEA, the Democrat-controlled Rules Committee structured the final outcome with a king-of-the-hill rule. It both allowed and rank-ordered four separate proposals from the least to the most severe: The Stenholm Amendment cut $45,000 out of the NEA's budget of $160 million plus, a symbolic amount equal to the Serrano and Mapplethorpe grants; the Stearns Amendment cut the NEA budget by 5 percent; the Armey Amendment cut the budget by 10 percent; and the

Rohrabacher Amendment abolished the agency.[1]

By placing the Stenholm Amendment first, the Rules Committee hoped to mitigate damage to the NEA. The strategy worked like a charm. The Stenholm Amendment passed by a 361–65 margin. NEA *supporters* voted for it to fend off harsher proposals to follow. NEA *opponents* also voted for it, figuring that harsher measures might not pass. Finally, members in the middle supported it as a way of sending a message to the NEA, without doing it any substantive harm. The 65 votes against the Stenholm Amendment represented an equally odd bloc: liberals who opposed any cut whatsoever to the NEA combined with conservatives who gambled that they would win deeper cuts if they voted down the symbolic Stenholm Amendment.

Once the Stenholm Amendment passed, support for harsher cuts evaporated, just as the Rules Committee anticipated. Members were on record as "slapping the wrist" of the NEA, and they considered it sufficient. Liberals and moderates joined forces against ardent conservatives to defeat the Stearns Amendment by a 328–95 margin. The Armey Amendment failed by an analogous 332–94 vote. The Rohrabacher Amendment terminating the NEA was rejected by voice vote.

The king-of-the-hill procedure spared the NEA for the time being, as its budget was cut by less than 0.0003 percent. However, the issue of federal funding for the arts remained visible into the 1990s. The Republican-controlled 104th Congress slashed the NEA's budget by 40 percent, and the future of the NEA remains uncertain.

---

1. Matthew C. Moen, "Congress and the National Endowment for the Arts: Institutional Patterns and Arts Funding, 1965–1994," *Social Science Journal* 34(2) (1997): 192–193.

last, depending on which position is most advantageous. A common tactic used by House Democrats when they were the majority, for instance, was to schedule a series of increasingly liberal amendments. The most liberal alternative that could pass in the House thereby won.

Republicans began using a *queen-of-the-hill rule* once they gained power. This rule also specifies a series of amendments, but the winner is the amendment that gets the most votes (so long as it is a majority), rather than the one passing last. In essence, the size of the victory margin replaces the ordering. Still another rules variation, known as the *self-executing rule,* specifies that a bill is automatically amended at the same time the rule itself is adopted. Substantive change is automatically incorporated in a "two-for-one" process.

HOUSE FLOOR ACTION

The House is usually in session for 200 or more days a year. However, most of its business is conducted from Tuesday through Thursday, so that members have the opportunity to return to their districts for long weekends. The procedures they follow on the House floor are regimented.[27]

The first step to passing legislation on the House floor is to debate and approve the rule issued by the Rules Committee. The rule normally passes because it was crafted to meet the wishes of the majority. Once the rule is approved, the House dissolves itself into the *Committee of the Whole House on the State of the Union,* to consider the bill. The "Committee of the Whole," as it is called, is a parliamentary convenience that allows the House to operate with a quorum of only 100 members. It is really simply the full House meeting under another name in order to expedite business.

General debate then ensues. The House usually debates a bill for as long as the rule allows, although it occasionally finishes debate before the allotted time is up. Available time is divided evenly between those for and against the bill. The *floor manager* for each side allocates small blocs of time to members supporting her or his position. Floor managers typically are the chair of the committee or subcommittee that reported out the bill. They try to get a cross-section of members, representing both parties and all ideological stripes and geographic interests, to speak on behalf of their side. Floor managers wish to convey overwhelming support for their position. They yield time for debate in small increments—from as little as fifteen seconds to a few minutes. The "general debate" is therefore less a true debate than a series of cleverly crafted sound bites or extemporaneous monologues.

If amendments to the bill are permitted by the rule adopted earlier, they are offered at this juncture. Under the so-called *five-minute rule,* the sponsor of an amendment is given only five minutes to defend his or her proposal, and an opponent five minutes to rebut it. Yet, here, reality differs from the rule. Members may take additional time to argue over the proposed amendment simply by making a motion to the Speaker "to strike the last word." It allows them time to make their individual statement. For controversial amendments, as many as one or two dozen members may move to strike the last word. Alternatively, if widespread agreement exists on an amendment, members may barely discuss it.

The amending process can be extremely complicated if the adopted rule permits it. Members may offer four types of changes to a bill: an *amendment,* an *amendment to an amendment,* a *substitute amendment,* or an *amendment to the substitute.* Although it may seem unnecessarily complicated, the process actually makes

---

BOX 8.5   Hershey Melts Into Hands, Because of a Mouth

In March 1997, about 200 members of the House traveled to Hershey, Pennsylvania—hometown of the famous chocolate bar. They brought along their families, at the behest of organizers Ray LaHood (R., Ill.) and David Skaggs (D., Colo.).

The purpose of the bipartisan Hershey retreat was to forge better working relationships among members. The 104th Congress had been a heavily partisan affair, and many members sensed a need to begin anew. They pledged more understanding of and better cooperation with one another.

Unfortunately, the spirit of collegiality did not last long. On April 9, 1997—in the midst of a heated debate on the floor over campaign finance—Majority Whip Tom DeLay (R., Tex.) and David Obey (D., Wis.) exchanged more than words.[1]

The fracas began when George Miller (D., Calif.) accused the Republicans of being hypocritical about campaign finance reform. He claimed that for all their talk, Republicans thought that the current system of financing elections was fine, as demonstrated by the fact that DeLay allowed lobbyists to use his office to draft legislation. DeLay was furious. He demanded that Miller's words be "taken down" (ruled unparliamentary). The presiding officer declined that request, and Miller continued by reading an article from the *Washington Post*

describing DeLay's interaction with several lobbyists. DeLay replied that the story did not name any lobbyists and that it was untrue.

Yet, the story did indeed name seven lobbyists who worked closely with the GOP. Obey crossed over to the Republican side of the aisle with the story in hand to remind DeLay that it named names. The two men apparently poked their fingers at each other, with DeLay pushing Obey away, and calling him a "gutless chickenshit." Obey grabbed DeLay's tie before the two men were separated.

On that particular day, the words exchanged by the members in the heat of floor debate turned into an actual shoving match. The event was highly unusual, and both members later apologized. Yet, the tussle showed the intensity of emotions that can arise during floor debate; it also illustrated a long-term trend toward a loss of comity in the institution.[2] In the short term, of course, the DeLay–Obey scuffle simply melted some of the progress achieved at the chocolate capital of the world.

---

1. The following account draws from Nancy E. Roman, "War on the Floor: DeLay–Obey Tussle Flouts Era of Civility," *Washington Times National Weekly Edition,* April 20, 1997, 4.
2. Eric M. Uslaner, *The Decline of Comity in Congress* (Ann Arbor: University of Michigan Press, 1993).

---

sense. Assume a member offers an amendment. It may be changed once with an amendment to an amendment; or it may be replaced entirely with a substitute amendment, which can then be changed once with an amendment to the substitute. The key point is that the amending process is finite. A provision cannot be endlessly amended.

Amendments with strong support will be agreed to by a voice vote, with the presiding officer simply instructing all those in favor to say "aye" and all those opposed to say "no." Contentious amendments usually proceed to a roll call vote. A roll call vote is required if a member demands it and if he or she is supported by twenty-five other members. Since 1973, representatives have been able to vote by "electronic device." Each member has a small card about the size of a driver's license that is inserted into one of many stations on the House floor. The member then presses yea, nay, or present (abstention). The vote is tallied electronically and displayed instantaneously on an electronic scoreboard. Fifteen minutes are allotted for members to cast their votes.

Once the amendments have been voted on, the Committee of the Whole rises; in effect, that parliamentary convenience ends. The Speaker then orders the *previous question,* which means that debate has ended and the final bill will be voted upon. Although the minority party has a right to a *recommital motion*—sending the bill back to the committee from which it originated—the motion is not always made and it rarely succeeds. The full House then votes on final passage of the entire bill, as amended in the Committee of the Whole.

SENATE FLOOR ACTION

In contrast to the House, the Senate proceeds informally. Typically, the majority leader brings forward a bill under the unanimous consent agreement struck with the minority leader. A floor manager for each side (pro and con) delivers an opening statement. Debate and voting occur on the amendments permitted by the unanimous consent agreement, and a roll call vote is taken on final passage. (The Senate does not vote electronically.)

This apparent simplicity is misleading, however, because it understates the Senate's hallowed tradition of unlimited debate. It is often impossible to obtain a unanimous consent agreement because some senator strenuously objects to it; in those cases, debate on amendments and final passage may be unstructured and interminable. Senators are free to offer as many amendments as they wish, and those bent on killing a bill may produce dozens of amendments for consideration. They may also attach *nongermane* (unrelated) *amendments,* such as antiabortion riders to human resource bills, simply to envelop them in controversy. Senator Jesse Helms (R., N.C.) earned the nickname of "Senator No" for his constant attempts to derail legislation by adding nongermane amendments on controversial social issues. Another obstructionist tactic is to demand a quorum call (which takes time in a chamber without electronic voting). A senator's "hold" on legislation is yet another dilatory tactic.

The ultimate weapon of the senator seeking to derail a bill, however, is the filibuster.[28] It is grounded in the principle of unlimited debate. One or more senators, in the absence of any unanimous consent agreement, are free to kill a bill by debating it endlessly so that it does not come to a vote. The mere threat of a filibuster may win concessions from the floor manager of a bill; an actual filibuster may derail a bill, particularly if it comes late in a congressional session when time is running out.

Senators periodically complain that the filibuster allows the few, or even the one, to derail the wishes of the many. But they also resist changes to the practice, because each senator realizes that it protects his or her individual prerogatives.

Filibusters may be ended by invoking *cloture,* which closes down debate on a bill. Under Senate rules, a three–fifths (60) vote is required to invoke cloture. The supermajority makes it difficult, particularly when the numerical strength of the

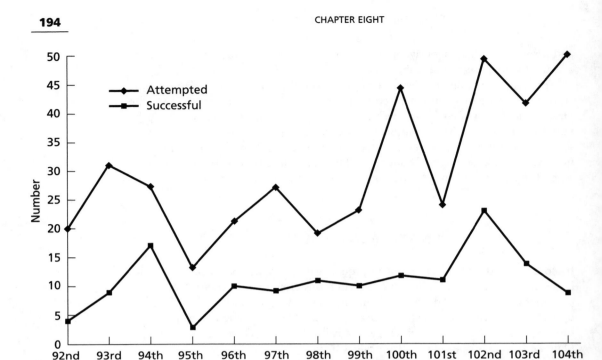

FIGURE 8.3   Senate Cloture Votes, 1971–1996

SOURCE: Norman J. Ornstein, Thomas E. Mann, and Michael J. Malbin, *Vital Statistics on Congress 1997–1998* (Washington, D.C.: Congressional Quarterly, 1998), 171.

political parties is fairly even, because most (not all) filibusters are launched by the minority party to derail legislation advanced by the majority party. The minority party requires only forty-one solid votes to deny cloture. As Figure 8.3 shows, only about one-third of cloture votes succeed, implicitly confirming the power of the filibuster.

When does Senate debate end? Observers joke that debate ends only when every senator has said everything she or he wishes to say. Senate proceedings are not scripted as they are in the House. The principle of unlimited Senate debate may have been what a foreign journalist had in mind when he quipped: "Congress is so strange. A man gets up to speak and says nothing. Nobody listens—then everybody disagrees."[29]

CONFERENCE COMMITTEES

Because only one version of a bill may be presented to the president for his signature or veto, the House and Senate must reconcile any differences on bills. Whenever possible, the two chambers do so informally by adding amendments to each other's bills and then shipping them back. In conjunction with informal discussions by the floor managers in each chamber, this process works to resolve some major and most minor differences.[30]

When the two chambers require a more elaborate procedure, they resort to conference committees.[31] Recall from Chapter 5 that conference committees are composed of representatives and senators appointed by chamber leaders. By custom, conferees are drawn from the standing committee/subcommittee that reported out the original bill. Under House rules, a majority of the conferees must have supported the legislation when it was considered on the floor. Conference delegations approximate party ratios in each chamber.

Conference committees fluctuate in size, depending on the complexity of the bill being considered and the number of House–Senate differences embedded within it. The House usually sends a larger delegation because it is the larger institution. Ordinarily, the conferees leave provisions already agreed to by both chambers off the table, although they sometimes put items back into play to provide more negotiating room.

Conference committees have been open events since 1975, when both chambers agreed to a rule requiring public meetings unless conferees voted to close a meeting. House Republicans went a step further in the 104th Congress, passing a bill forcing open meetings unless national security was involved. It was part of a public campaign to show a new era of openness in the House, but the provision was symbolic because meetings already were open.

Open procedures can give a false impression. The presence of lobbyists at conference committees can hamstring members who want to give ground in order to reach agreement. Conferees may haggle over their differences and strive to resolve them in small groups before the official conference even begins.

When chamber differences involve money, the middle ground is easy to identify, and the conferees usually split the difference. For example, a defense appropriation of $300 billion in the House and $250 billion in the Senate would be settled around $275 billion. When chamber differences involve substantive language, however, negotiations are more difficult. For instance, what happens when the House attaches the death penalty to certain crimes but the Senate does not? No firm answer can be given. Conferees try to trade, bluff, and persuade colleagues until agreement is reached. Conferees work to sustain the position of their parent chamber, because they will have to report back the agreement struck so it can be ratified. Scholars have produced an extensive literature trying to explain whether the House or Senate generally prevails in conference committees, without clear answers.[32] In more recent times, chamber leaders have regularly intervened in negotiations. Speaker Gingrich played a central role in 1997 negotiations aimed at balancing the budget.[33]

A conference committee ends when a majority of the conferees from each chamber sign a *conference report*. The report contains a comprehensive history of the bill, an estimate of its impact on the budget, and a synopsis of its provisions. Unlike a committee report, the conference report does not contain dissenting views; rather, it summarizes the agreement concluded.

Conference reports are rarely rejected. At that point in the legislative process, from the time the bill was first introduced, hundreds of people have worked thousands of hours on the bill. It is the product of chamber coalitions and bicameral negotiations. Conference reports are *privileged legislation,* which means that they can be brought up for a vote almost anytime on the floor. Most conference reports are accepted by voice vote. At this point in the process, opponents accept the inevitable.

THE FINAL STEP

Once the conference report is approved by both chambers, the bill is sent to the president. If he signs the bill, it becomes law. If he does nothing, but Congress remains in session, the bill becomes law in ten days; if he does nothing, and Congress adjourns, the bill is killed by *pocket veto.* If the president vetoes the bill, he sends it back to Congress with an explanation.[34]

Keep in mind that the legislative process does not end even after a presidential signature. The law passed by Congress still must be implemented by the bureaucracy, and it must withstand any legal challenges that arise in the courts. Congress may revisit a a law to convey its intent to those other political actors.

VARIATIONS ON A THEME

Political scientist Barbara Sinclair recently noted that the "textbook" legislative process described in this chapter is becoming less common.[35] Bills now wind their way through Congress in totally unpredictable ways, so that "variety . . . characterizes the contemporary legislative process."[36]

She points to various developments on the Hill. Many bills now receive multiple referral, thus bringing more than one standing committee into deliberations. Leaders increasingly use task forces to bypass committees. Changes have become commonplace after a committee has considered a bill. In the House, innovative rules are crafted to circumvent anticipated obstacles; in the Senate, individual senators force concessions by placing a hold or threatening a filibuster. Nongermane amendments are attached to bills in the Senate, causing consternation among representatives. Many bills face one or more of these legislative twists and turns. Bills seem to follow their own unique path.

Then, too, entirely new processes have emerged. Congressional leaders may strike an agreement with the president through closed-door summit negotiations and then introduce their handiwork into the legislative process for ratification.[37] Omnibus bills spending hundreds of billions of dollars are routinely assembled; they force members to give in order to get. Budget reconciliation—the process of requiring committees to make substantive changes in programs within their jurisdiction to fit within the budget framework established by Congress—creates opportunities for massive policy change under the pretense of budget balancing. These processes are being used more than ever before, but with some salutary effect, because they increase the chance that a bill will become law.[38]

The bottom line is that the legislative process defies easy description. Some bills pass quickly via shortcuts. Most follow a relatively standard (but often unpredictable) process. A growing percentage of major bills follow some customized route. The point to remember, in the words of former House Speaker Sam Rayburn, is that "too many critics mistake the deliberations of Congress for its decisions."[39] The legislative process is long, complex, and often divisive. Yet, the process requires a representative institution, consisting of two dissimilar chambers, to settle its differences in the public eye. The legislative process is the very essence of democracy.

NOTES

1. T. R. Reid, *Congressional Odyssey: The Saga of a Senate Bill* (New York: Freeman, 1980); Eric Redman, *The Dance of Legislation* (New York: Simon & Shuster, 1973); Paul C. Light, *Forging Legislation* (New York: Norton, 1992); Jeffrey H. Birnbaum and Alan S. Murphy, *Showdown at Gucci Gulch* (New York: Vintage Books, 1987); Timothy J. Conlan, Margaret T. Wrightson, and David R. Beam, *Taxing Choices* (Washington, D.C.: CQ Press, 1990); Janet M. Martin, *Lessons from the Hill* (New York: St. Martin's Press, 1994); Robert E. Dewhirst, *Rites of Passage: Congress Makes Laws* (Upper Saddle River, N.J.: Prentice-Hall, 1997); Steven Waldman, *The Bill* (New York: Penguin Books, 1995).

2. *Washington Post,* June 26, 1983, 14. A detailed discussion of legislative strategies is found in Edward V. Schneier and Bertram Gross, *Legislative Strategy: Shaping Public Policy* (New York: St. Martin's Press, 1993).

3. A good summary of the budget battle may be found in Richard E. Cohen, *Changing Course in Washington* (New York: Macmillan, 1994), 165–212.

4. Alexis de Tocqueville, *Democracy in America*, ed. J. P. Mayer, trans. George Lawrence (Garden City, N.Y.: Doubleday, 1969 [1835]), 118.

5. Norman J. Ornstein, Thomas E. Mann, and Michael J. Malbin, *Vital Statistics on Congress 1997–1998* (Washington, D.C.: Congressional Quarterly, 1998), 160–163, 167.

6. Ibid., 160–163; on issues of co-sponsorship, see Daniel Kessler and Keith

Krehbiel, "Dynamics of Cosponsorship," *American Political Science Review* (September 1996): 555–566.

7. Ibid., 167. Calculated from data presented.

8. A comprehensive discussion of television on Capitol Hill is Stephen Frantzich and John Sullivan, *The C-SPAN Revolution* (Norman: University of Oklahoma Press, 1996).

9. John McCaslin, "Armey of Letters," *Washington Times,* June 16, 1994, 7.

10. Suzy Platt, ed., *Respectfully Quoted* (Washington, D.C.: Congressional Quarterly, 1992), 56.

11. Roger H. Davidson, Walter J. Oleszek, and Thomas Kephart, "One Bill, Many Committees: Multiple Referrals in the U.S. House of Representatives," *Legislative Studies Quarterly* 13 (February 1988): 3–28.

12. Garry Young and Joseph Cooper, "Multiple Referral and the Transformation of House Decision Making," in *Congress Reconsidered,* 5th ed., ed. Lawrence C. Dodd and Bruce I. Oppenheimer (Washington, D.C.: CQ Press, 1993): 214.

13. Christopher J. Deering and Steven S. Smith, *Committees in Congress,* 3d ed. (Washington, D.C.: Congressional Quarterly, 1997), 156.

14. Ibid.

15. Walter Pincus and Guy Gugliotta, "A Day in the Life," *Washington Post Weekly Edition,* April 1–7, 1991, 6.

16. Donna Cassata, "Seeking Showdown With Clinton, Gingrich Gets on With

GOP," *Congressional Quarterly Weekly Report,* March 14, 1998, 673–674.

17. Jennifer Babson, "A Quicker Way and Special Day for Erasing Debatable Rules," *Congressional Quarterly Weekly Report,* June 24, 1995, 1807.

18. *Congressional Record,* August 5, 1987, S. 1293.

19. Jacqueline Calmes, "Byrd Struggles to Lead Deeply Divided Senate," *Congressional Quarterly Weekly Report,* July 4, 1987, 1422.

20. "Senate Holds Habit Stymies Oregon Dem.," Associated Press wire story, reprinted in the *Bangor Daily News,* November 12, 1997, A7.

21. Steven S. Smith, *Call to Order: Floor Politics in the House and Senate* (Washington, D.C.: Brookings Institution, 1989), 98.

22. Ross K. Baker, *House and Senate,* 2d ed. (New York: Norton, 1995), 187–188.

23. Barbara Sinclair, *Unorthodox Lawmaking* (Washington, D.C.: Congressional Quarterly, 1997), 96.

24. Leroy N. Rieselbach, *Congressional Reform: The Changing Modern Congress* (Washington, D.C.: Congressional Quarterly, 1994), 208–209.

25. James G. Gimpel, *Fulfilling the Contract: The First 100 Days* (Boston: Allyn & Bacon, 1996), 36.

26. A major study of the House Rules Committee in the postreform era is Stanley Bach and Steven S. Smith, *Managing Uncertainty in the House of Representatives: Adaptation and Innovation in Special Rules* (Washington, D.C.: Brookings Institution, 1988); see also Greg Thorson, "Committee Coalitions and Special Rules in the House of Representatives," paper delivered at the Annual Meeting of the American Political Science Association, San Francisco, August 1996.

27. For a thorough discussion of House and Senate floor proceedings, see Smith, *Call to Order;* and Walter J. Oleszek, *Congressional Procedures and the Policy Process,* 4th ed. (Washington, D.C.: CQ Press, 1996), 161–225.

28. An informative recent discussion of the filibuster is Sarah A. Binder and Steven S. Smith, *Politics or Principle? Filibustering in the United States Senate* (Washington, D.C.:

Brookings Institution, 1997); see also their article "The Politics and Principle of the Senate Filibuster," *Extensions* (Norman, Okla.: The Carl Albert Congressional Research and Studies Center, Fall 1997), 15–19.

29. Platt, *Respectfully Quoted,* 55.

30. Charles Tiefer, *Congressional Practice and Procedure* (Westport, Conn.: Greenwood Press, 1989).

31. For a comprehensive treatment of conference committees, see Lawrence Longley and Walter Oleszek, *Bicameral Politics: Conference Committees in Congress* (New Haven, Conn.: Yale University Press, 1989).

32. See Gilbert Y. Steiner, *The Congressional Conference Committee* (Urbana: University of Illinois Press, 1951); Richard F. Fenno, Jr. *The Power of the Purse* (Boston: Little, Brown, 1966), 616–678; David J. Vogler, "Patterns of One-House Dominance in Congressional Conference Committees," *Midwest Journal of Political Science* 14 (May 1970): 303–320; David J. Vogler, *The Third House: Conference Committees in the United States Congress* (Evanston, Ill.: Northwestern University Press, 1971); John A. Ferejohn, "Who Wins in Conference Committee?" *Journal of Politics* 37 (November 1975): 1033–1046; Gerald S. Stromm and Barry S. Rundquist, "A Revised Theory of Winning in House–Senate Conferences," *American Political Science Review* 71 (June 1977): 448–453.

33. Andrew Taylor, "Tax and Spending Bills Passed: Deal Now in Conferees' Hands," *Congressional Quarterly Weekly Report,* June 28, 1997, 1492–1494.

34. For a discussion of the conditions under which presidents are likely to veto legislation, see Gary W. Copeland, "When Congress and the President Collide: Why Presidents Veto Legislation," *Journal of Politics* (August 1983): 696–710.

35. Sinclair, *Unorthodox Lawmaking;* see also David T. Cannon, "Unconventional Lawmaking in the United States Congress," paper presented at the Annual Meeting of the American Political Science Association, Chicago, September 1992.

36. Sinclair, *Unorthodox Lawmaking,* 217.

37. For an overview of summitry, see John B. Gilmour, "Summits and Stalemates:

Bipartisan Negotiations in the Postreform Era," 233–256 in *The Postreform Congress,* ed. Roger H. Davidson (New York: St. Martin's Press, 1992); an engaging study of a specific summit on Social Security is Paul Light, *Artful Work: The Politics of Social Security Reform* (New York: Random House, 1985).

38. Sinclair, *Unorthodox Lawmaking,* 222–223.

39. Platt, *Respectfully Quoted,* 56.

9

Congress in the Political System

Throughout this book, we have emphasized that to view Congress as a single institution is to misunderstand it. The Congress is the House, and it is the Senate; however, it is also the House *and* Senate. In this final chapter, we make a related point: Congress is a discrete political institution, but it is also part of a set of political institutions and ongoing political processes. In Chapter 2, we introduced the place of Congress in our constitutional system, and in Chapter 3, we discussed the relationship between members of the institution and their constituents. In this chapter, we look at the more formal roles played by Congress as part of a governmental system that has three branches.

Specifically, we address how the government with its separated institutions operates and consider the trade-offs between unified and separated government. We also consider what kind of differences divided party control of the government makes. We discuss the relationship between Congress and the president, focusing on the president's success in promoting his legislative program in Congress and on House and Senate reactions to the presidential veto. We look at the Senate's confirmation role and the increasingly combative nature of that process, as well as at the relationship between the Congress and executive agencies. Finally, we examine how Congress anticipates constitutional challenges, how the courts practice judicial review, and how Congress reacts to declarations that one of its laws is unconstitutional.

CONGRESS IN A SEPARATED SYSTEM

Congress was created as a bicameral institution, in part, to ensure that it would not easily and efficiently act in haste. According to theory, the existence of two chambers ensures that legislation will receive two hearings and be considered by two groups of people with different perspectives prior to becoming law:

> Another advantage . . . of the Senate is the additional impediment it must prove against improper acts of legislation. No law or resolution can now be passed without the concurrence first of a majority of the people [expressed through the House of Representatives], and then of a majority of States [expressed through the Senate]. It must be acknowledged that this complicated check on legislation may in some instances be injurious as well as beneficial.[1]

The bicameral Congress is more deliberative than efficient. Further, it is part of a system of separated powers, with three different institutions capable of influencing the overall direction of governance. Some degree of cooperation among the branches is required for government to be very effective. Yet, each has both the responsibility and the ability to ensure that the others do not get out of line.

Reason Over Passion

Recall that when the Constitution was drafted, its authors were trying to meet the need for a stronger central government. The primary fear motivating the Founding Fathers in the summer of 1787 was that the Union was too weak and would collapse under the weight of internal strife or easily fall prey to outside forces. As we have seen, though, a strong central government raises other concerns—primary among them, effectively keeping its power in check. James Madison, in Federalist No. 51, characterized the dilemma in this way: "You must first enable the government to control the governed; and in the next place, oblige it to control itself."[2]

Madison's solution as to how to simultaneously achieve both goals is telling. He suggested that a dependence on the people is the best method for controlling the government, "but experience has taught mankind the necessity of auxiliary precautions."[3] His prescribed precautions included both bicameralism and separated institutions, each with some capacity to check the actions of the others. The Founding Fathers were concerned, of course, with factions, but also about the impact of a passionate citizenry on governmental actions. In fact, they argued that government should be the mechanism through which passions are made subordinate to reason.

Those who drafted our Constitution did not intend for the policy-making process to be easy. If reason was to replace passion, then deliberation rather than haste would need to be the focus; arguments that would be persuasive in different forums, and not inflammatory rhetoric, would need to rule the day. Our system requiring majorities in multiple settings resulted from a fear of tyranny of the majority. Lord Bryce, writing over a century ago, characterized the American system as one having friction. Using his terms, actors within various bodies of our government expend energy because of the friction produced by competition, which serves as a check on their activities.[4]

There can be little doubt that the efforts to slow the process of legislation and to make the enactment of laws difficult were largely successful. This does not mean that Congress is incapable of getting together with the president and moving quickly. But this is the exception rather than the rule. In fact, major legislation may be considered by any number of congresses prior to passage. Months, years, and even decades might go by before legislation is passed. Social Security, Medicare, and various youth service programs are frequently cited examples of policies that were decades in the making.[5]

The Challenges of a Separated System

The question we face is the same one that our founders faced: Is the system balanced so as to allow effective legislation after due deliberation, or is it out of balance? If out of balance, we might see easy and rapid legislating, with bills passed that are either unwise or poorly drafted. Although some state legislatures might have that problem because of limited session length, it is not a criticism often leveled at the Congress. Instead, we hear the opposite. If our system is out of balance, it is in the direction of inaction. Such imbalance, it is sometimes argued, undermines our ability to address serious public policy concerns in a timely manner.[6]

The criticism that our government is too inefficient takes many forms, but they tend to be related. One observation is that the world has changed in the last 200-plus years and that what worked then does not work now. In the modern world, change takes place more rapidly than in the past, and the problems we confront are more complex than ever before. A system designed to be inefficient no longer meets the needs of a society that consistently experiences rapid change. Both bicameralism and the separation of powers hinder our ability to confront the challenges of our contemporary society.

Other critics claim that we can legislate on little things, but that when it comes to addressing serious problems, our system fails. The challenges of race relations, income distribution, and environmental protection become insurmountable when Congress, the president, and the courts all have ample opportunities to weigh in on them. Action comes only after a sense of crisis develops.[7] The Civil War, it is argued, was simply the most extreme example of the consequences of a system not capable of addressing its serious problems in a timely manner.

The presidential candidacy of Ross Perot was partially the result of a different set of criticisms of our government's incapacity to act efficiently. Perot saw the failure to address the budget deficit and to reform various political processes as an indication of an unhealthy system. For many problems, he seemed convinced that there was an obviously right answer that the experts knew, but that politicians could not reach. That failure, according to the argument, is due to the fact that there are too many people representing too many vested interests.[8] The multiplicity of actors involved in policy-making in the United States gives too much voice to individual interests, according to these critics.[9] Gridlock occurs in separated systems, but not in efficient systems.

Related to the Perot-style critique is the common criticism that our government mainly reflects the influence of special interests.[10] Interested individuals, of course, have access to Congress. In fact, that access can be achieved in each house—through committees, individual members, parties, and various informal groups. But congressional access is only the start. Special interests can gain an audience in the executive branch through both political and bureaucratic processes. Interested parties can also gain a hearing in the court system. The policy process is doomed, then, to be nothing more than a constant attempt to accommodate a plethora of interests seeking access through a large number of venues.

The greatest difficulty with the bicameral, separated system, some argue, is finding the capacity to act when control of the government's various apparatuses is split between two parties. And what is worse, as Table 9.1 shows, is that divided party government has become the norm. Divided government can occur when the partisan control of the two houses of Congress is split, but more commonly, it occurs when Congress is controlled by one party and the presidency by the other. In either case, the concern is whether anything can get done under those circumstances, and if so, whether it will have any value.

Party Government in a Separated System

Some observers favor some variation of party government as a way to increase both efficiency and accountability in our system.[11] Ideally, unified party government would enhance the quality of representation, the quality of legislation, and the efficiency with which it was enacted.

As mentioned in Chapter 3, party government requires clear party positions on issues, party differences on these issues, and voter selection of the preferred platform. Electoral competition determines the majority, but then the winning party must have the capacity to enact its program. In other words, the party must control the government sufficiently to enact and implement its plan. The subsequent election is both a referendum on the sitting government and an evaluation of who is more likely to meet voters' hopes for the future.[12]

A system of party government, combined with a two-party system, is clearly efficient. The voters speak, and the winning party acts. Many argue that it also enhances representation primarily by clarifying lines of accountability and responsibility. If voters are satisfied or dissatisfied, they know who deserves credit or blame—the governing party. Contrast that with the current circumstances in the U.S. government: Who gets the credit or blame? The president, one's own senator and representative, and the majority party in Congress may all be found culpable, but none are clearly so.

Some advocates even claim that the quality of legislation would be enhanced under party government. Parties would have every incentive to write legislation that worked (rather than balanced interests) because they would gain credit if it did work and be blamed if it did not. Moreover, something of a natural selection process would work over time. Legislation that failed would be amended or repealed by the new majority party upon taking office.

Table 9.1   Divided Party Control of the U.S. Government, 1860–1996

Election Year	Congress	House	Senate	President
1860	37th	Republicans	Republicans	Lincoln (R)
1862	38th	Republicans	Republicans	Lincoln (R)
1864	39th	Republicans	Republicans	Lincoln (R)
1866	40th	Republicans	Republicans	A. Johnson (R)
1868	41st	Republicans	Republicans	Grant (R)
1870	42nd	Republicans	Republicans	Grant (R)
*1872	43rd	Republicans	Republicans	Grant (R)
*1874	44th	Democrats	Republicans	Grant (R)
*1876	45th	Democrats	Republicans	Hayes (R)
*1878	46th	Democrats	Democrats	Hayes (R)
1880	47th	Republicans	Tied	Garfield (R)
*1882	48th	Democrats	Republicans	Arthur (R)
*1884	49th	Democrats	Republicans	Cleveland (D)
*1886	50th	Democrats	Republicans	Cleveland (D)
1888	51st	Republicans	Republicans	Harrison (R)
*1890	52nd	Democrats	Republicans	Harrison (R)
1892	53rd	Democrats	Democrats	Cleveland (D)
*1894	54th	Republicans	Republicans	Cleveland (D)
1896	55th	Republicans	Republicans	McKinley (R)
1898	56th	Republicans	Republicans	McKinley (R)
1900	57th	Republicans	Republicans	McKinley (R)
1902	58th	Republicans	Republicans	Roosevelt (R)
1904	59th	Republicans	Republicans	Roosevelt (R)
1906	60th	Republicans	Republicans	Roosevelt (R)
1908	61st	Republicans	Republicans	Taft (R)
*1910	62nd	Democrats	Republicans	Taft (R)
1912	63rd	Democrats	Democrats	Wilson (D)
1914	64th	Democrats	Democrats	Wilson (D)
*1916	65th	Republicans	Democrats	Wilson (D)
*1918	66th	Republicans	Republicans	Wilson (D)
1920	67th	Republicans	Republicans	Harding (R)
1922	68th	Republicans	Republicans	Coolidge (R)
1924	69th	Republicans	Republicans	Coolidge (R)
1926	70th	Republicans	Republicans	Coolidge (R)
1928	71st	Republicans	Republicans	Hoover (R)
1930	72nd	Republicans	Republicans	Hoover (R)

Table 9.1   continued

Election Year	Congress	House	Senate	President
1932	73rd	Democrats	Democrats	Roosevelt (D)
1934	74th	Democrats	Democrats	Roosevelt (D)
1936	75th	Democrats	Democrats	Roosevelt (D)
1938	76th	Democrats	Democrat	Roosevelt (D)
1940	77th	Democrats	Democrats	Roosevelt (D)
1942	78th	Democrats	Democrats	Roosevelt (D)
1944	79th	Democrats	Democrats	Roosevelt (D)
*1946	80th	Republicans	Republicans	Truman (D)
1948	81st	Democrats	Democrats	Truman (D)
1950	82nd	Democrats	Democrats	Truman (D)
1952	83rd	Republicans	Republicans	Eisenhower (R)
*1954	84th	Democrats	Democrats	Eisenhower (R)
*1956	85th	Democrats	Democrats	Eisenhower (R)
*1958	86th	Democrats	Democrats	Eisenhower (R)
1960	87th	Democrats	Democrats	Kennedy (D)
1962	88th	Democrats	Democrats	Kennedy (D)
1964	89th	Democrats	Democrats	L. Johnson (D)
1966	90th	Democrats	Democrats	L. Johnson (D)
*1968	91st	Democrats	Democrats	Nixon (R)
*1970	92nd	Democrats	Democrats	Nixon (R)
*1972	93rd	Democrats	Democrats	Nixon (R)
*1974	94th	Democrats	Democrats	Ford (R)
1976	95th	Democrats	Democrats	Carter (D)
1978	96th	Democrats	Democrats	Carter (D)
*1980	97th	Democrats	Republicans	Reagan (R)
*1982	98th	Democrats	Republicans	Reagan (R)
*1984	99th	Democrats	Republicans	Reagan (R)
1986	100th	Democrats	Democrats	Reagan (R)
*1988	101st	Democrats	Democrats	Bush (R)
*1990	102nd	Democrats	Democrats	Bush (R)
1992	103rd	Democrats	Democrats	Clinton (D)
*1994	104th	Republicans	Republicans	Clinton (D)
*1996	105th	Republicans	Republicans	Clinton (D)

NOTE: Asterisks identify those years in which the government was divided.

SOURCE: Harold W. Stanley and Richard G. Niemi, *Vital Statistics on American Politics*, 2d ed.
(Washington, D.C.: CQ Press, 1989), 112–114.

Of course, all of these notions regarding party government are idealized. Moreover, they are quite impractical in the system of government found in the United States. Throughout this book, we have pointed to factors that prevent this kind of concerted party governance: the different term lengths for House, Senate, and president; the different constituencies for each; the lack of party control over nominations; and the lack of party control over the behavior of its members. Still, many observers argue that our system works best when one party controls all the branches of the government so that we can at least approximate party governance.[13] The question of whether the quality of governance in the United States would be higher with party governance is largely moot (barring a major constitutional overhaul). We do not and cannot have it with any reliability.

The question of the quality of governance with divided party government, however, is far from moot. To repeat, it is the norm. Assessing how well we govern ourselves with divided government is quite relevant. Moreover, the answer to the question is far from settled. In the next section, we will address some of the research that has examined that question.

DIVIDED PARTY GOVERNMENT

Many heralded the 1992 elections as something of a return to normalcy in terms of unified party government. Finally, the United States, as a nation, would be able to effectively address the various intractable problems that had accumulated under divided party government. Issues like the budget deficit, welfare reform, and health care could be addressed with coherent policies crafted within the Democratic party, passed by the two Democratic-controlled chambers of Congress, and signed by the Democratic president. But the system does not work like that. As President Clinton and the Democratic leadership in Congress learned, their party was too diverse to try to legislate based solely on votes from among its membership.

The most glaring example of this failure was the inability to enact health care reform, but other issues also were turned back or survived only after serious lobbying and vote trading. A mere two years later, in 1994, voters roundly rejected unified government and sent a majority of Republicans to both the House and the Senate. If unified party government could not handle the deficit, welfare reform, and other contentious issues, what would happen next? Among other things, it turned out, there would be rancor and deadlock—including two government shutdowns. Early in the 104th Congress (1995–1996), it may have seemed that advocates of unified party government were correct. That is, perhaps unified party government was not very pretty, but divided government could be worse. Before the session ended, however, welfare reform was passed, the Kennedy–Kassebaum bill on medical care was enacted, and a deficit elimination package was approved. Many political scientists were not surprised by the legislative achievements toward the end of the 104th Congress. Increasingly, congressional scholars argue that the American political system was designed to work without party dominance and that unified party government is not necessary for our system to function effectively.[14]

The underlying premise is that legislating is never easy—and should not be. In this manner, advocates of this viewpoint are much like the Founding Fathers. They believe that the ability to pass legislation easily and quickly is potentially dangerous.[15] Legislative quality is often enhanced by deliberation.[16] There is often an implicit assumption that legislation is better when compromise is required and when various interests are accommodated to find the multiple majorities necessary in the process. Difficulty in passing legislation thus is a virtue rather than a system flaw.

A body of research seems to demonstrate that the system is, in fact, fully capable of functioning under divided party government. For example, David Mayhew concludes after a careful analysis of legislation over a fifty-year period that neither the amount of legislation nor the enactment of major pieces of legislation is hampered by divided party government.[17] Nor, he argues, does it contribute to the propensity to engage in deficit financing.

Other research that places the process of lawmaking within the context of a separated system reaches the same conclusion.[18] Part of the argument made by these scholars is that parties are factional to begin with, and policy-making requires the construction of a majority out of various factions. As the 103rd Congress (1993–1994) demonstrated, this process can rarely be accomplished within the confines of a single party. Reaching across party lines happens routinely within the context of a bicameral legislature and a strong president. Divided party government provides little in the way of additional obstacles beyond the entrenched structural ones.

Moreover, research on recent elections suggests that divided party government might be the precise intention of some voters.[19] Clearly, divided party government is not an aberration, nor does it occur only after the midterm elections. We frequently see divided party government at the start of a presidential term. When asked their views of divided government, large numbers of voters endorse it in principle. And enough voters cast votes that result in divided government to suggest that they also endorse it in fact.

So, what lessons have we learned about divided versus unified party government? First, the United States seems quite capable of governing itself with reasonable effectiveness either way. Second, there are biases in outcomes depending on the situation. Under unified party government, we are more likely to see clearer legislative intent. Although such legislation is likely to be passed more expeditiously, it may also be less carefully scrutinized and therefore more prone to error.

With divided party government, deliberation should be more extensive, and so errors should be fewer. Such legislation may more carefully balance a wider range of interests, thereby obscuring both the intent and the ultimate beneficiaries of the legislation.

In the end, one's ideological biases influence how one feels about this issue. More cautious voters (and scholars) may prefer divided party government to keep the president (or Congress) from going too far; those who want to see problems addressed more aggressively are likely to prefer party government.

BOX 9.1   Beyond Gridlock to Shutdown

When the voters sent a majority of Republicans to both chambers of Congress in 1994 to counter the Democrat in the White House, there was little reason to expect that inter-branch relations would be smooth. The divided party control of the government was exacerbated by the Republicans' belief that they held a public mandate to lead a revolution. Among the key components of that mandate was balancing the federal budget. As if the mandate was not enough, many Republicans believed that balancing the budget was both a moral and electoral imperative.

After the 1994 election, President Clinton, by many accounts, was looking for a way to redirect the course of his presidency. He quickly recognized that it is easier to prevent the passage of objectionable legislation than it is to push programs through Congress. As budget negotiations began for fiscal year 1996, then, Clinton recognized that he could not write the budget, but he could prevent what he characterized as Republican excesses.

Fiscal year 1996 began (on October 1, 1995) without a budget and appropriations package in place. For the next two weeks, most of the government operated under a temporary spending package, but when Republicans tried to include provisions unacceptable to the president in an extension of the temporary package, Clinton balked. As a result, most of the government closed down, and federal workers were sent home, for only the fifth time in history. A record six days later, the White House and congressional Republicans agreed on a framework for a final agreement leading to a balanced budget within seven years. As part of that plan, they passed another continuing resolution that would keep the government open through December 15.

Republicans in Congress were exuberant. They felt they had won the war—in fact, had won several wars. They had achieved the balanced budget they sought and, they believed, on their terms. They also thought they had won the hearts of the American people. They were convinced their revolution would march forward.

However, within the confines of that agreement, there was still plenty of room for disagreement.[1] The president found this to be a prime opportunity to illuminate differences between the parties in terms of Medicare, tax cuts, and other issues. As a result, in the middle of December, the government shut down once more, this time for three weeks. Although Social Security checks were mailed and a number of other critical functions continued, most significant activities came to an abrupt end. Passports were not issued, meals to the elderly were not served, and vacations were ruined as the Statue of Liberty and other federal parks, the Smithsonian museums, and even the capitol building were closed.

Although it is reasonable to conclude that divided party government does not prevent effective legislating, its ramifications are nevertheless diverse and felt throughout the political system.[20] In the next section, we look at an additional area in which Congress and the president must work together: the legislative process.

THE LEGISLATIVE SUCCESS OF THE PRESIDENT

While Congress and the president interact in a variety of ways, one critical indicator of how well the branches are working together is how they come together on legislation. As we have seen, the legislative process is sufficiently complex that

BOX 9.1   continued

In this epic battle, with rival governmental philosophies, two parties, and two institutions pitted against each other, public sentiment ultimately determined the winner. More accurately, the loser was pinpointed—Republicans in Congress. As the public began to take sides, Republican party unity began to splinter. Republicans ultimately offered to pass a relatively clean resolution that would allow the government to reopen; the president had only to submit a plan to balance the budget in seven years in accordance with the previously agreed-upon framework.[2] The president submitted such a plan, but its specifics were not acceptable to the Republican Congress. Negotiators continued their work, not completing action on all fiscal year 1996 spending measures until the end of April, with the fiscal year more than half over.[3]

The stakes in this battle between the president and the Congress were quite high, with the conflict addressing fundamental issues of governance. No one should have expected it to be easy to find common ground. In any case, the outcome of this battle tells us much about the nature of presidential-congressional relations. First, neither institution fully got its way, as both were forced to compromise. Neither president nor Congress really won, but neither completely lost. Government was reshaped, but not exactly as either side had hoped.

The tools of the president in this type of conflict are few. He cannot simply pull out a checkbook and keep government running. Unlike Congress, he cannot pass legislation that achieves his goals. But the president can say no—and in this case, he did. Because Congress could not find two-thirds agreement to override the president's opposition, they were stymied. In the end, members were forced to act together, but only after pressure to do so had reached a sufficiently high level. The shutdown served to generate that pressure.

The final lesson is that it is difficult for Congress to win a public relations battle with the president. The president is single-minded and can command public attention; Congress is split and of many minds. Divisions within Congress prevent a concerted effort and hinder it in any public relations battle.[4] This time, Congress blinked first. Blinking may not be indicative of complete surrender, but it can suggest the direction of negotiations and the compromises that ultimately will be necessary.

---

1. Alissa J. Rubin, "Reality of Tough Job Ahead Dampens Joy Over Deal," *Congressional Quarterly Weekly Report,* November 25, 1995, 3597–3599.
2. George Hager, "A Battered GOP Calls Workers Back to Job," *Congressional Quarterly Weekly Report,* January 6, 1996, 53–57.
3. George Hager, "Congress, Clinton Yield Enough to Close the Book on Fiscal '96," *Congressional Quarterly Weekly Report,* April 27, 1996, 1155–1157.
4. Robin Toner, "Split and Bruised in Polls, G.O.P. Weighs New Tactics," *New York Times,* National Edition, January 5, 1996, D18.

---

it is difficult to judge clearly how effective presidents are in the process. One thing is certain: The president quite effectively places items on the public and the legislative agendas. A president who decides that an issue is important likely can ensure that Congress gives the issue attention. Getting an item on the agenda does not necessarily mean legislative success, but it is a critical first step.

Resources in Setting the Agenda

Presidents have a number of devices that help them set the agenda.[21] Foremost is the presidential campaign. If a president campaigns on an issue and wins, Congress is virtually certain to consider it. In fact, although the president might work with congressional leaders or even individual members to develop the agenda, much of his effort is focused on planting the issue in the public con-

BOX 9.2   The Budgetary Process

If one thinks of a budget as a plan—how much money will be taken in, how much will be spent, and for what purposes—then the U.S. government arguably had no regular form of budgeting prior to 1921. Federal agencies submitted requests for funds to congressional committees, which acted on those requests in a piecemeal fashion. Because of the obvious problems with that approach, however, pressure grew early in the twentieth century to enact a federal budget. Many factors contributed to the perceived need for a federal budget, including the gradual growth in the size of the federal government, increasingly common deficits, and the development of improved methods of public management.[1]

After considerable deliberation, Congress passed the Budget and Accounting Act of 1921. This act created the Bureau of the Budget (the precursor to the Office of Management and Budget) and required the president to submit annually a unified budget to Congress. Although this act might seem to be simply a reasonable step toward more efficient government, it was also a pivotal point in the shifting of power from Congress to the executive branch.[2]

Previously, the power of the purse had been firmly in the hands of Congress. Now, however, the president used his office and access to the public to establish the contours of budgetary debate by submitting an initial proposal to Congress. Congress did not, of course, abdicate its powers, but it increasingly reacted to presidential initiatives.

Throughout the mid-twentieth century, control over federal funds continued to flow toward the presidency. A pattern developed whereby the House would trim the requests of the president and the Senate would serve as an appeals board to hear pleas from the president or his agencies to avoid those cuts.[3] In this sense, both chambers were reactive rather than proactive. Congress did not pass a budget, but rather passed appropriations legislation—thirteen separate bills—approving spending plans for the various executive departments. In no way did Congress challenge the president for supremacy.

During a period of divided party government in the early 1970s, however, members of Congress began to fear that budgetary power had shifted too far. President Nixon had developed the practice of impounding funds; that is, he simply refused to spend monies that by law were to be authorized and appropriated. At the same time, deficits appeared to be surging out of control, and many in Congress felt that they had lost the capacity to effectively control spending.

In 1974, Congress passed the Congressional Budget and Impoundment Control Act. The act had many significant components aimed at increasing the capacity of Congress to budget effectively and to counter the growing power of the president. It created budget committees in both chambers and required Congress to pass its own budget resolutions. It also established the Congressional Budget Office to provide its own expertise. Additionally, it established clear guidelines for impoundments in various forms.

The original process required Congress to pass two budget resolutions each year. The first would establish targets for other committees to work with as they developed their spending and revenue bills, and the second would lock firmer numbers into place. A critical component of the resolutions process was the possibility of reconciliation—that is, mandating changes in existing legislation between the first and second resolutions to meet spending and revenue targets. That process was not used until the fiscal year 1981 budget. It has since developed into a focal point of the process as a potent force for controlling the budget, even as the second budget resolution has faded from use.

sciousness before placing it on the congressional agenda.[22] The annual State of the Union address is an effective device allowing the president to communicate with the public and Congress simultaneously. But any public statement by the president will receive press attention and might be used to influence the agenda.

BOX 9.2 continued

Since 1981, the United States has experienced unified party government for only two years. Further, during most of that time, there was extreme budgetary pressure due to enormous deficits. As Box 9.1 indicates, those two components represent a formula for gridlock and acrimony. Budgets are, after all, the ultimate statement of political priorities and should divide the parties. When coupled with institutional interests, the struggles we have seen really should not be surprising. Although Congress and the president agreed—usually only with great difficulty—on a variety of plans in the 1980s to address the budget deficit, none seemed to make much difference. Deficits continued to grow, and responsibility was impossible to pinpoint. However, that difficulty in affixing blame suggests that Congress has succeeded, at least in part, in reclaiming a role in the budgetary process.

The general process as it stands today still begins with presentation of the president s budget early in the calendar year. In the meantime, the Congressional Budget Office develops its own economic forecasts and budgetary projections, including a current services budget (what revenues and expenditures would be if nothing changed). From there, the budget committees in both chambers begin work on a budget plan in the form of a concurrent resolution. Recall that although concurrent resolutions do not require the president s signature and do not have the force of law, they must pass both chambers in identical form. Conference committees, then, become a focal point of bargaining and compromise. Once an agreement is reached, the authorization and appropriations committees understand their targets and can begin their business in earnest.

More substantially, the budget resolution routinely contains reconciliation instructions—instructions that will require changes in laws. The president becomes more involved as

Congress begins to pass its appropriations bills and as the reconciliation bill moves forward, because all these require his signature. These acts, rather than the budget plan, determine what the government will actually do in the coming year. Routinely, neither the reconciliation bill nor all of the appropriations bills are passed by the start of the fiscal year on October 1. After this deadline, a continuing resolution normally is used to keep the government operating until agreements can be reached. (Of course, as Box 9.1 relates, these can be controversial in their own right.) Ultimately, and usually well after the fiscal year has begun, many (previously not passed) appropriations bills, along with the reconciliation bill, are passed in a large omnibus bill that encompasses the agreements and compromises reached within Congress and between Congress and the president.

In reality, though, the process is neither routine nor easy. Partisan, institutional, and policy differences all complicate the decision-making process. With fiscal year 1998 leaving the United States with a record surplus, however, we may have entered a new era of budgeting. It remains to be seen what the politics of budgetary surpluses might be and how power will shift under these new circumstances. Should the United States enter a period of unified party government, that, too, would open a new set of circumstances for the budgetary power play. In the meantime, it is probably safe to expect that surpluses will neither erase partisan differences nor alter the fact that both Congress and the president have institutional interests to protect.

---

1. Howard E. Shuman, *Politics and the Budget,* 2d ed. (Englewood Cliffs, N.J.: Prentice-Hall, 1988), 24–31.
2. James L. Sundquist, *The Decline and Resurgence of Congress* (Washington, D.C.: Brookings Institution, 1981), 39–45.
3. Richard Fenno, *The Power of the Purse: Appropriations Politics in Congress* (Boston: Little, Brown, 1966).

Although the president is generally able to ensure that issues critical to him are on the legislative agenda, it does not necessarily follow that the president is influential in setting the overall agenda. Many issues, for example, have been on the agenda for a long time and will continue to be regardless of anything the president does. Campaign finance reform was on both the public and the legislative agenda long before Bill Clinton became president, and there is every reason to believe it will be on the agenda long after Clinton has left the White House. Other issues become part of the legislative agenda due to events occurring outside of the Capitol—events that might leave both the president and Congress reacting as opposed to shaping. An act of domestic terrorism or a natural disaster are examples.

Getting the attention of Congress is only the first part of the battle. Next, the president has to shape the content of the legislation and influence the final outcome. To help the president in this regard, the White House contains an office that serves as a liaison with Congress. This office is critical for effective communications, as well as for enhancing the influence of the White House. But as we saw in Chapter 8, many things besides the president's viewpoint influence the votes of members of Congress. Still, the president has many weapons in his arsenal.[23]

With the resources of the executive branch behind him, the president often is able to persuade members that his position is "right" and to gain votes on the merit of this position. When that fails, the president has abundant resources with which to bargain. The veto power, which will be discussed shortly, provides the president with a major bargaining tool. In fact, bargaining may take many forms: vote trading on policy issues, presidential support of benefits for a member's district, campaign support, or informal perks such as preferred seating at an important state dinner. Presidents may also base appeals in terms of the well-being of the country. At the start of the Clinton presidency, the president twice received the final vote needed for a majority on budget and economic issues from a senator and a representative who feared the consequences of their defeat even while dubious about the wisdom of the policy.

The president has some indirect tools as well. Foremost, the president can go public to develop grassroots support for his position.[24] Partisan appeals and the use of other segments of the party support system might be invoked to help persuade reluctant fellow partisans. The White House also maintains active liaisons with a number of groups within American society (for example, African Americans, women, and labor groups). Through these groups, the president can bring indirect pressure to bear on members of Congress.

When all of these forces are combined, presidents still do not win all the time, but they tend to do quite well. They also do noticeably better when their party controls Congress. Although there is no foolproof way to evaluate a president's effectiveness, *Congressional Quarterly* has developed a useful system for gaining some insights.[25] Researchers examine all roll calls in the House and Senate and determine if the president has taken a clear position on each vote. If he has, they then determine whether his position prevailed. This evaluation system ignores voice votes, defeats in committees, and the possibility that the president may have bargained away key elements of his policy preference. It also does not take into account that some presidents might be more aggressive in taking and sharing their position on a range of issues. But it does provide a baseline by which we might judge presidential effectiveness and its variation over time.

As Figure 9.1 shows, presidents routinely are fairly successful when they take a position. Only five times since 1953 has the president prevailed on less than 50

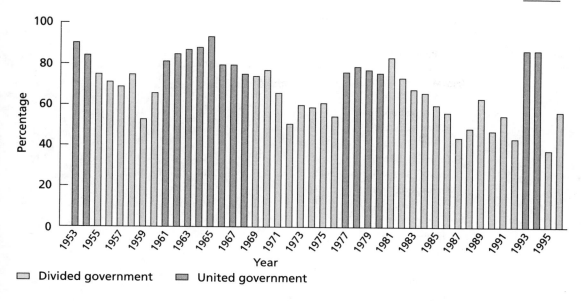

FIGURE 9.1   Presidential Success, Average Score for Both Chambers of Congress, 1953–1995

SOURCE: *Congressional Quarterly Almanac, 1996.*

percent of the issues on which he took a position. By contrast, in nine years, the president has succeeded over 80 percent of the time. As the figure also shows, presidents are far more effective when their party controls Congress.[26] President Clinton's first term is instructive on that matter. In each of his first two years in office, with a Democratic-controlled Congress, his success rate was 86.4 percent. His success dropped to an all-time low of 36.2 percent during the first year of the Republican-controlled 104th Congress. The next year, it rebounded but was still a relatively low 55.1 percent.

In many ways, the success of presidents is impressive given the obvious gulf between Congress and the presidency. Of course, many executives around the world have close to a 100 percent success rate. Our divided institutions and competitive two-party system prevent that kind of record. Presidents, though, have learned how to influence Congress. When they establish priorities and are willing to work for them, they can be reasonably effective. When they belong to the minority party, opt not to invest resources, or are less effectively organized, success rates typically drop.

The Veto Power

The major source of presidential influence over lawmaking is the capacity to veto legislation. Article I of the Constitution spells out the veto power of the president. When legislation has passed Congress, it moves to the president, who can sign the bill, veto it, or do nothing. If the president signs the bill, it becomes law.

Table 9.2   Bills Vetoed, 1789–1997

President	Regular Vetoes	Pockets Vetoes	Total Vetoes	Vetoes Overridden
George Washington	2	0	2	0
John Adams	0	0	0	0
Thomas Jefferson	0	0	0	0
James Madison	5	2	7	0
James Monroe	1	0	1	0
John Q. Adams	0	0	0	0
Andrew Jackson	5	7	12	0
Martin van Buren	0	1	0	0
W. H. Harrison	0	0	0	0
John Tyler	6	4	10	1
James K. Polk	2	1	3	0
Zachary Taylor	0	0	0	0
Millard Fillmore	0	0	0	0
Franklin Pierce	9	0	9	5
James Buchanan	4	3	7	0
Abraham Lincoln	2	5	7	0
Andrew Johnson	21	8	19	15
Ulysses S. Grant	45	48	93	4
Rutherford B. Hayes	12	1	13	1
James A. Garfield	0	0	0	0
Chester A. Arthur	4	8	12	1
Grover Cleveland	304	110	414	2
Benjamin Harrison	19	25	44	1

If the president vetoes the bill, it goes back to Congress with an explanation of his objections to the bill. If members so desire, Congress may attempt to enact the legislation over the president's objections, but doing so requires a two-thirds majority of both chambers. Finally, if the president does nothing for ten legislative days, the bill becomes law without a signature. The exception is when Congress has adjourned and the president cannot return the bill to Capitol Hill with a veto. In that case, in what is called a *pocket veto,* the legislation does not become law.

Although vetoes attract a lot of attention when they are used, as Table 9.2 shows, they are generally used quite infrequently. The veto has been exercised only about 1,000 times on public bills over the entire history of the United States, or about 2.4 percent of the total. (The number of vetoes of private bills is closer to 1,500, but they have become rare in contemporary congresses.) Moreover, vetoes are rarely overridden because it requires a two-thirds vote of both the House and the Senate to do so; overrides succeed only about 4 percent of the time.[27] Thus, when presidents decide to stop the legislative process, they

Table 9.2 continued

President	Regular Vetoes	Pockets Vetoes	Total Vetoes	Vetoes Overridden
Grover Cleveland	42	128	170	5
William McKinley	6	36	42	0
Theodore Roosevelt	42	40	82	1
William H. Taft	30	9	39	1
Woodrow Wilson	33	11	44	6
Warren G. Harding	5	1	6	0
Calvin Coolidge	20	30	50	4
Herbert Hoover	21	16	37	3
Franklin D. Roosevelt	372	263	635	9
Harry S. Truman	180	70	250	12
Dwight D. Eisenhower	73	108	181	2
John F. Kennedy	12	9	21	0
Lyndon B. Johnson	16	14	30	0
Richard M. Nixon	26	17	43	7
Gerald R. Ford	48	18	66	12
Jimmy Carter	13	18	31	2
Ronald Reagan	39	39	78	9
George Bush	31	15	46	1
Bill Clinton	20	0	20	1

NOTE: Clinton's numbers as of 1997.

SOURCES: *Congressional Quarterly Weekly Reports,* 1995–1997; Gregory Harness, *Presidential Vetoes 1789–1988* (Washington, D.C.: U.S. Government Printing Office, 1992).

usually succeed. Of course, in many cases, that success is, in fact, a failure. The president may favor legislation, but not in the form in which it arrives on his desk. Periodically, though, the president strongly objects to an initiative, so that stopping it meets his legislative objectives. More often, the veto reflects the inability of Congress and the president to find common ground on an issue. In those cases, the veto represents a failure or loss for both the president and Congress.

Historically, presidents have used the veto for a variety of reasons.[28] Our first presidents only vetoed legislation that they deemed to be either unconstitutional or poorly drafted. President John Tyler was the first president to use it as a matter of policy preference. Some presidents have used the veto as a method of emphasizing partisan differences between themselves and Congress. President Harry Truman was most successful with this strategy, but both President Gerald Ford and President George Bush utilized it to some extent as well. (Note also from Table 9.2 that Truman and Ford were among the presidents most likely to be overridden.) Franklin Roosevelt was reported to have periodically commanded his aides to "find me a bill I can veto" so as to remind Congress who was in charge.

Although use of the veto does affect public policy directly, its prime effect is that it provides a formal tool to presidents, allowing them to be involved in the legislative process all along. Without the veto, the president would be little more than a lobbyist, but with the veto, he has a strong bargaining position. If one wishes to enact a piece of legislation, the legislation must be drafted so as to anticipate the reaction of the president or gain the votes of two-thirds of both chambers. But the veto does not give the president the ability to dictate to Congress, because advocates of a bill might be just as constrained by the need to find majorities in both the House and the Senate. If the president does not work with proponents of legislation to find common ground with a congressional majority, the legislation may never reach his desk.

The veto is a powerful weapon in interinstitutional conflict. Variations of the traditional presidential veto have been promoted to affect the balance of power between Congress and the president. After years of discussion, advocates of a stronger executive, especially in regard to appropriations, have enacted a version of the line-item veto. Those working to strengthen Congress have utilized a legislative veto as a tool to provide Congress with better oversight of the executive branch.

The Line-Item Veto

The line-item veto, in its general form, allows the president to veto specific portions of a bill without vetoing the entire bill. Presidents have long advocated for that authority, pointing out that forty-three of the nation's governors have that tool. But many arguments have been raised against the line-item veto. Some fear that it gives the president too much power. Others point to research suggesting that the line-item veto does not contribute to fiscal restraint, but rather enables the president to more effectively barter pet projects with legislators.[29] Finally, many believe that the only way to give the president a line-item veto is through a constitutional amendment.

Republicans included the line-item veto in their Contract With America and passed a version of it that they hoped could withstand constitutional scrutiny. Under the plan enacted at the start of the 104th Congress, the president could veto specific portions (or lines) of legislation under certain conditions. Provisions subject to the line-item veto included tax breaks benefiting fewer than 100 people, new or expanded entitlement programs, and dollar amounts connected to a specific project in an appropriations law. After signing the law, the president had five days to exercise this line-item veto and return the provision to Congress with a veto message. At that point, under special and expedited rules, Congress could pass a new law containing the vetoed items. If Congress did so, the president could still exercise his regular veto on the entire package. Then standard veto provisions became operative, and Congress could override the veto with a two-thirds majority of both chambers. If not overridden, the veto stood. The law providing for the line-item veto (PL 104-130) was set to expire automatically on December 31, 2004, unless extended.[30]

President Clinton exercised the line-item veto a number of times, vetoing both a tax break (for a Republican contributor) and specific expenditures. The most substantial legislative test of this device came when Clinton vetoed thirty-eight military construction projects totaling $287 million out of the $9.2 billion 1998 military construction spending bill (PL 105-45). After the line-item veto, Congress passed new legislation with the money for those projects in it. President Clinton then vetoed that legislation, necessitating a two-thirds vote of both the House and the Senate to override it. In February 1998, the long battle came to an end as Congress did, indeed, override that veto.

The question remained, however, whether the actions taken by the president under the line-item veto law were constitutional. Immediately after it was passed, a number of members of Congress filed suit, claiming it was unconstitutional. The Supreme Court, though, rejected the claim, arguing that members of Congress had no grounds to sue because they had not been harmed. A second case, based on a line-item veto of Medicaid funds in New York, eventually made its way through the courts. A federal district court initially ruled that the line-item veto is unconstitutional because it is an "unauthorized surrender to the president of an inherently legislative function." In June 1998, the Supreme Court agreed and dismissed the law as unconstitutional. Justice John Paul Stevens, writing for the Court, concluded that "this Act gives the President the unilateral power to change the text of duly enacted statutes."[31] It is safe to assume, however, that the outcome of the line-item veto has yet to be finally determined.

Senate Confirmations

Another key area in which Congress and the president must work together is in the staffing of the government. The Constitution gives confirmation authority to the Senate for a number of presidential appointments, including the entire federal judiciary, ambassadors, and other top executive department officials. Throughout much of American history, this advice-and-consent function was routinely fulfilled without acrimony. The Senate found it appropriate to prevent incompetent and unfair people from gaining appointment but also believed that the president was entitled to choose the people with whom he would be working. The process of confirming appointments, by and large, was regular and predictable. In recent years, however, the process has changed substantially. What is predictable now is that nothing is predictable and that acrimony will arise.

The process of confirming a nomination follows regular legislative channels in the Senate, but the process also differs from that for legislation in substantial ways. For example, after the nomination (or during the presidential decision-making stage), there is a background investigation, the extent of which will vary depending on the nature of the appointment. Judicial nominees, for example, are investigated by the FBI and then evaluated by the American Bar Association Committee on Federal Judiciary for competence.

After the background work is complete, the appropriate Senate committee typically holds a set of hearings on the nominee. The nominee, as well as supporters and opponents, testifies, and the nominee may be asked to identify positions or actions that he or she will take (or not take) upon assuming office. While normally reasonable, this type of questioning is particularly problematic for judicial nominees who, after confirmation, must try each real case on its own merits.

Nominees recognize that answering hypothetical questions about how they will decide a certain type of case raises questions about their fairness when such a case later comes before them.

After holding hearings, the committee votes on whether to recommend that a nominee be confirmed. If there is a confirmation recommendation, that nomination normally goes to the Senate floor for a vote. Periodically, the committee votes against recommending confirmation but also votes to submit the name to the full Senate for possible confirmation.

In reality, the process is often much more challenging than this description might suggest. In recent years, the presumption of confirmation has given way to a culture that allows and even encourages opposition to presidential nominees.[32] One source of opposition is interest groups, which utilize the confirmation process to raise their own visibility, to promote fund-raising, and to publicize issue positions.[33] Finding nominees to oppose and depicting those nominees in the most negative light becomes key to organizational success for some interest groups. Once it decides to oppose a nominee, the interest group then uses whatever techniques it can to raise the case's profile and to destroy the nominee's reputation. In some cases, the attempt is almost incidental to who the nominee is.

A case in point is Judge Margaret Morrow, who took nearly two years to gain confirmation. The Senate Judiciary Committee took only about six weeks to unanimously support her, but thereafter, she was targeted by a conservative group for defeat. The efforts of this group convinced Senators John Ashcroft (R., Mo.) and Jeff Sessions (R., Ala.) to oppose her. However, support for Morrow was both broad and deep—those who knew and respected her crossed most political boundaries and covered most of the ideological range of American politics. Not until the group opposing her found another target was Judge Morrow confirmed.[34]

A second force in this pattern of opposition can be traced to the increased partisanship on the Hill. The opposition party may oppose a candidate and leak damaging information to embarrass the president. The incentives for engaging in this tactic are particularly strong at the start of a president's term, when the opposition fears being steamrolled by a popular president. One way to slow down the president's momentum and to undermine his authority is to oppose nominees through exposure of various personal or political shortcomings.

Parties also may oppose nominees for electoral purposes. A confirmation battle might be used either to embarrass the president's party or to draw distinctions between the two parties. In fact, it is unfair to suggest that only Congress uses confirmation hearings to highlight partisan differences. Presidents also use the hearings to send various messages to interested groups about their status in the administration.

Finally, of course, the parties may legitimately disagree on the direction of government. Traditionally, the opposition party gave wide discretion to the preferences of the president. In this more partisan era, however, the opposition is simply less inclined to allow the government to go unchallenged in a direction they oppose. And even if unable to defeat nominees, the opposition might be able to damage their reputation so that they are less effective upon assuming their positions.

A third source of opposition is individual senators. This culture of opposition has enabled senators to use the confirmation process for a variety of purposes that have actually served to further undermine the process. By tradition, senators may request that a *hold* be placed on a nominee. The hold originally enabled a potential opponent to seek more information or to slow down the process to determine if sufficient opposition might be found to defeat a nominee. Now, holds are used to block confirmations indefinitely, as well as for purposes unrelated to specific nominees. Placing a hold on a nominee may put the senator in a position to bargain with the president or her or his colleagues on some other matter.[35]

Individual senators can make their opposition known by threatening to filibuster a nominee. Filibuster threats are reasonably effective because there is little reason for the Senate leadership to invest great effort to gain the confirmation of a presidential appointment, especially under divided party government. In fact, appointees may need to find a Senate sponsor to take a personal interest in the nomination in order to keep it on track and to marshal it through the committee and to the floor.

Individual senators also have a strong say in the nomination of judges within their judicial districts if they are members of the president's party. Senatorial courtesy requires that presidents gain the acquiescence of senators in their party before submitting a nominee to the bench in the senator's home state. If the president fails to do so, the senator merely needs to announce opposition to invoke this "courtesy." At that point, his or her colleagues rally to the defense of the senator, generally preventing action on the nomination. The other senators, of course, have a vested interest in protecting this prerogative for all.

Finally, senators in leadership positions have an unusual capacity to stop or delay confirmations. The Senate Committee on the Judiciary simply moved very few Clinton judicial nominees to hearings. Chair Orrin Hatch (R., Utah) seemed to feel that great discretion in filling these vacancies was important, presumably in part because a two-term president has great potential to shape the character of the judicial branch. Senate Foreign Relations Committee Chair Jesse Helms (R., N.C.) blocked the nomination of William Weld as ambassador to Mexico by refusing to hold hearings and calling the Senate parliamentarian to his committee to quell any doubts about his authority to stall the process in this manner.

An additional factor that has shaped recent confirmation practices is the media.[36] The media have been quite unfriendly to the confirmation process. They pay little attention to the serious questions regarding competence and fairness, focusing instead on the sensational claims that the opposition will inevitably make. When they are not covering sex, drugs, money, or nannies, the media are likely to focus on the political aspects of the controversy. Whatever opposition, support, or gamesmanship that is taking place will gain attention over the substance of the issue. In an attempt to add some dignity to the confirmation process for judges, the Senate has modified its rules so that some testimony is heard in closed sessions.

As a result of the changes in the norms surrounding the confirmation process, many aspects of it have deteriorated. Background investigations no longer serve the simple purpose of ensuring that a mistake is not made by placing a nominee into a position of trust. Rather, they are used to uncover damaging information

---

BOX 9.3   One Senator Versus William Weld

When U.S. Ambassador to Mexico James Jones announced in 1997 that he was stepping down, an important position opened for President Clinton to fill. At the start of Clinton's second term, many dynamics were at play. The president maintained an interest in assuring the success of the North American Free Trade Agreement (NAFTA). Continued cooperation between the U.S. and Mexican governments in the war against illegal drugs was important to American antidrug efforts. The Mexican economy continued to rebound from a monetary crisis. The nomination would also be a signal about his second term: What approach would Clinton take now that he was free of any future electoral concerns? Moreover, Clinton was still confronting a Republican-controlled Congress with a tendency to examine his nominees very carefully.

William Weld seemed like the answer to all of Clinton's needs and interests. Recall from Box 3.3 that Weld was the popular Republican governor of Massachusetts who narrowly lost a race for U.S. senator to John Kerry. Weld was highly regarded by most individuals in both parties, as well as by those in the business world—important for the position of ambassador to Mexico. As a Republican and friend of Speaker Newt Gingrich, Weld was expected to be confirmed easily.[1]

But Weld's social liberalism, which made him palatable to Clinton and Democrats in Congress and to voters in his native Massachusetts, would prove to be his undoing. Still, Weld could only be undone by the rules of the Senate that grant individual senators, especially those with seniority, the capacity to obstruct the will of the majority.

If Weld was toward the extreme left of his party, then Senator Jesse Helms (R., N.C.) is toward the extreme right. Helms also chairs the Senate Foreign Relations Committee, through which ambassadorial appointments must travel. After the nomination, it became clear that Helms had strongly negative feelings about Weld. Helms announced that he would oppose Weld because he considered Weld soft on drugs—a position not suitable for the U.S. ambassador to Mexico. Weld favored the medicinal use of marijuana and had supported needle exchange programs. Among other positions that distinguished Weld from Helms was Weld's support of a woman's right of choice to have an abortion. Moreover, Weld seriously criticized Helms during his Senate campaign. It is not clear why Helms so firmly opposed Weld, but as time went on, it became clear that his opposition was firm and that he was willing to expend much political capital to fight this confirmation.

---

that may induce further opposition to a candidate who has encountered some resistance for political reasons.[37] Additionally, these background checks are used to embarrass nominees of the president, often through leaks of information to the media.

Hearings often are used to build a case for opposition or simply to embarrass nominees. Frequently, the proceedings are sensationalized, having little relevance to any judgment of the competence of the nominee at hand. Hearings provide an opportunity for interested parties to flex their political muscles and demonstrate their effectiveness to their constituents. Senators may use floor votes to put themselves on the record for the purposes of keeping score and obtaining future funding from interest groups.

The consequences of this are many. One key consequence is that it is becoming more difficult to find qualified people who are willing to put themselves forward for service in the executive branch. Also, it is more difficult for presidents to put their people in place. It is often the people close to the president who are

---

BOX 9.3   continued

What could one senator, no matter how adamantly opposed, do to derail this confirmation? It seemed unlikely that Helms could command a majority of his committee in opposition, so a "Do Confirm" recommendation seemed likely to come from the committee. It was also doubtful that he could command even the forty votes needed to sustain a filibuster if he opted to go that route. As the chair of the committee, Helms opted simply to do nothing.

Doing nothing, though, meant not holding a hearing to bring the matter to a vote. Supporters would have to find another way to gain a vote. Exercising one of the protections given to committee members, Senator Richard Lugar (R., Ind.) petitioned to hold a special committee hearing.[2] Helms would either have to call a meeting or face the possibility that a majority of his committee might call a meeting without his approval. A majority seemed likely to support such an effort.

Helms circumvented that effort by calling a meeting. With the Senate parliamentarian providing support, Helms convened the committee and asserted his right as committee chair to not hold hearings. For half an hour, he offered precedents, even citing examples involving his opponents in this matter. Any time another senator tried to speak, he slammed down his gavel and ruled the senator out of order. Even a point

of parliamentary inquiry, a privileged request by the rules, was ruled out of order. At noon, he brought the gavel down once more, indicating that by Senate rules, committee members were required to adjourn.[3]

The matter might have gone directly to the floor, but that would have required the support of the Majority Leader Trent Lott. Lott instead backed the prerogatives of his committee chair and refused to support a direct-to-the floor effort.[4] The handwriting on the wall was clear, and shortly thereafter, Weld withdrew his nomination. Helms, backed by the unique rules of an institution that places great powers into the hands of its individual members, walked away victorious.

---

1. Margaret Feldstein, "Clinton's Choice for Mexico," http://pathfinder.com/time/magazine/1997/int/970512/diplomacy.clintons-choi.html.
2. Donna Cassata and Carroll J. Doherty, "Three Senators Side With Lugar, Demand Meeting on Weld," *Congressional Quarterly Weekly Report,* September 6, 1997, 2091.
3. Donna Cassata, "Helms Lashes Back at Critics, Holds Firm on Blocking Weld," *Congressional Quarterly Weekly Report,* September 13, 1997, 2159–2160.
4. Katherine Q. Seelye, "With Iron Gavel, Helms Rejects Vote on Weld," *New York Times,* National Edition, September 13, 1997, 1, 10.

---

most vulnerable. Moreover, if President Clinton's record is one from which we can generalize, we may see presidents increasingly opt to nominate centrists rather than risk the consequences of or commit to fighting for someone who is more ideological.

Finally, vacancies are piling up in both the executive branch and the judiciary. An investigation conducted by G. Calvin Mackenzie concluded that between 25 and 30 percent of appointed executive branch positions were vacant at any given time in 1997. Many other positions are filled with temporary appointments. The circumstances in the judiciary are even worse. In 1997 and 1998, approximately one in ten judicial positions was vacant at any given time. And at one point, fully one-third of the Ninth Circuit Court of Appeals was vacant. Further, about one-quarter of the judicial vacancies had been that way for over eighteen months.[38] Chief Justice of the United States William Rehnquist used *The 1997 Year-End Report on the Federal Judiciary* to plea for help because both the speed and the quality of justice in the federal judiciary was being adversely affected. He urged the president to make nominations more quickly and the Senate to move more rapidly to make decisions. At this point, however, the judiciary is caught in the middle of conflict between the other two branches of the government.

TOOLS OF EXECUTIVE OVERSIGHT

Beyond confirming appointments to the executive branch, Congress has a constitutional responsibility to ensure that the executive faithfully carries out the law. Intentionally or not, legislation might not be executed as Congress desired or intended. Members of Congress thus have reason to be increasingly concerned about executive oversight as Congress drafts legislation that provides great discretion to executive agencies. The reasons for this pattern of legislating are many, including the complexity of contemporary issues and the difficulty of finding a majority when developing detailed laws. As a result, the rules and regulations promulgated by these agencies have begun to take on greater and greater importance.

We have already explored one device used in executive oversight—the legislative veto—in Chapter 2. You will recall that in the 1930s, Congress began to include legislative veto provisions in many of its laws. But the Supreme Court, in *Immigration and Naturalization Service* v. *Chadha* (1983), ruled that the legislative veto as exercised in this immigration case was unconstitutional. In fact, it seemed that legislative vetoes are unconstitutional in *all* cases. Even with that judgment, however, Congress periodically inserts legislative vetoes into legislation. For now, the legislative veto lives on in a gray area of dubious constitutionality.

While the legislative veto is one of the most controversial tools of executive oversight, it is neither the most commonly used nor the most effective. The most substantial, albeit blunt, tool of oversight is the congressional power of the purse. The appropriations process is a way for Congress to establish priorities. Agencies engaged in activities valued and appreciated by Congress tend to fare well in the budgetary process; those less valued or evidencing poorer performance suffer in the process.

Beyond control of the checkbook, Congress oversees the executive branch in any number of both formal and informal ways. Some forms of oversight involve addressing problems or reacting to alleged deficiencies as they become public; others are ingrained in the ongoing congressional routine; still others fall into the category of reasonably systematic program evaluation. In a valuable piece of research, Joel Aberbach identifies fourteen distinct oversight techniques.[39] In order of use, the fourteen are:

1. Staff communication with the agency
2. Program evaluations by congressional support agencies
3. Oversight hearings
4. Staff investigations and field studies
5. Program reauthorization hearings

BOX 9.4   Overseeing the IRS

If there is anybody Americans love to hate, it is the Internal Revenue Service (IRS). Given the jobs of collecting taxes and ensuring compliance with the tax code, the IRS is bound to have its critics. Recent investigations of the IRS, however, suggest that some individuals and some policies and practices have gone beyond unpleasant to abusive.

Over the years, the IRS has received its share of criticism from Congress in its oversight role. Among the criticisms were that the IRS was slow to process returns, that IRS advisors were difficult to reach, and that IRS personnel often provided incorrect information to citizens calling in with questions. Concern about how the IRS was treating taxpaying citizens led to new legislation, the Taxpayer Bill of Rights, that among other things created a taxpayer advocate within the IRS.[1]

One specific area where the IRS received increasing criticism was its failure to modernize its technological capacity. The IRS was provided funds to put a new computer system in place, but the agency consistently failed to provide the results expected by Congress. Finally, disgruntled members of Congress decided to use their appropriations tool to deal with the issue. For fiscal year 1997, the House Appropriations Committee voted to cut the IRS budget by over 10 percent from the previous year and by about 20 percent from the president's request.[2]

However, the most visible demonstration of oversight came during late 1997, when both chambers of the Congress held dramatic hearings highlighting allegations of abuse by the IRS. Agents from the IRS testified that they feared the consequences of undertaking an audit and getting no new revenues, that regions were score-carded by how much they collected during audits, and that audits increasingly targeted lower-income taxpayers who were less likely to be able to fight back. In conjunction, citizens complained about abuse at the hands of the IRS.[3]

The hearings undoubtedly made for both good politics and effective oversight. Some observers complained, however, that the hearings were unbalanced and that the defects of the IRS were greatly exaggerated. Regardless, the hearings left few observers doubting that the IRS had serious problems. For instance,

incentive structures at times encouraged abuse of taxpayers; oversight of agents often was inadequate; the overall level of competence was substandard; and the unusual powers of the IRS to seize property or paychecks and to place liens on the possessions of individuals represented invitations for abuse. Overall, the IRS appeared to be an organization without appropriate leadership and direction.

Many members of Congress tried to take advantage of the criticisms of the IRS to achieve other policy goals, such as a simplified tax structure.[4] Others used these oversight hearings to push for a fairer IRS. The primary reform proposal that emerged from the hearings suggested moving management of the IRS out of the Treasury Department and into the hands of an independent board. While the president would nominate most of the board (subject to Senate confirmation), the president would no longer appoint the head of the IRS or have direct authority over it.[5]

In a preemptive move, President Clinton issued a series of directives to improve the operations of the IRS.[6] In the summer of 1998, legislation was passed to overhaul much of the way the IRS conducts its business. Provisions included both a taxpayer bill of rights and improvements to internal operations. Whether any of the broader goals of some members will ultimately be achieved remains to be seen, but several lessons are evident. First, Congress exercises a range of tools in the oversight process: appropriations, new legislation, and hearings. Second, even if the reorganization does not take place, there is little doubt that congressional oversight has and will continue to play a major role in how the IRS conducts its business.

---

1. "Taxpayer Bill of Rights II Signed Into Law," *Congressional Quarterly Weekly Report,* August 3, 1996, 2178.

2. Andrew Taylor, "Panel Votes to Slash Budget for IRS Computer Overhaul," *Congressional Quarterly Weekly Report,* June 22, 1996, 1756.

3. Pat Widder, "Traumatized by the IRS," *Chicago Tribune,* September 25, 1997, 1.

4. John Mintz, "Hearings on IRS Practices Open: Democrats Question GOP Motives, Claim Allegations Misleading," *Washington Post,* September 24, 1997, A4.

5. "Commission Calls for Creation of a Board to Oversee IRS," *Congressional Quarterly Weekly Report,* June 28, 1997, 1500.

6. John M. Broder, "Clinton Presents Proposals to Improve IRS," *New York Times,* October 11, 1997, A9.

6. Program evaluations by committee staff personnel

7. Amendment hearings

8. Analysis of proposed regulations

9. Member communication with the agency

10. Agency-produced reports

11. Agency-produced program evaluations

12. External program evaluations

13. Review of casework

14. The legislative veto

In terms of effectiveness, Aberbach found that staff and member communications with the executive agency in question were perceived to be most effective, followed by program reauthorization hearings and oversight hearings. That the list of effective techniques includes both the informal and formal suggests much about the process. Many criticize Congress for not giving enough attention to oversight, but those criticisms may reflect, at least partially, a misunderstanding of how it takes place. Critics are certainly correct that program creation is more exciting than oversight and that incentives for oversight are not always sufficient. Still, Congress does not abdicate responsibility for its programs once enacted. To the contrary, it utilizes a wide range of diverse techniques to continue to try to bend public policy toward its preferred outcomes.

CONGRESS AND THE COURTS

Beyond the advice-and-consent role played by Congress in the selection of federal judges, most of the institutional interactions between Congress and the courts revolve around policy questions. Because the courts are the arbiters of real conflicts, they are routinely placed in the position of applying the law to specific circumstances. In fact, the realities of both the legislative and judicial processes force the courts to move beyond applying law to actually interpreting law. As a result, the courts are increasingly under criticism by legislators and others for overstepping their bounds.

The interpretation of statutes is a complicated issue for both the courts and the Congress. When the courts consider legislation to be vague or unclear, they may find themselves trying to determine what Congress actually meant. In fact, there is considerable controversy within the community of legal scholars and among judges as to the appropriate role that legislative intent should play in court decisions. Legislators are aware that their laws will be interpreted by others outside of Capitol Hill and may strive to establish how it should be applied. Committee reports and floor debates ultimately may become part of the record used to determine how to interpret a law. Congress, through its public record, sometimes attempts to anticipate the possible reaction of the courts to its legislation.

Beyond the interpretation of statutes, the courts have the authority to declare laws of Congress unconstitutional—a power that is used only rarely and reluctantly. But the fact that the courts have the power of review requires Congress to anticipate how the courts might react. In many ways, this power of the courts is similar to the president's veto power. The implications of judicial review are often quite significant for congressional action.

One case in point is campaign finance reform. Efforts to reform the campaign finance system are seriously constrained by the *Buckley* v. *Valeo* decision of 1975. In that case, the Supreme Court declared a part of the Federal Election Campaign Act Amendments of 1974 unconstitutional because it infringed on the free speech guarantees of the First Amendment. The Court ruled that campaign expenditures constitute a form of expression or speech and cannot be infringed upon under normal circumstances. Attempts to limit campaign expenditures, then, are normally unconstitutional attempts to limit speech. Anticipation of how the courts will react to new efforts at campaign finance reform has been one of the factors preventing Congress from taking effective action in that area.

The power of the courts to review statutes for constitutionality was only vaguely granted by the framers of the Constitution. Because courts have no independent control over monies or enforcement, they are in a precarious position when ordering others to act. President Andrew Jackson recognized the Supreme Court's weakness when he came into conflict with it over the Cherokee cases in the 1830s. When the Court ruled, he is reported to have said, "Well, [Chief Justice] John Marshall has made his decision, now let him enforce it."[40] Marshall, of course, could not, and Jackson continued as he pleased.

As a result of the limits on the courts' power, the first exercise of judicial review was critical to the balance of power among government institutions. The opportunity came in *Marbury* v. *Madison* in 1803. William Marbury had received a last-minute appointment to the federal bench by the outgoing Federalists in 1801. However, his commission was never delivered to him, so he appealed to the Supreme Court to compel James Madison, the in-coming secretary of state, to deliver it. The Court appeared to be in a lose-lose situation. If it ordered Madison to deliver it, he would ignore that order and undermine the prestige of the Supreme Court. If it failed to issue the order, it would appear to be an admission that the Supreme Court had no authority over the executive branch.

Chief Justice John Marshall found a way out of this dilemma. Marbury had directly petitioned the Supreme Court to issue the order (known as a writ of mandamus) because the Judiciary Act of 1789 had given it original jurisdiction in such a matter. On behalf of the Court, however, Marshall concluded that the portion of the law that gave the Supreme Court original jurisdiction in this matter was unconstitutional. It was a grant of original jurisdiction beyond that provided in the Constitution, and therefore, the Supreme Court did not have the authority to hear this case. From the Court's perspective, the beauty of the decision was that it asserted its right to declare a law unconstitutional, and no one had to act for the decision to be respected. The Court, however, remained cautious, not venturing to declare another act of Congress unconstitutional until the Dred Scott case in 1857.

BOX 9.5   Internet Indecency and the Constitution

After years of trying, the Congress finally passed the Telecommunications Reform Act at the end of 1995. But as those deliberations moved toward a close, the bill was amended to include what was called the "Communications Decency Act."[1] The aim of the legislation was to outlaw so-called cyberporn and other allegedly indecent material on the Internet. Under the act, those publishing indecent materials on the Internet where the material might be accessible to anyone under eighteen years of age could serve up to two years in prison and be fined $250,000. The problem was that the law was unconstitutional.

How is it that an unconstitutional law passed the Congress? To begin with, the Senate held no hearing on the legislation and passed it after only two hours of debate. Many of the key advocates of the legislation even confessed to having spent little or no time on the Internet and joked that they could not even program their VCR, let alone surf the Web.[2] Even then, Senator Patrick Leahy (D., Vt.) argued that the legislation was unconstitutional and offered an alternative approach to the public policy problem. Other senators and many outside the

chamber also argued that the act was clearly in conflict with the First Amendment.

Sometimes Congress passes laws on the fringe of constitutionality hoping that the Supreme Court can be persuaded to see things its way; other times Congress seems not to care. Recall that the Founding Fathers advocated both bicameralism and the separation of powers with its system of checks and balances, in part, to cool the rages of passion. In this case, many in Congress felt that they needed to respond to public pressure for action. Moreover, even though the action in the House was originally less extreme than that in the Senate, House conferees largely deferred to their Senate colleagues on this issue.[3] In this case, bicameralism proved to be inadequate protection against the forces of passion, necessitating the check of the judicial branch.

The Supreme Court heard the case, and all nine justices agreed that the act was unconstitutional (although two justices signed an opinion with a somewhat different argument). Using very strong language, the Court concluded that the act was "wholly unprecedented" in its

In the end, the Supreme Court is not the final arbiter of what is constitutional because Congress can and often does respond to Court decisions. Congress can, of course, concede the constitutional question and try to reverse the Court decision by amending the Constitution. A number of amendments—including the Sixteenth, authorizing an income tax, and the Twenty-Sixth, allowing eighteen-year-olds to vote—fall into that category. But less drastic measures also are possible. Lawmakers frequently redraft legislation to accomplish the same goals with a slightly different approach. Many pieces of New Deal legislation initially were declared unconstitutional but were upheld in the courts after being redrafted.

Many factors influence how Congress will react to the ruling that a piece of legislation is unconstitutional. Legislation that was enacted close to the time the Supreme Court declared it unconstitutional is more likely to result in a congressional effort to reverse the Court's decision. Those who drafted and supported the original legislation may still be in the Congress and continue to care about the issue. Further, the majority needed to pass legislation may more easily be recaptured if little time has passed.

Additionally, if Congress feels outside pressures, it is more likely to respond when a law has been declared unconstitutional. Interest groups adversely affect-

BOX 9.5 continued

breadth and that it placed an "unacceptably heavy burden on protected speech."[4]

Having had one of its acts declared unconstitutional, it was time for Congress to react. Original opponents of the bill saw the Court's action as an opportunity to promote their own point of view. Senators Patrick Leahy and Russell Feingold (D., Wis.) immediately called for Congress to replace the Communications Decency Act with less intrusive measures, such as software solutions to the hardcore issue.[5]

Senator Dan Coats (R., Ill.), one of the original authors of the Communications Decency Act, rewrote the legislation in response to the Court decision. Coats' new legislation took into account the Court's specific objections to the previous act and, he claimed, would pass constitutional muster.[6] Trying a different approach, Senator John McCain (R., Ariz.) offered legislation that would require any recipients of federal support, such as schools or libraries, to use Internet content-filtering software.

Ultimately, Congress will have to find a way to achieve its public policy goals in a way that meets the Court's standards of constitutionality. If it does not, no action will be taken on Internet indecency. This example is a clear case of how government institutions can come into conflict on important issues as a result of their unique character and interests. Congress wants to protect citizens and feels great public pressure to do so. Its proximity to constituents encourages expeditious and decisive actions on salient issues. The courts, though, are more insulated from the public and feel pressured to defend the Constitution. Normally, the two sets of pressures find a resolution that meets both policy needs and the constitutional test. When they do not, the Constitution itself is changed or the stalemate is continued.

1. Dan Carney, "Indecency Provision Attacked as Clinton Signs Bill," *Congressional Quarterly Weekly Report,* February 10, 1996, 359.
2. Kathryn Jones, "An Unplugged Congress Stumbles into Cyberspace," April 3, 1996, http://www.nytimes.com.
3. Dan Carney, "Court to Look at Government's Role in Policing 'Cyber-Indecency,'" *Congressional Quarterly Weekly Report,* March 15, 1997, 627–628.
4. *Reno v. ACLU* (1997), No. 96–511.
5. Carney, "Court to Look," 627.
6. Jeri Clausing, "Sponsor of Communications Decency Act Introduces a Sequel," November 13, 1997, http://www.nytimes.com.

ed by a Supreme Court decision may petition the Congress for a redress of its grievances, and Congress may respond. Similarly, if constituents react negatively to a Supreme Court decision, they may successfully pressure the Congress to respond. Congress also is more likely to respond when the Supreme Court is divided in its opinion. The likelihood of a redrafted law being upheld is enhanced when fewer justices need to be convinced that the new approach is constitutional.

The ultimate reaction of Congress is unpredictable.[41] But the declaration of a law as unconstitutional, like a presidential veto, is a dramatic instance of institutions in conflict. Although rules and precedents govern how such conflicts will play out, this type of conflict is unique in that it moves beyond policy differences to include institutional interests. Here, we see one institution, the Congress, quite responsive to public opinion, and another, the Supreme Court, relatively isolated from public opinion.[42] As a result, the conflict may take decades to be resolved, as it has, for example, on the issue of prayer in public schools.

As a result of the court's unique position in the American political system, many critics, both in and out of Congress, argue against judicial activism. At the extreme, critics contend that too often, the courts create law, develop their own meaning for laws, and interpret and reinterpret both statutes and the Constitution to achieve their own policy preferences. Although there is no necessary relationship between whether one's judicial philosophy is activist or restraining and whether one is a liberal or conservative, criticism has come primarily from conservatives who perceive that most judicial activists are liberal.

Critics in Congress have been vigilant against judicial activists. The attack on Judge Morrow, discussed previously, was based on the perception that she was an activist. Similarly, the vacancies on the Ninth Circuit Court of Appeals can be partially attributed to the desire of some senators to check those courts that are perceived to be too activist. In fact, some evidence suggests that Congress lets the judiciary expand and contract based, in part, on its satisfaction with the courts.[43] This reaction by Congress makes sense. If the courts are being too activist, then one way to constrain them is to provide less personnel for them. Finally, when Congress is really unhappy, it may attempt to restrict the courts from hearing a particular kind of case.[44] Such an attempt to limit jurisdiction, traditionally, is more important as a threat than as an effective way to curb the courts.

In many ways, the tools Congress and the courts have to address interinstitutional conflict are rather blunt. The courts can only interpret cases of actual conflict brought before them. They have the powers of interpretation and of judicial review, but both of these powers are reactive. Congress has some capacity to influence who sits on the bench (although not having the power to nominate is a severe constraint) and can influence the capacity of the courts in some very general ways. It can also react when the courts interpret one of its laws in a negative way. But that reaction does not represent the final say because the courts will likely have the opportunity to speak again. Conflicts often are quite protracted, with neither institution capable of effectively gaining the upper hand against the other—as the Founding Fathers intended.

THE BICAMERAL CONGRESS
IN A SEPARATED SYSTEM

Each of our political institutions—legislative, executive, judicial—has its own unique powers and resources. As the Founding Fathers intended, none of them seems capable of dominating the other two, and each seems capable of assuring its relevance into the foreseeable future. When there is consensus, government functions smoothly. When the polity is divided over a course of action, it is difficult for the government to develop and sustain a policy, but the branches must somehow come together if progress is to be made.

The same observations can be made about Congress. That is, Congress is really two bodies with unique circumstances, cultures, and histories. Much can be accomplished within the House and the Senate. Individual chambers, committees, and even members can effectively oversee the executive branch, and within limits, members control their own reelection success. But the primary functions of Congress are legislating and effectively representing citizens in the process. To legislate, the two chambers must come together.

As members try to work together, the character of each body becomes more evident. The Senate obviously provides its 100 members with wide latitude as legislators. Its rules reflect that bias in any number of ways, including the right of everyone to the floor, the reliance on unanimous consent agreements, the tradition of unlimited debates, and the practice of holds. It is a body that operates on its own rhythm, one that is quite distinct from the two-year cycle found in the House and that does not require conformity to an arduous process to get legislative proposals to the floor.

The House is constrained in many ways by its size. Unlike senators, many representatives toil in relative anonymity—even among one another and their own constituents. Numbers constrain initiatives and access to the floor. The formal, rules-driven atmosphere is a sharp contrast to the casual and personal nature of the Senate. Political parties and other groups, both formal and informal, that can deliver blocs of votes become important to finding a majority in the legislative process. Leadership is more formal, and leaders have a more substantial set of powers. The relentlessness of the election cycle adds further pressures to the daily responsibilities of representatives. At the same time, smaller districts allow some members to be less concerned about the range of opinions found in American society.

Beyond policy differences, representatives and senators also tend to become frustrated by the unique ways of each other's chamber. The big-picture approach of the Senate to public issues exasperates the House, whose members are more likely to defer to expertise and to focus on details. The House has a difficult time understanding how the Senate can let one person get in the way of the legislative process. The Senate's lack of responsiveness to public mandates and seeming insensitivity to the two-year cycle of the House threatens representatives. In turn, senators see the herd mentality sometimes found in the House as frightening and as justification for their toleration of colleagues acting on their own. The inability of the House to deviate from its rigid procedures strikes the Senate as absurd. The Senate sees a large number of ideological or narrowly focused members of the House who do not seem to understand that legislating requires compromise and bargaining.

Still, for over 200 years, the two chambers have managed to come together hundreds of times each year. The differences between the chambers normally are enriching rather than unhealthy, and thus represent strengths of a bicameral system. To the extent that one values access, deliberation, and compromise, the bicameral body is appreciated. Moreover, the place of the bicameral Congress in a separated system compels the institution to ensure that its diversity is a positive force rather than one that leads to too much divisiveness. When Congress fails in its tasks, the other institutions step up. For example, if Congress is unable to develop sufficient detail in its legislation, then both the executive and the courts will intervene. If Congress begins to feel institutionally threatened, then it will react. Over the years, Congress has reformed itself many times to meet external challenges to its authority, and it is likely to do so many times more.

A bicameral Congress in a separated system does not operate by formula. Incentives vary over time, and institutions evolve. The American political system may not be pretty, but Congress does enjoy the capacity to remake itself on a regular and ongoing basis to meet the needs of American society. Evolution of the House and Senate, separately and together, is inevitable. The founders' success came through ensuring that the bicameral Congress has the incentive and the capacity to protect itself, and that each chamber adds something unique to American governance. What is the future of the bicameral Congress in our separated system? One answer is certain—it will be different in detail. But 200-plus years of history also suggest that its assets will assure its centrality to the American system of representative government.

NOTES

1. James Madison, "The Federalist No. 62," in *The Federalist Papers,* ed. Garry Wills (New York: Bantam Books, 1982), 314.

2. Madison, "The Federalist No. 51," in *The Federalist Papers,* ed. Garry Wills, 262.

3. Ibid.

4. James Bryce, *The American Commonwealth* (London: Macmillan, 1888), esp. Vol. 1, 271–304.

5. An excellent examination of the long struggle to enact youth service programs is found in Jean Shumway Warner, *A Policy Study of Youth Service: Synthesizing Analysis of Policy Content and Policy Process Over Time* (doctoral dissertation, University of Oklahoma, 1995).

6. A careful analysis of power in American politics that reflects this point of view is found in Clifton McCleskey, *Political Power and American Democracy* (Pacific Grove, Calif.: Brooks/Cole, 1989).

7. Ibid., 184–186.

8. For example, Lester C. Thurow, *The Zero-Sum Society* (New York: Penguin Books, 1981). Also see Mancur Olson, *The Rise and Decline of Nations* (New Haven, Conn.: Yale University Press, 1982).

9. A full set of criticisms is found in Theodore J. Lowi, *The End of Liberalism* (New York: Norton, 1969).

10. Kay Lehman Schlozman and John T. Tierney, *Organized Interests and American Democracy* (New York: Harper & Row, 1986).

11. Political scientists promoted that perspective in 1950 in American Political Science Association, *Toward a More Responsible Two-Party System: A Report of the Committee on Political Parties* (New York: Rinehart, 1950). More recently, see James L. Sundquist, *Constitutional Reform and Effective Government,* rev. ed. (Washington, D.C.: Brookings Institute, 1992).

12. Bryce, in his *The American Commonwealth,* developed these themes over 100 years ago in a chapter entitled "Comparison of the American and European Systems," 271–290.

13. McCleskey, *Political Power,* 234–235.

14. Most prominent among these works are David R. Mayhew, *Divided We Govern: Party Control, Lawmaking, and Investigations, 1946–1990* (New Haven, Conn.: Yale University Press, 1991), and Charles O. Jones, *The Presidency in a Separated System* (Washington, D.C.: Brookings Institution, 1994).

15. Jones, *The Presidency,* 286–287.

16. Ibid., 292–293.

17. Mayhew, *Divided We Govern.*

18. Jones, *The Presidency.*

19. Morris Fiorina, *Divided Government* (New York: Macmillan, 1992), esp. 62–85, and Gary Jacobson, *The Electoral Origins of Divided Government: Competition in U.S. House Election* (Boulder, Colo.: Westview Press, 1990).

20. For example, Fiorina, *Divided Government,* 86–111.

21. Paul Light, *The President's Agenda* (Baltimore: Johns Hopkins University Press, 1982).

22. Samuel Kernell, *Going Public: New Strategies of Presidential Leadership,* 2d ed. (Washington, D.C.: CQ Press, 1992).

23. An excellent treatment is found in Jon R. Bond and Richard Fleisher, *The President in the Legislative Arena* (Chicago: University of Chicago Press, 1990).

24. "Going public" is Kernell's term; see his *Going Public.*

25. See Bond and Fleisher, *The President in the Legislative Arena,* 53–80, for a discussion of these scores.

26. For more detail on this point, see Bond and Fleisher, *The President in the Legislative Arena,* 81–121.

27. For a review of these figures and an exploration of the factors that contribute to vetoes, see Gary W. Copeland, "When Congress and the President Collide: Why Presidents Veto Legislation," *Journal of Politics* (August 1983): 696–710.

28. Robert J. Spitzer, *The Presidential Veto: Touchstone of the American Presidency* (Albany: State University of New York Press, 1988), 1–70.

29. Research on the line-item veto in the states includes Glenn Abney and Thomas P. Lauth, "The Line-Item Veto in the States: An Instrument for Fiscal Restraint or an Instrument for Partisanship?" *Public Administration Review* (May/June 1985): 372–377; and James J. Gosling, "Wisconsin Item-Veto Lessons," *Public Administration Review* (July/August 1986): 292–300. For the views of governors, see James W. Douglas, "Former Governors' Perceptions of a Presidential Line-Item Veto," *Presidential Studies Quarterly* (Fall 1997): 745–759.

30. For a summary, see "President Gets a Budgetary Scalpel," *1996 CQ Almanac* (Washington, D.C.: CQ Press), 2-28–29.

31. "U.S. Judge Says Line-Item Veto Unconstitutional," AllPolitics, February 12, 1998, http://allpolitics.com/1998/02/12/line item.veto/. Andrew Taylor, "Few in Congress Grieve as Justices Give Line-Item Veto the Ax," *CQ Weekly Report,* June 27, 1998, pp. 1747–9.

32. Excellent discussions of both recent trends in the confirmation process and their consequences are found in The Report of the Twentieth Century Fund Task Force on the Presidential Appointment Process, *Obstacle Course* (with background papers by G. Calvin Mackenzie and Robert Shogan) (New York: The Twentieth Century Fund Press, 1996), and its follow-up paper, G. Calvin Mackenzie, "Starting Over: The Presidential Appointment Process in 1997" (New York: The Twentieth Century Fund Press, 1997). Also available at http://www.tcf.org/Mackenzie/.

33. Interest group mobilization also seems to decrease the likelihood of confirmation. See Lauren M. Cohen, "Warring Factions: Senators, Interest Groups, and the Politics of Appointing Federal Judges," paper presented at the Annual Meeting of the Midwest Political Science Association, Chicago, 1998.

34. Neil A. Lewis, "Attack on Clinton Nominee May Backfire on the G.O.P.," *New York Times,* National Edition, February 10, 1998, A12.

35. Mackenzie, "Starting Over," 8–10.

36. Robert Shogan, "The Confirmation Wars: How Politicians, Interest Groups, and the Press Shape the Presidential Appointment Process," in *Obstacle Course,* 87–168.

37. Mackenzie, "Starting Over," 10–11.

38. Ibid., 1–8.

39. Joel Aberbach, *Keeping a Watchful Eye: The Politics of Congressional Oversight* (Washington, D.C.: Brookings Institute, 1990), esp. Chapter 6.

40. Lisa Paddock, *Facts About the Supreme Court of the United States* (New York: Wilson, 1996), 20.

41. For a good overview, see Joseph Ignagni and James Meernik, "Explaining Congressional Attempts to Reverse Supreme Court Decisions," *Political Research Quarterly* 47 (June 1994): 353–371.

42. Thomas R. Marshall, *Public Opinion and the Supreme Court* (Boston: Unwin Hyman, 1989).

43. John M. De Figueiredo and Emerson H. Tiller, "Congressional Control of the Courts: A Theoretical and Empirical Analysis of Expansion of the Federal Judiciary," *Journal of Law and Economics* 39 (October 1996): 435–462.

44. Dan Carney, "Vote to Limit Judges' Powers Indicates Rocky Path Ahead," *Congressional Quarterly Weekly Report,* June 14, 1997, 1379.

Appendix

Legislative Information
on the Internet

Information on the World Wide Web about Congress continues to expand. Sources of information about the legislative process and congressional politics include the following:

THOMAS
http://thomas.loc.gov
This comprehensive source maintained by the Library of Congress provides a summary of bills, congressional debates, committees, and the legislative process.

House of Representatives
http://www.house.gov
The home page of the U.S. House of Representatives provides a directory of members, a summary of committees and leadership posts, and a synopsis of the House schedule. It also offers a section on roll call votes.

Senate
http://www.senate.gov
The home page of the U.S. Senate provides a directory of members, a summary of committees and leadership posts, and a synopsis of the Senate schedule. It also offers a section on Senate history.

C-SPAN
http://www.c-span.org
The home page of the cable television network C-SPAN provides a summary of House and Senate schedules, information on committee hearings, and a "question-and-answer" section on Congress.

Roll Call

http://www.rollcall.com

This site maintained by *Roll Call* magazine provides the "inside scoop" about life on Capitol Hill. It offers commentary, policy briefings, and a directory of the membership.

Congressional Quarterly

http://www.pathfinder.com/cq

This site provides a "report card" on members of Congress. It offers a searchable index of key votes by representatives and senators.

Capweb

http://www.capweb.net

This site provides a comprehensive multimedia look at the organization and politics of Capitol Hill. It also offers the "Capitol Hill Diaries," which are amusing stories and anecdotes posted by congressional staffers.

Index